A LIFE OF DECEPTION

The Truth by Mae Cardinal

To
Peter Kerr Jarrett
Best Wishes
Mae Cardinal

A LIFE OF DECEPTION:

The Truth by Mae Cardinal

TABLE OF CONTENTS

Chapter 1: Gram's Passing 4
Chapter 2: The 1929 Depression 10
Chapter 3: World War II, 34
Chapter 4: Our Marriage Beginning 55
Chapter 5: My Business Venture 64
Chapter 6: Camping Out, 76
Chapter 7: Jewelry Business 90
Chapter 8: Tension Release 131
Chapter 9: Copenhagen 145
Chapter 10: Blueberry Season 162
Chapter 11: Easter 179
Chapter 12: Spain 1987 188
Chapter 13: Dad's Birthday 194
Chapter 14: Josh 215
Chapter 15: Trailer 234
Chapter 16: My Sibling 239
Chapter 17: Marriott Newport 254
Chapter 18: The Reunion 266
Chapter 19: Incarceration 283
Chapter 20: Pat's Life 301
Chapter 21: Intracoastal 324
Chapter 22: Becca and Dean 338
Chapter 23: My Forever Friend 350

Gram's Passing

It never occurred to me to write a book. I have no real education, but I need to share the failure in my life. I desperately want it to be heard.
So I sat down at my computer, really out of boredom at first, to, write about the life I once had. And as you can see, I just kept going. I was obsessed, haunted by my past. I needed to release the unbearable pressure I was suffering.

My life growing up was a happy one. I was the last born of three girls and one boy. Arna and Sue were born just eighteen months apart. Pat, our only brother, came next, two years later, then I was born five years after Pat.

Our family—aunts, uncles, and grandparents—all lived side by side in three different houses on the same street. We were always in close contact. Our doors were never locked, so friends and neighbors could just pop in.

Our simple, pleasurable life meant planning family gatherings that we called outings. Everyone cooperated, bringing their special dish and games. Holiday dinners were usually shared too. Sometimes we had as many as twenty-five gathered around a makeshift table.

Our two-family house had three small bedrooms, a large kitchen parlor, and one toilet, all on one floor. It held all the comfort we needed at the time.

Guistina (we called her Elsie) lived on the second floor with her husband and two daughters, Jenna and Patrice. Guistina was Mom's only sister. She was much younger and very devoted. She had a special bond with Mom. She was a carbon copy of Grandma, slender, beautiful, petite, and serene.

We all loved Elsie dearly; we considered her our second mother. She was very generous and kind, always there to take on any responsibilities Mom was unable to handle. I looked forward every week to sweeping down her stairs for the twenty-five cents she gave me!

Grandma Pasqualina passed away on September 17, 1931. She was a petite, frail woman. I was six years old but the memory is still vivid in my mind. I remember her being laid out in the parlor dressed in pink. She looked just like a Madonna. There was the scent of flowers throughout the house, a black wreath on our front door, and an open window ready for the casket removal.

I remember sleeping in the next room with my older cousin, Bella. She gave me the courage to accept Gram's passing.

Grandma was gentle, kind, beautiful, and extremely fussy. Her skin was like velvet. She kept her home immaculate. It was spotless even though it was barely furnished with the bare necessities.

Her wooden floor was washed every Saturday. She never anticipated the danger of placing hot water on the floor. Five months earlier, as she got ready to wash the floor, she placed a pan of hot water down in front of her. As she turned around to grab the mop, her beautiful eighteen-month-old daughter Gina ran in front of her and tripped, falling directly into the pan of scalding water, she died instantly.

Grandma went ballistic. Her life had no meaning after that, even though she had three more children who needed her. She felt she had killed her baby, and spent the rest of her short life in bed, never forgiving herself for letting it happen. She mourned continuously. She refused to live, just waiting for her time to die. It was said that Grandpa could hear her screams of sorrow down the street as he walked home from work.

I don't remember Grandpa at all; I was too young. However, I do remember the closet in Mom's room where she kept Grandpa's memorabilia. His sword and uniform from the First World War, so impressive, I can still see them in my mind today.

Mom was the eldest of her siblings. She cared for Grandma and begged her to get out of bed and resume her life with them, but Grandma turned a deaf ear. She desperately wanted to relieve the pain she was suffering. She died a short time later of a broken heart.

Uncle Tom, Mom's only brother, refused to forgive Grandma for abandoning them. He refused to have any contact with her, even though Mom begged him to make just one visit to see her. He was very bitter, so much so that he refused to set foot in her room until the day she died. Mom made all the arrangements after she passed. Friends and neighbors came to pay their respects, they brought food, goodies, and donations.

Although mom made it understood that we were not to touch anything on the table until after everyone left, to be respectful of others, we could hardly wait for the neighbors to leave so we could dig in to the goodies.

Grandma being laid out in the parlor for five days was frightful for us. It was harder for Mom and Aunt Elsie to stay awake to mourn. Very often they would fall asleep sitting comfortably in their chairs!

We felt a sigh of relief when the funeral director finally came to take her away. It was impressive seeing the casket being lifted and taken out through the open window.

What a relief it was when, a short time later, all wakes were held in funeral parlors. Mom and Aunt Elsie wore black every day for the next year, to symbolize their loss and show respect to the deceased.

Mom, being the oldest, assumed the responsibility of taking care of Grandma's kids. Aunt Elsie kept close ties with Mom, and living together in the same house, they became inseparable. Their devotion to each other was unusually special; there was never an unkind word between them.

Luckily, Dad loved her family too. He accepted them as if they were his very own, and we all included them in our daily lives.

The after-effects of Grandma's passing caught up. Uncle Tom was consumed with guilt, and any mention of Grandma was out of the question. Mom could feel his pain. She was worried about his frustration and the effect it would have on his already disturbed condition. His days were spent studying at Brown University or isolated in his room reading for hours and talking to himself.

Tom was a brilliant and troubled man, almost to the extent of being mentally disturbed. His lonely life concentrated on writing poems, some of which were very amusing.

Although Tom was a good-looking man, he had no interest in making friends or dating women. He suffered from an obsessive-compulsive disorder, afraid of coming in contact with germ-related objects, refusing to touch any of us without using napkins or tissues. He idolized the children in our family. It was clear he desperately wanted to show affection, to kiss them and love them, but the best he could do was touch their nose with a tissue, which was his way of showing affection. How sad that this handsome man lived a very lonely life. He died at the age of seventy never experiencing a pleasurable, affectionate embrace, or a loving relationship with a woman. His final days were spent working and gambling away his money at the horse track.

After his passing, Mom needed to vacate his room in the complex he rented. She was totally shocked to see the conditions he had lived in. Newspaper covered his bed, which apparently he slept on, there were papers of every kind throughout the room. He always washed his hands but never used a towel, yet his clothes were clean and he never had an odor.

I always felt rather special being the youngest of my siblings. Come bath time every Saturday, I was the first to be bathed. Mom, the sweetest woman who ever lived, would fill the huge tub down in the cellar and, one by one, she would bathe us, adding warm water as it cooled down. Our black cast iron stove always had a huge pan of heated water ready whenever it was needed.

As we got older, on Saturdays (bath day) we would walk with our towels in hand to the public bathhouse in Silver Lake, then wait our turn.

Dad had such a feeling of guilt seeing us walk to our weekly bath, he remodeled our toilet and installed a tub and shower.

1929 Depression

The 1929 Depression was disastrous for most people. I remember the discussions and concern among the neighbors. It was said that people were taking their own lives after losing their life savings in the stock market crash. The banks had closed their doors and people without deposit insurance were totally destroyed. Lines of people formed at the banks' front doors, waiting for hours hoping to hear some good news. Families were hurting. People were selling apples and pencils on street corners begging for help to support their families.

We, however, never felt any effect during the Depression years because Dad was successful in the oil business at that time. He was a hard working business man, kind, generous, and full of compassion. I remember a poor man with no legs, his torso resting on a flat board with wheels and a block of wood in each hand pushing himself up and down streets begging for donations. Full of compassion, Dad would often remind Mom to be generous whenever the legless man wheeled by.

Dad was well liked and had a good reputation among his friends. No one ever said an unkind word about him.

Our family was fortunate to live a more-than-adequate life during those years. Dad made sure we were never deprived. He believed in living and eating well.

Sunday was our special day—the only day we would have a full breakfast together as a family. Dad insisted on having the works: meat (usually meatballs that mom would prepare for her gravy), potatoes, and eggs. He had a sweet tooth, so delicacies finished the breakfast.

A specialty bakery nearby was a family treat. Their breads were special made, with a hard crispy crust on the outside and delicately soft on the inside. All their pastries were delightfully tempting. Sunday was leftover day so Arna was always chosen to walk to the bakery for the special day-old doughnuts.

As I said, Dad was kind and generous. He had compassion for the less fortunate, who included many of his poor customers who could not afford to pay for their oil deliveries. His black book was filled with the names of creditors. He felt so thankful for the luxuries he possessed; he devoted his life to helping the needy. I remember the many times his customers called Mom and praised him for his generosity. He made sure they never went without food or heat.

On the other hand, although he was a clever man, he was a sucker for a bargain. You could sell him a straw hat in a blizzard.

I remember many times we were visited by a strange-looking man. He had a long, curved scar across the left side of his face, which was pitted. He came from Federal Hill, the mafia part of town. He usually carried jewelry, liquor, or coats of all kinds. The neighbors referred to him as the con man. He spoke very little, avoiding small talk. He would conclude his business briefly, then leave.

One day this man brought an armful of furs. My sisters thought the furs were beautiful and they tried on different styles. Mom picked out a black beaver, which fit her perfectly. I wasn't impressed since I didn't like furs, but I took advantage of the offer and chose a leopard skin. I was still young then, and when I wore it to school, my friends didn't seem to notice it, or if they did, it was never mentioned.

We felt very safe in our town. In spite of their reputation, the mafia protected the people. Petty crimes were not allowed. They made sure our town was free of riffraff.

Dad had two long-time customers named Kate and Christina Quinn. They were spinsters, both elderly and devoted sisters, who were living off their sizeable inheritance from a soap fortune. (The company still operates in Rhode Island.) Their only relatives were two great-nephews who were complete strangers.

Kate, the older of the two, was well schooled in finance. She had the knowledge to control her wealth but she needed Dad to help her make the right decisions. She looked up to him and trusted him. When Christina passed away at the age of eighty-five, Kate (who was nearly blind) felt alone, so she begged Dad to take her in to live with us. It put Dad in a difficult position. It would require giving up one of our bedrooms, and it would be a steady imposition on Mom, but how could he refuse her? His conscience was overpowering; he had to make it work. Full of compassion, he prepared for Kate's moving in.

The kind lady that Mom was, assumed the responsibility of caring for her. Kate was happy being with us, she enjoyed the family discussions and sometimes the distasteful chatter. There were days when Dad, full of compassion, would take time off from his work and take her for a ride, just to break the monotony.

As the months passed, it was becoming too stressful for Mom. Kate was failing, and she needed special care. Dad, feeling the pressure, moved her back to the home she had left. He never abandoned her. He visited her frequently, making sure she was comfortable. Mom too was relieved, although she never complained.

I was considered special in Kate's eyes. She had a special liking for me, maybe because I gave her special attention, or because I was sympathetic and felt pity for her.

It hurt me to see her living alone and nearly blind in that huge Victorian house. It was filled with antiques, paintings, and furniture. I tried to visit every day to help with her needs.

Most of her food was ordered and delivered, but

often she would ask me to pick up her special cravings, like fish and chips, or lobster sandwiches.

Although she had a vision loss, she knew exactly how to take care of her money. She had her bills separated into dollars, tens, and twenties. She knew exactly how much she was to give me for her food orders, and she had no problem making change.

She delighted in telling me stories about her life with Christina. She would reminisce about their life together and how much she missed her. She always had tears in her eyes.

The days were tiring for her. It was obvious she couldn't continue living alone. She had difficulty getting around and, to be honest, I was beginning to tire of my visits. Dad felt sad, he convinced her that she needed special care, and she would be much happier living in an elderly complex. It was sad to see the hurt in her eyes. We tried to tell her about the pleasant surroundings, the people, and the activities she would experience there.

She finally understood. With Dad's help, the arrangements to get her into the nearby old folks' home were made. She was sad when she asked me to help her with the preparations, and the necessities she would need.

Before she left her home, she said, "Mae, everything will be left behind so take whatever you want." How sad to think a lifetime of accumulated wealth and collections just left behind for others to enjoy. I helped myself to some of her precious silver and some beautiful paintings, whatever we could fit in Dad's car at the time. She had no idea of the many years of pleasure I got from her prized possessions.

We felt good when we visited that we had done a good deed for her. Her attitude changed too. She showed signs of contentment.

Busy with our own lives, we visited less. Actually, she wasn't at the home long, our last visit was just a few weeks later. Mary was almost 100 years old when she passed away. We didn't know her nephews, we had no contact with them. But her memory lives on. Now we can only pray and give her our blessings.

It was the start of winter and Dad's business was booming. Oil deliveries were needed and burner repairs were in demand. The calls came day and night, and he was always ready to accommodate their needs. His women customers were impressed with his good looks and his generosity. All that attraction pumped up his ego. He spent considerable time away from home, but Mom never complained. She would wait anxiously for him to walk in the door.

Helen and Dom, his customers for many years, were overly friendly. Helen was a heavyset woman, rather attractive, and very pleasant. Dom was meek. He had a short vocabulary and was very reserved. They very often visited our house, usually on weekends. I was young, however even I noticed the attraction that Helen had for Dad, and it became apparent that he was spending a lot of time at their house.

Later we found out Helen had divorced Dom and was keeping company with my dad. Mom was very aware of the attraction, but she chose to ignore their closeness. Rather, she accepted Helen's friendship completely. I always wondered why she was so blind to the fact, never showing concern for his behavior. Her only interest was keeping her family together. She always felt that since she was never deprived, it didn't matter. Her children were her first priority. She had faith in her marriage; she knew how much Dad loved his family and that he would never leave us.

Eventually the affair with Helen ended—and a new one began. Although he was kind and caring, we kids felt a certain amount of resentment toward him. Whenever we would discuss his behavior, Mom would become very angry, reminding us that he was our father, that we must have respect. Foolishly, she believed that since he never slept outside of our home, it was just a passing thing.

Many nights he would work late, so we hardly ever got to see him at bedtime. His first instinct when he did come home was to peek in our room. We particularly looked forward to those special nights when he would wake us from our sleep and ask, "How would you kids like to take a ride?" I think he was consumed with guilt over his womanizing, so to help clear his conscience he would try his best to please us. Still, without hesitation, we'd spring up from bed, without dressing, and jump into the car.

We knew that a ride took us to the modern ice cream shop on Federal Hill.

The outdoor market was the shopping plaza for every variety of food and household goods. The streets were lined with vendors selling vegetables, fish, poultry, clothing, and almost anything your heart desired from their pushcarts. The specialty ice cream store was our favorite. Ice cream in the 1930s was only purchased at ice cream parlors, since the ice boxes at that time had a compartment for blocks of ice, it was impossible to store ice cream. We kids were never satisfied with just one flavor. We always asked for double scoops of two different kinds. Refrigerators were a blessing when they were later introduced to the public.

The 1939 World's Fair was a popular attraction at the time. The word was out that the fair was to be held in New York, featuring special inventions that could be seen for the first time.

Dad was impressed. He surprised Mom with the suggestion that they should make the trip to see the fair that weekend.

Without a second thought, Mom excitingly began to prepare some cooked food so there would be enough for us to eat during her absence. Food was important to her. She was always afraid we might go hungry.

Her daily routine was always the same. After breakfast, she would start her soup for the evening meal and leave it on the stove until suppertime.

Bacteria? It was unheard of in those days. I never remember us getting sick from food left out all day.

Mom didn't waste time. She excitedly packed a bag. You'd think she was preparing for a two-week trip! It was her special treat spending time alone with Dad. She always gave in to his wishes; she loved him dearly.

To visit New York was considered a special occasion. We kids managed very well while they were gone. Pat, being the man of the house while they were gone, felt superior controlling his sisters. He kept watch over us.

That weekend ended suddenly. "We didn't have enough time," Mom said, "to really enjoy other attractions in New York."

When they were back, she eagerly described the inventions of the future they saw. Television impressed her the most. She explained how images were transmitted, converted, and shown on a screen. We couldn't understand at the time how you could watch people performing live, but later we were convinced.

Dad was also impressed with what he had seen at the fair—and promised us a television as soon as they became available. He kept his promise too! How exciting it was to watch the programs on our black and white 8-inch TV. We used the radio mostly for news and music. Technology had a big influence on our childhood. We were continually impressed.

Dad was two years old when he came from Roccomonfina, Italy. There, his family harvested chestnuts, one of his favorite foods. In America chestnuts were only available during the Christmas holidays. He was so proud of his heritage he made sure that Mom included them in our diets. We ate chestnuts many different ways—roasted, baked, in soups, and in pastries.

Dad, the oldest of his five siblings, wanted desperately to attend school when he was a boy, but his father was a stern, ignorant man who felt that children should help with the chores around the property where they lived. He didn't feel any need for education.
Dad ignored his father's demands. He was determined to learn, so whenever possible, he would sneak away to attend classes. Although his education was limited and deprived, his defiance paid off. He was self-taught and well read, always able to answer any questions asked. Many nights he would tell us stories about his father's strict rules and the fear he had instilled in his children.

Sometimes his dad would play games where he tried to trick them. He was looking for the right answers so he tested them to satisfy his curiosity. If they gave the wrong answer, he would punish them by letting them work extra hard or have them move piles of dirt from one place to another on their property.

They had a strict, fear-based upbringing, but they all

lived a satisfied and contented life.

I really didn't know my grandpa. I was too young when he passed away. But I was old enough to remember the kind of business they were in. Their property was quite large, with ample space for almost any business. A hint: Gram was referred to as the "chicken lady."

They raised chickens in their backyard. The neighbors came to buy them freshly killed, which was dreadful to watch. Using a sharp knife, gram would cut their throat and hang them from a rope tied from one column to another. I remember how I cried the first time I saw it. Watching them shiver and bleed left an impression on me long after. The backyard was set up for feathering, dressing, and washing the blood down the drain.

When there was a lull, she would preserve her garden tomatoes, immersing them in large vats of warm water to remove the skins. After peeling them, Gram would pack them in Ball jars she had stored for the winter.

She was a strong woman, full of energy. She was also very aware of her heart condition. She always carried a small bottle of brandy with her. Often I saw her pull the small bottle out from her bosom and take a swig. She eventually died of a heart attack at the ripe old age of eighty-four.

Dad took care of his mother until the day she died, even though she detested his womanizing and chastised him every chance she got.

Our home was situated across from a playground where there were many activities for youngsters. The city pool was a treat since the ocean was much too far away to go to often. After supper, all of us boys and girls, would play kick the can, hopscotch, hide and seek, and lots of other innocent, fun games. Those were the most popular in those days.

Our games were usually interrupted when the waffle or ice cream man rang his bell when he pulled up to us. Everyone would stop playing and run to the truck, trying to be first in line. The waffles were especially delicious. They were served hot, with lots of sugar. What a treat!

Our thoughts at that time were clean and innocent; we had no knowledge of sexual activities. I was called "champ" by most of my friends in those days since I had a tough, tomboy image. I took part in all the boys' sports, but in reality I was very much a girl. As I grew older, I deeply resented being called "champ." I eventually corrected that image by simply refusing to answer.

Mom's days were programmed like a pattern. Certain days for special chores. I dreaded coming home from school on Thursdays. That was wash-the-kitchen-floor day, and I was the washer, which she never let me forget. Now I think back how weird her thoughts were. After the floor dried, she would spread newspaper to keep the floor from getting dirty. Then she would sometimes pass a wet mop, "just to pick up the spots" she explained.

We didn't look forward to fall and spring cleaning either. That was when we cleaned the entire house, we changed curtains, and rearranged the furniture. It never changed, but that paid off later because all of us followed the same pattern through our entire lives too.

Shopping for food was easy and convenient because the traveling fruit peddler made a daily run. The neighbors would congregate around the truck with its large display of fruits and vegetables. Our neighborhood store was nearby. It was very small and it mostly carried meats of all kinds. There never was a specific day for food shopping. Every day mom would walk and buy what she needed to cook for that day's meals.

One day she sent me to buy a pound of cheese. As I skipped and hopped home, I accidentally dropped the package, scattering the cheese all over the ground. I remember how frightened I was to tell her. What a surprise when she handed me a dime and told me to go back and this time to be more careful. Imagine, five dollars bought us food for an entire week.

There was no need to leave the house to shop. Specialty stores were few and far between, and of the rest was delivered daily, like ice, coal, milk, and other necessities.

I was impressed watching the coal slide down the

chute through the cellar window. I don't know why that sight left such an impression on me. I can still hear the rumble it made while being poured.

Anthony, a traveling salesman with a truck full of domestics, would make his visits on Friday, going house to house. Mom bought and prepared what was needed for our bridal trousseau, just in case we would one day get married. She usually paid Anthony twenty cents or more each week.

There were one or two other stores in our neighborhood, but they mostly sold candy, bread, and small necessities. Woolworths was the only store that carried most of what we needed, but you had to travel to Olneyville to get there, which was where the places of interest were.

It was a safe environment for us in those early days. Neighbors visited each other daily. We never had to worry about intruders invading our property or even having to keep our doors locked. I often think back about the special treatment and respect we received. Men had high regard for women, tipping their hat, opening the car door, and standing to offer a lady a seat on the bus. How comforting it was. We were never afraid of walking the streets alone at night.

Sunday was a special day for us kids. We looked forward to spending the day at the movies and meeting with our friends from the neighborhood. It was an all-day affair and we really got our money's worth. The cartoons settled us in, two movies followed, and it ended with the coming attractions—

all for a dime.

We would walk to Olneyville, about two miles away, and Dad gave us fifteen cents each—ten cents for the show and five for candy. Sometimes he would be overly generous and give us an extra nickel!

Every Thursday, the Royal Theatre offered one piece of dinnerware to each patron, so Mom and Aunt Elsie never missed a Thursday movie. Every house in our neighborhood had a complete set of green and white movie china.

Mom's dear friend Mary Mazzo (for whom I was named) was working in the Atlantic Mills in Olneyville. It seemed everyone in our neighborhood was working there.

Mary encouraged Mom to apply for work. She boasted about all their friends congregating, chatting, and being together. It was a temptation Mom could not resist—she was gullible and easily led. She got very excited about the idea, she applied, and she got the job.

Every day was special for her. We could see the pleasure she felt, leaving home and being with her friends. It wasn't very hard to convince her. She worked as a doffer. Many days we would visit her at work and watch as she controlled the spools of thread as they spun around a cylinder. I was proud of her continuously working the spools. It was obvious that she enjoyed what she was doing.

Friday was payday—our special day to meet Mom after work. That was always a special treat. Mom remembered how often I begged my friend Nina for a ride on her bike. (I thought of Nina as a rich kid. She seemed to have everything. She was even a champion swimmer at the Olneyville Boys Club.)

I suppose at the time I was envious of her but still, she was my best friend, school chum, and neighbor. I liked being with her, although I have one regret that has haunted me since that time.

After school Nina spent every day alone until her parents came home from work. One day in particular we were playing a game in her living room. As I walked by the kitchen, I noticed a nickel on the counter. On impulse, I took that nickel. I've been punished with guilt for that all my life. I have never been able to get it out of my mind. I tried to convince myself that I was young and that kids sometimes do stuff like that at that age.

Our friendship seemed to fade after that incident. I was consumed with guilt, so, out of shame I avoided her. I later thought, why would I be so stupid to lose my friend for a nickel?

The Western Union store, a block away, was our first stop that particular day. Lined up against the wall were several two-wheel bikes. I had no idea that Mom would ever buy me a bike, so you can imagine how shocked I was when she said, "Pick out the bike you would like to have." I was speechless. How very special she was. Of course I chose red, my favorite color. I was so happy. I couldn't wait to show my friends.

Mom walked home while I proudly rode my bike. That was one of my happiest days.

My sister Sue was a clothes freak. All she ever wanted were new clothes, so Mom always had her choose at her discretion since she was very particular, and preferred designer clothes. I never remember my other sister Arna asking for anything. She was content and easily pleased with whatever was offered to her.

But Sue was a fanatic. She had an expensive appetite—her clothes were special. She always left for work before me. One particular day, while getting ready for school, I admired her Angora sweater and decided to take a chance and wear it to school.

While waiting at the bus stop, I saw Sue! For whatever reason she had returned home. Of course she saw me wearing her sweater. I will never forget that day. She was so angry when she threatened me, I promised never to touch her clothes again. The admonition hit home: honesty is the best policy.

Mom was always ready to please us. She never refused us in any way. I think she chose to work just to satisfy our material desires.

Dad wasn't happy with her working. He complained about his business calls being neglected. However, Mom was happy and felt a sense of freedom. Being with her friends at the mill was the best thing that could have happened to her. But that pleasure was taken from her. Her working days were over. She was forced to leave her job, to devote her days to the old routine, cleaning and preparing meals for her family.

How very proud she was of her four children. She always praised us with kind words. I never remember her raising her voice or getting mad. She rarely sulked. Whenever my sisters and I became unhappy over frivolous things, she would praise us, lifting our spirits up with her famous words, "but I made you beautiful." Her thoughts were always based on our happiness.

Cold winter nights were spent sitting in front of our stove with our feet up on the oven sill for comfort. Each night Mom warmed the bricks from the oven, covering them with a towel and placing them between the bed sheets. What a treat it was snuggling into our warm beds.

God forbid we should get a chill or a fever. Out would come her famous remedy, *moliva*, an Italian concoction made from apples, honey, and a mixture of herbs boiled together in a pot. She would insist we drink it hot to capture its full effects. Miraculously, it did work. Whenever we suffered a headache, she would take a dish containing a small amount of water, then let droplets of oil drip into the water, one at a time, while praying. It was believed that should the oil separate, it was a sign that we were being cursed with the evil eye. It was an old Italian tradition that was handed down from generation to generation and taught specifically on Christmas Eve.

Superstitions were common among the Italians. They believed in night ladies who secretly brought evil into their homes. Mom believed it so strongly she placed scissors above all entrance doors to keep out the evil spirits.

1938 Hurricane

We didn't experience too many tragic events in those days; the most dreadful that remains with me was the 1938 hurricane.

I was twelve years old and it was truly frightening. I remember the dark sky, the wind howling at over 100 mph, our house shaking, and the electric wires, telephone poles, roofing shingles, and debris falling everywhere. The huge elm tree crashed down on our house and blocked our front entrance. I was shaking with fright; afraid we were all going to die. Dad tried his best to comfort us but he too showed concern.

The next day, the destruction we saw was horrifying. Water from the rising river flooded downtown, people were stranded in office buildings, cars were buried in water, and shut off all the streets. It particularly affected the oceanfront homes. Beaches were wiped clean of all shore property. All of New England was affected by the storm and many, many lives were lost. After the flood and the waters subsided, looting was uncontrollable.

In the days that followed, there was no communication, no electricity, and no gasoline for automobiles. Everything came to a standstill. Some of our drinking water was contaminated. It took weeks before they began restoring the devastated city of Providence.

We were a happy family. We had many special times together.

Singing was one of Mom's favorite pastimes. You could hear her humming as she went about her chores. She had a fine voice and loved all the old tunes. She harmonized and felt proud to accompany me in a duet. I seriously believe that her fine voice was carried down from generation to generation. We had many great voices in the family.

Dad decided to retire in April, 1940. He had an abundance of energy. He purchased some property in York, Maine, established a restaurant, and constructed a small cottage with just enough space to accommodate our needs.

He was a conservative man, kind, but far from extravagant. He always took short cuts in everything he did. The loft was our sleeping quarters. He and Mom used the only first floor bedroom.

Our summer days were spent enjoying the ocean while they ran the restaurant.

Mom was an excellent cook and a master in Italian cuisine, so she did all the cooking. She really enjoyed preparing special foods for her many customers. Her menu, strictly Italian, featured a variety of pasta dishes and Italian soups. Pasta and *fagioli* were favorites among her customers.

After closing hours, we would try to get her to walk the beach with us, but her excuse was always the same, "I'm too tired." We knew what she really wanted most was just to rest on the porch with Dad.

Those were days of excitement. Aunt Elsie and her family usually surprised us with sudden visits. Mom would quickly prepare her famous macaroni and meatballs to serve everyone, an easy dish to serve the gang.

Dad was an adventurer, just as ready to take risks with one mission after another. After many years, the restaurant became stressful and he decided to give it up. He placed a "For Rent" sign in the window, and rented it out to an antique dealer.

After their hard work, he thought a vacation was needed, so they drove to Florida by car. He preferred driving so he could see the scenery. As we expected, while in Florida he purchased land in Port St. Lucy and Tamiami Trail, with plans to again build a vacation home for our family.

When Mom gave us the good news, we were ecstatic and had visions of living near the ocean. But that never materialized because the State of Florida stepped in and Tamiami Trail became a two-lane highway.

Energetic and industrious, Dad was a master in screw machines. As time passed, his last job before retirement was manufacturing mechanical pens.

Arna and Sue both married but they always remained close to our family. Mom felt she had gained sons and never her lost daughters. I sometimes thought that Arna and Sue married to escape Dad's control. He made certain his daughters would grow up self-contained and well respected in spite of his philandering.

Sue was very daring and venturesome—curfew meant nothing to her. She pleased herself and ignored the demands Dad put upon her. I remember one school day when she was still a teenager when she came home from school with lipstick on her lips and blonde streaks in her hair. She evidently had forgotten to wipe the lipstick off, which she usually did before coming home. But there was no way she could hide the streaks. It was obvious. Dad saw the new look and got so angry he got scissors and tried to cut her hair off. Sue was so frightened she promised never to use peroxide on her hair again.

Arna, being the first born in our family, suffered the most control from Dad. Her one and only date, Alan, was one of our brother Pat's closest friends. Alan was clean-cut, tall, and good-looking. His excuse to chum with Pat was to see Arna. The attraction between them was obvious. Alan was aware of the strict rules and was careful not to cause any suspicion. Every visit he made was with caution.

Then he approached Dad and asked permission to court Arna.

It was just what Dad needed to hear. He immediately gave his approval, with one stipulation that, at all times, he must have full respect for her, and stating specifically that she was not allowed to go out with him alone.

With Dad's own reputation, trust was hard to come by. It was a strange relationship. Whenever Alan would come courting, they would sit across from each other in our parlor. Their privacy was limited since Dad was very observant, sometimes prancing back and forth across the kitchen and glancing occasionally in the parlor. Intimacy was impossible. They married after a short courtship and had two wonderful sons. As time passed, Dad became less and less controlling.

Pat was a fine musician, and again, being an only son in an Italian family, he was special. He received exceptional treatment from my parents, to the extent that whatever Pat said or did was accepted. He felt it was his duty to control and watch over us girls. Rather spoiled, he had to have the last word.

The four-piece band he formed spent three nights a week practicing at our house. Pat played his trumpet all the time, trying desperately to imitate Harry James's *The Flight of the Bumblebee*. He tried, but it was impossible to compete with the famous legend.

I was fifteen at the time and had a crush on Jay, who

played sax with the group. He had a special look. He was tall and extremely handsome. He came from a prominent family that owned one of the finest restaurants in Rhode Island.

I think he had a small feeling of admiration for me, at least I wanted to think so. Occasionally, while playing, he would look at me with a slight grin. Whether it was intentional or not, my ego would skyrocket. I could feel my face flush with excitement. I pretended to be interested in their performance but I really focused my eyes on him.

Pat was no fool and could read my mind. He figured I had a crush on Jay. He advised me to stay clear of his friends. I learned later that his friends were only interested in girls for sex and unworthy purposes.

Their practicing soon came to an end. Mom couldn't take the deafening noise. Our home wasn't very spacious and they required a much larger, soundproofed area.

World War II

On December 7, 1941, the scary news came over the radio: The Japanese had bombed Pearl Harbor.

Recruiting began almost immediately. All boys eighteen and older were compelled to register for the draft. I saw Mom hold her head with both hands and cry out "Oh my God" repeatedly. She was afraid of her only son being called into the service. She was resentful, knowing the danger he faced.

The Second World War had broken out. Pat, just nineteen, was inducted and sent to the Pacific. The Battle of Iwo Jima was one of the worst battles fought. Mom spent her days worrying and praying to God to watch over her son, to keep him safe. There was little correspondence but Mom never missed a day waiting for mail delivery. Dad had promised me Pat's car while he was away—why let it sit unused? I was so happy I was on cloud nine. I felt special driving at sixteen since children my age were riding bicycles. I hadn't realized at the time how expensive it would be to maintain. I couldn't afford it, but nothing was going to stop me.

During the winter months, whenever the temperature fell below freezing, I crawled under the car and drained the water from the radiator to prevent it from freezing. When it was necessary for me to use the car, I would replace the water and be on my way. I never let the snow or rain stop me from enjoying that pleasure. A container of water was always stored in my car in case it was needed. I

never let Dad know the struggle I was having with
the expenses for fear he would take the car away
from me.

I spent some of my time after school helping with his
business just to earn enough for the car expenses,
that was the most important part of my life at the
time. Nothing mattered more.

School was becoming a bore. I was so overwhelmed
with the excitement of my driving I dropped out
before finishing the twelfth grade. Of course I
realized later how dumb it was of me to put the
pleasure I got from my car before my education.

I wasn't happy working on a screw machine, but it
was what I had to do to earn enough money to meet
my expenses. Dad was disappointed with me for not
finishing school. He suggested I at least take a
course in business since he was in need of a
secretary, but I was in denial. I had learned some
bookkeeping in my studies before I left school.
Enough that Sue and I were able to handle the
records and routine office work quite well.

The winters in the 1940s were sometimes severe,
with snowfall often three or four feet high—with slick
roads. It didn't bother me at all. It didn't stop me
from driving in spite of the bad experiences I had. I
was fearless.

One night, while driving home from my friend's
house, I had a frightening incident I will never
forget. While crossing a wooden, ice-slick bridge I

had no control and began spinning, in fear of crashing through the wooden side rails and dropping into the water below. Miraculously, with my foot off the brake, my car came to a sudden stop. I'm sure God was watching over me.

Idra was my dear, devoted friend. I looked forward to spending the weekends with her, crossing that bridge to get to her house wasn't going to stop me. Her unusually kind and gracious family had an effect on me too. To be with them was very special. Her four brothers were very devoted and kind to each other, they had an earnest attachment to Idra. They also kept their eyes on my car's water situation!

Saturdays were special for us. We waited patiently for the boys to invite us to go out Saturday night with them. It was doubly exciting because we had to plan our night so carefully, her dad had a firm restriction where she was concerned, no late hours. A curfew didn't set very well with her either. Luckily, his nightly routine was always the same. He retired just after dark.

We always made sure the bedroom window was left unlocked before we went out, climbing back in and sleeping with our clothes on didn't matter. We had Saturday night fun.

Sundays at Idra's were a delight too. We had No dull moments, discussions, family conversations, and talks about everyday happenings. It was busy and exciting. Their mom, a dear sweet lady who spoke Italian, was always busy preparing dinner for the crowd.

Dinnertime was a treat. When everyone sat at the table ready for dinner, her mom placed a large wooden tray of polenta—had to be three feet square—in the middle of the table; everyone cut their portion and all ate directly from the tray. I was very impressed, they explained that it was a special custom from Italy. I looked forward to being with them every weekend. They treated me with so much kindness that I could not resist traveling twenty miles every weekend just to be there with them.

The war finally ended in 1945. After serving four years in Iwo Jima, Pat was on his way home. Mom, teary-eyed and grateful, was happy that her son was still alive. The pictures he brought home, taken during the battles, were gruesome—dead Japs scattered about, some with missing limbs, faces, etc. It was a horrifying sight. It almost made me sick.

Mom couldn't imagine what he had been through after she saw those photos. Pat picked one out of the group and said, "Look, Mom, how special is this?"

She was confused and asked, "What does it mean?"

He answered proudly, "After we captured the Island, we raised the United States flag on Mt. Suribachi as a symbol of our victory."

She didn't quite understand but she took his face in her hands and kissed it, full of so much pride. So thankful and fortunate to have their son back, they welcomed him with a homecoming party. Everyone was invited.

Families were finally being reunited with their military sons and daughters. The celebrations seemed endless.

Pat showed a slightly different attitude when he returned. He was somewhat bitter and overly nervous. He was sensitive in conversation. There were times he would get angry over minor things; sometimes he misconstrued everything that was said. Mom warned us to be very pleasant and understanding because "he's been through hell."

In 1946, our family was invited to a celebration dedicated to the end of World War II. I had a fine singing voice at that time. A lad named Mickey, who played the accordion and lived in our town, founded and directed a six-piece orchestra that was very popular there. Any functions planned among the Italians were sure to include Mickey's orchestra. I was somewhat shy but was always called upon to sing.

My first performance singing on stage was at my school play when I was thirteen. I remember how special I felt when Ms. Padien asked me to sing a solo of "Down in the Valley." I loved country music and had a passion for yodeling. Many times during the summer I would walk around the house yodeling, unaware that my voice escaped through the open windows. The result was that the neighbors often teased me about my singing.

Mickey saw me sitting with my family and insisted I come up on stage and sing a tune. I was nervous but I accepted. I wanted to leave after finishing my song but Mickey coaxed me into doing another. As I stepped down from the stage, I saw that I was being stared at by a young man. His eyes followed me to my seat. I felt uncomfortable during the dinner too because each time I looked up, he still stared.

After the event, as we were leaving, I noticed him following us and waving a gesture for me to come ahead. I ignored him but I felt flattered. Dad, always very protective, made sure I did not leave his side.

The next day I got a call from Fran, our neighbor and dear friend. She asked me to come visit. She had something to tell me. I didn't hesitate because her voice sounded like it was urgent. I walked over to her house, not very far away, wondering why the sudden call.

Fran gave me a hug before I could ask what was up, and to my surprise, there he was sitting at the table, that admirer who had followed me after the event. I was startled. Fran introduced Norata, her nephew.

Fran purposely arranged the meeting for him. I was impressed with his good looks—he was a dead ringer to John Garfield, the handsome movie actor. I was shy. We conversed briefly. Without hesitation, he asked to date me. I never cared to date Italian men because they had a reputation of being very possessive. But, because Fran was a special family friend, I felt an obligation. Plus, I was overwhelmed by his good looks.

I fell into a trap. We were immediately attracted to each other. Norata had recently been discharged from the army and he was ready to enjoy some of his homecoming.

We began dating soon afterward, and quite extravagantly. I had the feeling he was determined to win me over with his lavish spending. He showered me with fun and exciting times—museums, plays, live shows in Boston, ferry rides to Block Island, fine dining—it was a new beginning of pleasure for me. I was on cloud nine. I had never experienced this kind of luxurious freedom. I was an overwhelmed, naive nineteen-year-old with little experience in dating. Most of the boys at that time were in service. My few dates before meant meeting at the movies or the park.

Our town was overrun with sailors from the Quonset Naval Air Base. Most of the girls my age had been foolishly inspired by their uniform. I wasn't attracted to them at all.

Although I was infatuated and enjoying the good life with Norata, I was turned off by his drinking. I made no mention of it to him, but it did irritate me. He never stopped with one drink. He would almost always have two or more. I related it to his having been in the service.

His company had provided equipment and firearms

to the soldiers on the front lines. He was not in actual combat, which gave him more opportunity to drink. As time passed, his habit became less and less consuming.

Money seemed to be no object for him. Every date was planned for new excitement. I had never had the pleasure of traveling to see special attractions, but he kept aware of all the coming events. I was having a great time, almost looking forward to every date.

I was beginning to have feelings for him. He too was showing concern, and he certainly was determined to please me.

After a few months of dating, he had a sudden transformation from being a gentle, loving guy to having bitter, angry outbursts. I suddenly realized that the Italian personality was being revealed. He was becoming judgmental. In conversation, he had to have the last word. He had to control every discussion; in his eyes, he was never wrong.

I sensed a streak of jealousy. He would sometimes make an insulting remark if I made some nice comment about one of the male actors or if I suddenly made some kind gesture in company. It seemed that he envied all men in my presence. I was losing confidence in myself and creating a low self-esteem. His jealously was overbearing. I continued to date him, despite his strange mental attitude, but every date was becoming less and less exciting.

I realized then that I had made a mistake. It was exactly what I had promised myself I would never do, I had involved myself with an Italian. I felt a moral obligation to leave this relationship but I somehow couldn't end the luxurious pleasure of fun I was enjoying.

I remember one Sunday afternoon, while we were waiting in line at the theatre, my neighbor John noticed me, came over, and greeted me warmly with a peck on my cheek.

Norata became furious. "How dare you make a fool of me?" He blamed me for the incident. I took offense at his remark, thinking that he is too insecure if he mistakenly interprets a friendly act as aggressive or amorous. Where am I heading? There was no way I could continue with this relationship.

I thought at the time, he's just overcome with jealousy. His words came from his mouth, not from his heart. I wanted to overlook his behavior, thinking that he's just demanding complete devotion from me.

In truth, he had two personalities. He would often remind me that I was his and he would never let me go. Explanations never came easy for him. I was confused, not knowing what I should do. He was wrong-headed. We discussed this behavior many times but with little resolution. He never felt his actions to be out of order.

I had second thoughts. A part of me said leave, walk away, don't look back. But my own insecurity and the extravagant pleasure I was experiencing kept me there, indebted to him. As time passed, I had a change of thought: I can't continue with this false feeling, that, it is what it is. Accept him as he is or leave him without concern.

Norata was suspicious. He was aware of my intentions to leave him. Suddenly, just after dark on the night of October 12, 1946, he drove around as if looking for someplace to park. I asked him "What's going on? What are you looking for?"

He didn't answer. He was quiet and acting rather strange. The smell of liquor on his breath convinced me he had been drinking. I was scared that something was about to happen. He never acted this way before. He was not a violent person in spite of his Jekyll and Hyde personality.

I was frightened. He finally drove to a remote area and stopped the car. Without saying a word, he started unzipping his pants. I said frantically, "What are you doing?" I fumbled for the door, trying to get out. My heart was pounding. It made me sick that he was determined to overpower and rape me. I was helpless to resist him. I begged "No, no!" I kept fighting and trying to pull away until he did overpower me. I gave up. He was no match for me.

It was over very quickly. All he could say was "I'm sorry, I'm really sorry, but if I can't have you, no one else will."

In a state of panic, threatening to reveal this nightmare, I screamed for him to take me home immediately. I was furious. I yelled, "Get out of my life! I never want to see you again. Don't you ever call me."

But, in my heart I knew I was doomed. This man had taken my virginity. He will have to be the only man in my life. He kept silent the entire ride home. I couldn't stop shaking. All I could think was, 'How am I going to survive this nightmare?' He knew I was innocent, naive, and ignorant about sex. I was angry, in pain, hurt, embarrassed, and full of a sense of worthlessness.

I never slept that night, shamed and wondering what I should do, how could I possibly explain this appalling experience to my parents? I believed when I was growing up that a one-time sexual encounter would result in a pregnancy. My fears mounted. I was too young to be a mother.

Our parents never told us about the facts of life. We knew almost nothing. To talk about such things was wrong. We were taught that sex was shameful, dirty, and vulgar.

It was instilled in me that sex was for a man's pleasure—and only after marriage. How am I going to live with myself? Who will want me? I kept thinking. I was doomed. Virginity was very important to men in those days. Unless you were a virgin, you were rejected. We were brought up with respect. We were afraid to be labeled cheap or to be called a tramp. That guided our sexuality.

I tossed and turned in bed thinking about what had just happened. If I have conceived, how am I going to care for a baby at my age? What am I going to do? I felt a physical sickness that was indescribable. How will I tell anyone what had happened? How angry I was, and how much it hurt.

As I tried to get a grip on my fears, I remembered the startling experience that Aunt Carry had been through.

Aunt Carry was Norata's aunt. She was a highly intelligent woman who was confined to a wheelchair because of her elephantiasis. Her legs were enormous, with rows and rows of hanging fat that restricted her ability to walk. She had contracted the disease after marriage.

Aunt Carry was my trusted friend. She was always there to fill me in on Norata and his family's traits. She was extremely strict, with no tolerance for disobedience. Many times, while caring for Norata as a young boy, she confessed that whenever he got out of hand she would prick him with a needle for punishment. She felt he needed discipline because being an only boy among three sisters, he was badly spoiled by his parents and he needed to be corrected. I thought that was cruel and abusive, in spite of her intelligence. I often wondered if her strict discipline had an effect on him and his low opinion of women.

We had many interesting conversations. One in particular that is firmly rooted in my mind: her honeymoon scare. Her first night as a married woman was frightful. While preparing herself for bed, she saw Uncle Jack place a gun under his pillow. At first, she thought perhaps he was keeping it there for protection. So she asked him, "What are you doing with a gun? Why are you putting it under your pillow?"

He answered, "If you're not a virgin, I will kill you."

She answered right back, "I'm not worried. I am a virgin."

At 8:30 the next morning, I heard Mom shuffling around in the kitchen. I lay in bed sick and confused after the sleepless night. Then I heard voices. Mom came into my room and asked me to get up. She said, "Norata and his mom are here."

His mom? Why had she come? My legs wouldn't move. How could I possibly face her? They've come to apologize. How embarrassing. My mom is unaware of the incident and now I'm being exposed.

It took all the strength I had to get myself out of bed. Oh how I dreaded facing them. I was almost sick with shame.

I just stood there when I met them. Norata looked haggard and drained. His only words were "I'm sorry." As he said that I was certain Mom knew what had happened. Luckily, both moms were in my bedroom making my bed. I could hear them conversing very faintly.

I am sure Mrs. C. (as she was called) was apologizing for her son's behavior. I feared the reaction from his mom. How could I face her? What was I to do?

I looked at Norata with a feeling of contempt. I asked, "What are you doing? Have you no shame? Why have you brought your mom here?"

He seemed dumbfounded, like he was in a trance, not knowing how to respond. His only answer was, again, "I'm sorry."

I was humiliated, disgraced, and speechless. We both looked at each other not knowing what more to say when I suddenly felt relieved. Mrs. C. came out of the bedroom, looked at me (trying to ease my embarrassment), and smiled. With that, Mom offered to make some coffee. Mrs. C. refused, explaining that she had to report for work. (She also worked at the Olneyville Mill.)

After their short visit, the tension eased. Little more was said before the two left. Mom made no mention of the visit. I thought, she too, was embarrassed.

I remember my first menstrual period. I was thirteen years old. It was at school, and what was happening to me was frightening. With no explanation I was sent home. I ran most of the way, petrified. Mom seemed uncomfortable but she described in a few words what girls go through every month. I often wondered why she would rip up old sheets and pack them lightly in a drawer. I guess at the time there were no such thing as Kotex. My sisters never explained the menstrual cycle to me either. They too felt too embarrassed to talk about it.

Norata visited every day asking for forgiveness. I was still in shock. "It will take time," I said, "for me to trust you."

I was haunted by the fear that I would become pregnant. Norata obviously confided in his older sister. He said, "Please, let me take you to see Verna. She will know what to do." Verna was very intelligent, a district nurse, and Norata's confidant.

I was somewhat embarrassed confronting her, but she was my only salvation. Who else could I turn to?

Verna was very understanding. She asked no questions. She didn't have to. I'm certain she was aware of what happened. She gave me two tiny pills to swallow and a glass of water, and assured me that everything would be all right. I felt at ease and thanked her. At least I felt I had someone to confide in if I had to.

Early Saturday morning the following week Norata called and said, "I'm on my way. Be ready." He hung up real fast before I could ask him why he was coming. I wondered what could be so urgent? In less than twenty minutes, he was at my front door.

Imagine my wonder when I saw Mrs. C. sitting in the back seat of his car.

I didn't know what I should say. She was a nice person but a little withdrawn. I had the feeling that she was embarrassed at not being able to speak English very well. She had come to America at eighteen and had little schooling.

I greeted her warmly, "Hi, how are you, Mrs. C.?"

She gave me a warm smile and replied, "I'm good." I was confused at why he had his mother with him.

I asked, "Where are we going?"

Norata said, "It's a surprise." He seemed excited.

We stopped at a jeweler not far from town. It was so unexpected I started to tremble. I was full of uncertainty. The diamond she picked out was a beautiful three-quarter caret solitaire. I was dumbfounded and shocked. I didn't know what to say.

After paying cash for it, I heard Mrs. C. ask the clerk for assurance that the stone was clear. What came to mind was that with only a few months into our relationship, this ring would be my commitment Was I really ready for this?

Norata proudly took the ring, turned to me, and put it on my finger. He smiled and whispered in my ear, "Now you will never leave me."

I was overwhelmed with excitement looking at this beautiful diamond on my finger. At that moment all feelings of uncertainty disappeared.

We continued to date but inside I still had a feeling of resistance. He continued to control me, even about what I should wear. Red was one of my favorite colors. One day I wore a red skirt. At the sight of it he fumed, "Why are you wearing red?"

I said back, "Why would you ask me such a stupid question? This is my favorite skirt."

He replied, "Don't ever wear it again. Don't you know that red is a come-on color with whores? Just don't wear it." In some ways he was ignorant and old fashioned. But I never wore red again.

We dated almost nightly. Norata was getting anxious. He was trying to convince me that I had to consider his sexual desires. I was embarrassed and afraid of getting pregnant. I simply refused to talk about it.

I suppose he realized there was no way that I could be convinced where sex was concerned. Then he began making excuses as to why on some nights he couldn't see me. I became suspicious, remembering some of the wild stories he had boasted about with his friends in his younger days.

Once he told me stories about his longtime friend Lisa, from Olneyville. He mentioned that, in spite of her being a lesbian, she was in love with him and would do anything for him. I wondered if that was true. I hadn't heard from him at all that day. Something wasn't right; he never let a day go by without calling. I was ready for bed when I wondered if he could be with Lisa. That made sense, and if he was I wanted to prove a point.

I got dressed and drove to Olneyville, though I wasn't sure which apartment she was living in. Did it matter? There was Norata's car parked in front of the complex. It was a warm summer night and when I looked up there was an open window. What was I to think? I was as mad as hell. I started honking my horn thinking that he'll have to see me. How could he not notice my car with so much noise? There was no response.

When he came to make amends the next day I was not about to hear any excuses. I said, "I want to return your ring. We're done." He hesitated, then said nothing as I handed the ring back to him. He casually walked away.

I was surprised when he didn't try to make excuses. He knew there was no mistaking his cheating.

I didn't hear anything for four days. I began to wonder? doesn't he care? Is it really over for him? Or is he testing me? But I also thought, why am I so naïve and proud? Why am I unable to accept the fact that he's a man with sexual desires? My self-esteem was tearing me in half. How was I going to change? I was so innocent growing up. I knew so little.

The separation however did not last. He finally called and asked if I wanted to talk. I thought his rejection was definite, that he'd probably given up on me. So my shock was complete when his first words when he saw me were, "Here, put this on" as he handed me my ring. There was no mention of the previous, deceitful days.

Inside, I was so excited at having my ring back. We spent that night talking about marriage and our future

Every girl dreams of having a beautiful wedding. I wasn't sure if I was ready for marriage then, but in the excitement of making plans for that special day I did just that, I dreamt about the wedding.

Shopping for my gown and making the arrangements was exciting. I was still uncertain, wondering if I was making the right decision. I wasn't sure if I was in love or it was just infatuation. Whichever it was, I was trapped. There was no turning back, so I kept on with planning.

Mom had a two-dollar subscription shower for me at the Richmond Hotel. Our wedding took place one month later at the Knights of Columbus Hall, on November 1, 1947. There were 150 friends and family attending. The day went smoothly, but I was not a happy bride.

I still had that same sense of uncertainty. Was I doing the right thing? Then I answered myself: it's done, there's no turning back.

The photographer constantly reminded me to smile. At one point, he commented that this was supposed to be a special day. My finished pictures showed an unhappy bride.

Most marriages in those days were approved by the parents. Dad was impressed with Norata's extravagance and new car. He gave his approval, thinking Norata was financially set. In truth, he was using his mustering out pay for fun and excitement.

Dad always felt that money would bring you happiness. I found out later that money only pacifies.

Our plans for marriage were so sudden that we hadn't prepared for living quarters. I was hoping Dad would offer to let us use one of his apartments, but I know how he thinks: offering us an apartment would mean that the rents would not be secure each month. Anyway, Dad's rental property was completely occupied, plus Norata was very proud and he thought asking for one of Dad's apartments would be degrading.

Mrs. C. was kind enough to offer us the extra bedroom in her home—temporarily. We took her offer even though it restricted our freedom.

The only furniture we had purchased was an elegant bedroom set we had specially made by the famous Turilli. The hand-carved four-poster bed with the canopy top, double dresser, and two-piece highboy was my prized possession.

Italians believed in money offerings at all weddings. Before we left on our honeymoon, we opened our envelopes, took what we thought was needed, and left the balance for the bedroom furniture delivery. There wasn't much money left for our use so we traveled by car to New York and Washington. It was my first time traveling away from home.

Norata knew how to make a trip worth taking. He studied the map and picked out all the special attractions. The days were filled with fun activities. The most memorable were the White House tour, visiting the U.S. Treasury, and seeing the Washington Monument. At that time there were no restrictions on touring all the government buildings.

I remember the lovely red plush carpeting throughout the White House. I felt the excitement standing under the huge dome with the guide explaining how it was possible for one person standing at one end to hear conversations clearly from the opposite side. It was an unexplainable mystery.

The tour at the U.S. Treasury, open to the public to view, was impressive. Who could forget watching the flow of money being printed before their eyes?

Our Marriage Beginning

After a week of fun, we returned home to begin our married life together. Mrs. C. tried her best to make us comfortable. She had us occupy the first floor bedroom with the adjoining living room and kitchen. It was like we had our own apartment. Her home had a second floor with two extra bedrooms and a small kitchen. She tried to give us as much privacy as we needed by spending most of her time upstairs.

I said to Norata that occupying his parent's house wasn't fair. We had to find another place to live. Norata asked, "Aren't you comfortable living here?"

I told him, "Not really, your mom and dad are being confined in their own home. That just isn't right." I felt a sense of guilt, that we were imposing, but Norata didn't have the same feeling.

After living with his folks for almost three months, we decided that it was time for us to start out on our own. My mom wasn't happy about our plans to look for a new place to live. She felt guilty knowing we could have one of their rentals. She asked, "Why should they have to rent from a stranger when we could very easily provide them with a stable place to live?" She let Dad make all the decisions in their lifetime but there were times when her spoken word had impact.

We finally got the break we needed. We moved into one of Dad's apartments, rent-free. Norata promised Dad that if he renovated and corrected all the needed repairs to the property, it would be to both our advantage, and would compensate for the rent. Dad agreed, but not wholeheartedly. He later said, "I didn't expect the rent anyway."

Living rent-free gave us a financial head start in our marriage. Norata was a hard worker, a good provider, and a jack-of-all-trades who was not afraid to take on any task or challenge.

Dad was in the mechanical pen business. Since Norata was part of our family it would be fair to introduce him to the business. Dad offered him a job working the screw machines.

Proud and with high expectations, Norata gave it a try for three weeks, then he decided to go out on his own. He couldn't accept taking orders from his father-in-law. He preferred to work for himself. He did odd jobs, mostly in carpentry.

The start of our marriage was built on a shaky foundation. I was still unsure, but as I said, there was no turning back.

As time passed Norata continued to show his controlling and dominating ways. He had sudden outbursts of resentment, sometimes without a cause. What bothered me most was his attitude in company. He loved to tell stories of his past experiences. It seemed that he had to control every conversation. Any contradictions while he was talking would irritate him, causing him to be intolerable, and make rude outbursts.

I felt embarrassed. I was tense when we had company. I had to pick with whom we could socialize. It was usually family since they understood him and were aware of his negative attitude. Strangely, though, people did like him. He had another side to his personality and others found him interesting.

I wanted our marriage to work so I convinced myself that we needed time to adjust to our dissimilar ways. We were both young and needed to accept each other as we were.

Norata was an only boy growing up with three sisters. He was born with bowed legs which made him wear leg braces most of his childhood. Because of his affliction, it was said that he was favored by his parents. The three girls resented his special treatment. His sister Verna's stories about growing up with a spoiled Norata were very amusing. She said that whenever he was awarded candy or goodies, she was so envious that she would push him backward to the floor, leaving him helpless and immobile. We laughed at stories of the resentment as told by his siblings.

As time passed, tension grew. We had an off-and-on-again marriage. I couldn't accept his controlling. Getting along with him meant giving in to his every command. It wasn't until I realized how naive I was giving in to his possessive behavior that I changed my attitude. I insisted on a change. I simply refused to give in to his demands. It was a difficult battle because we argued constantly. It just didn't work.

In those days, we were taught to marry for better or worse. Our parents stressed upon us that when we made our bed, we must lie in it. Those words kept us tied to our vows. Divorce was a no-no.
After some counseling, and in spite of our many confrontations, we worked it out. But it would only last for a few short months. There was no way he was going to change. I thought seriously that either I leave him or I must learn to live with him, because as long as I give in, our married life would be stable. I understood how much his parents had spoiled him when he was growing up. I had to make a decision. Did I want to live with his domineering or leave him altogether? I was convinced that trying to change his disposition was never going to happen. So I learned to live with it.

I was ambitious and felt a need to work to help with our finances. I also needed to feel independent.

Aunt Lara, a lovely lady and businesswoman, encouraged and helped me establish a cleaning business. I had some knowledge about sewing, which helped me to specialize in alterations. Aunt Lara's business consisted of linens, bedding, and accessories. The store she rented had two sections, side by side. Fortunately, the second half was vacant, so she convinced me to take that half.

Norata helped me set it up and make it presentable. Aunt Lara was always there to brief me about managing my daily routine. Each day, after closing hours, I would gather all the clothes brought in to be cleaned and take them to the cleaning factory nearby. There wasn't much responsibility running my business since all I had to do was tag and transport clothes to and from the factory. Still, I looked forward each day to spending my time at the store. I was happy greeting and conversing with the customers. Some of them even disclosed their financial and marital problems.

Aunt Lara, besides having a great personality, was very well liked. She had a fine clientele. It was exciting watching people come and go. We never had time to be bored.

Two years later, I became pregnant, and as the time for delivery came I had no choice but to close the shop.

Robert was a beautiful, nine-pound, husky boy, but I noticed when he was brought to me after birth that he looked rather strange. His complexion was blotchy and blue. I was afraid something was wrong with him.

When the doctor arrived, he explained that Robert needed a complete blood transfer. My blood type was Rh negative and Norata's, B positive, and, with that combination there was no way Robert could possibly survive. He needed to have a complete blood change.

The procedure was done twice, but his tiny body could not take the trauma. After seven days he passed away.

How can I describe the pain I was feeling? Nine months of eagerly waiting for my precious baby, then the frustration of only getting to hold him so briefly.

Norata took advantage of my stay in the hospital. It gave him free time to stray. Doctor Romano was furious at his not returning calls made to him about little Robert's condition. He almost shouted, "What kind of man did you marry? This child is fighting for his life."

I was too embarrassed and humiliated to reply sanely. I was simply wordless. I never thought Norata could be so uncaring. I'd never seen (or recognized) that side of him.

I was fully aware of his fear of needles, whether it was the punishment he received from Aunt Carry when he was a kid or from the experience he had while in service. I remember him telling me about the traumatic experience in service. He said that all servicemen had to line up for their tetanus shot, but he was a coward and was afraid of needles. After getting the shot, he walked away so fast that he noticed blood dripping down his arm with the needle still sticking in! Since that, the thought of being pricked with a needle now made him cringe.

I wasn't convinced that was why he avoided the hospital. There was no excuse for his disgusting behavior. He needed to be there for his son.

His only excuse was "I was too drunk." A cowardly excuse for not taking part in Robert's desperate transfusions. I figured out that he took the opportunity to party with Evelyn, a neighbor who tried her best to lure him into a relationship.

She was married to Norata's friend, but somehow that made no difference to her. Though I was aware of the attraction she had for my husband, I looked the other way since he had never given me cause to distrust him. Evidently I was wrong. Putting his pleasure before me and the child we created was what he needed most. I was devastated.

I left the hospital, sad and mentally distressed. My resentment lingered. I was much more concerned at losing my beautiful baby than caring about his foolish behavior. Norata was consumed with guilt. He tried to be nice, hoping for forgiveness, but it didn't work. My pain turned into hatred for him.

Since he was a self-made carpenter working for himself, he accepted any work available. He took Evelyn's calls willingly. I held him responsible for his actions. He simply took advantage of my hospital stay to enjoy his freedom. But I was so depressed, so hurt at having to leave the hospital without my baby, that I put his actions aside.

Even worse, I had to leave Robert without knowing where he was at. Dr. Romano explained that babies born at the hospital who had not survived were sent to a special burial ground for infants. He gave no specifics. I wanted to know where he was buried. I still do.

I had been disgraced. Having to sleep in the same bed with Norata made me cringe. I was determined to hurt him, to make him realize how deceitful he was. I lost all feelings for the man I had married. I told him to leave, that our marriage was over. He was in denial; he refused to move out.

I was serious so I spent the next few days packing his clothes while he was out working. I took advantage of him being gone and I called a cab. I loaded the back seat with his belongings and told the cab driver to take them to his mom's address. He called and offered excuses, but they had no effect. My hurt wouldn't go away.

Mrs. C. had never interfered in our marriage—until I refused to take her son back. After a few days she surprised me with a visit. I greeted her respectfully and never mentioned our separation. She handed me an envelope and said that Norata wanted me to have it. I suppose the $300 enclosed was a bribe. With that she turned, ready to leave, and said, "You know what you have. But you don't know what you are going to get." I assumed that she thought her son was a gem and I was a fool to let him go. I was at a loss.

Norata kept in touch, asking for forgiveness. After almost two months I realized that I had commitments and I needed him for support. So despite his denial and the hurt I was suffering, I allowed him to come home. The relationship was cold. I was full of resentment. It was like two people living together as strangers.

It is said that "time heals all wounds," but Robert still lives on in my thoughts and prayers. I was so full of sorrow for the baby I had lost that Norata's excuses and lies had no meaning. It was almost like he didn't matter. I'd lost faith in him and I never let him forget it.

The weeks passed and our living conditions didn't change; the resentment lingered. It created a cold feeling between us. Norata tried to make amends but it meant nothing. I could not forgive him the humiliation was too great.

He sensed my depression and I assumed he thought he could please me with a sudden change. He suggested we use some of the proceeds from the business to take a trip to Canada. I thought that it might ease some of my bitterness. I went along with his plans only to relieve myself of the anguish I was suffering.

In Montreal we made a special visit to St. Joseph's Oratory where I made a novena to Father Pio, a very special deceased priest who was known to answer all prayers. I lit a candle and prayed for Father to watch over our little angel.

My Business Venture

I thought about the pleasure I got from the cleaning business and began searching for new adventure. That's when the china business came to mind.

I needed to start somewhere. Norata thought that if anyone could help, it would be Dad's salesman Leo, from New York. Leo was a wonderful man, rather short and pudgy, and with a Jewish accent. He was always ready to please.

Leo was very devoted to Dad and especially fond of Mom, who would invite him to dinner whenever he was in town. Italian food was a special treat for him so he always looked forward to her invitation.

Dad was never extravagant. He never thought of spending money on a gift for Mom. Leo changed all that. He was determined to make Dad do a special deed for his wife.

At one of his visits, he gave Dad a very expensive gift—plus the bill! Dad was shocked. He was shamed into paying for something he never would have agreed to. Leo couldn't have cared less. He was determined to make Dad realize the wonderful woman to whom he was married.

When Dad saw the bill, he nearly flipped. It was a whopper. Leo wasn't going to let him be a cheapskate. He had chosen the very best.

Mom was thrilled when she opened the package and

saw an eighteen-caret gold bracelet with a diamond-covered watch enclosed. It was so special Mom was afraid to wear it. Only occasionally would she take it out from her prized possessions.

I approached Leo and explained how much I wanted to establish a china and gift business. He thought it was a great idea and eager to help. At one time I had worked for a company in Taunton, Massachusetts, demonstrating their goods at house parties. It gave me the exposure and experience I needed.

Leo made all the necessary arrangements, and Norata and I made the trip to New York. Leo was waiting for us at his office. I was eager to get on with business, but he insisted we have lunch at his favorite restaurant before we made our runs. We hailed a taxi that took us to a very exclusive restaurant overlooking Times Square.

The menu was totally Japanese and very gourmet. We weren't familiar with Japanese food so we asked him to order for us. Leo ordered the complete meal, including persimmons for appetizers, sukiyaki for the main course, and a very lovely dessert that I didn't recognize. Leo spoke Japanese fluently and ordered a very special Japanese wine. It was a wonderful experience.

After lunch we went to the wholesale district in town. Leo knew exactly which wholesalers would fit our needs. At each establishment we visited, we were introduced to the executives. We were totally impressed with how well Leo knew his associates.

We made the necessary notes that were important for later use. Leo also prepared a letter of introduction that made it possible to order merchandise from other companies as well.

It was a tiring day but we left New York full of confidence.

Since our customers were mostly interested in silver and fine china, most of our orders were from International Silver. The Royal Doulton line was one of our specialties. Our business became a big success, selling at house parties on a weekly payment plan. Norata and I would take turns making deliveries and collections.

Leo kept in touch with our progress and also kept us informed about new adventures. We were indebted to our dear friend Leo, who later passed away at the young age of sixty-five.

Two years later we were again blessed with a son, an eight-pound six-ounce bundle of love. My first sight of him was like seeing Robert come to life. He had the same exact look, a chunky full body and handsome round face. Norata was excited at having a son. He was so different in attitude since little Robert was born. He insisted we name him Junior.

In his young days Norata was called Nathan. I wondered how Norata came from Nathan. It was interesting that all three of his cousins who lived in

Poughkeepsie, New York, were also named Nathan.

It seems that their grandfather made a promise to his three sons that should their first born be given his name, Norata, they would inherit all his possessions and wealth. Unfortunately, their grandpa lived until he was ninety-eight, and had very few possessions. The boys all grew up with a name they detested so they labeled themselves Nathan.

I refused to embarrass my son with the name Norata. He would be   ashamed being called that, so Junior was out of the question. I named him Ned.

Norata was full of pride with his precious son. He believed strongly that a son born to an Italian family was a great honor. He promised that Ned would have all the luxuries he had been deprived of in his childhood. He followed through on that belief; Ned was the king. He was never deprived. In fact, he got anything his heart desired.

I often wondered why Robert wasn't acknowledged the same as Ned. Could the name have that much effect? Or was the advantage of freedom too tempting at his young age? I'll never know.

Although Norata showered his son with luxuries growing up, he wasn't spoiled. Ned was very respectful and always ready to help, in spite of the special attention he received from us.

I tried to devote as much time as I could to him in spite of my work schedule, but I had to make sacrifices. Mom was always ready to look after him whenever it became necessary.

At four years old I noticed Ned playing with an imaginary friend. I felt that he needed to mix more with other children, so I enrolled him in a convent. He seemed happy being with other children, but he preferred being home.

The nuns were very pleasant. They devoted all their attention to the children, especially teaching them religion and prayer.

Each day, after work, I would pick him up. At the sight of me, he would stop what he was doing and come running. He always had a smile on his face. He was happy to come home.

Norata pampered his son. He relished spending as much time as he could with him. One day, after work, he came home proudly with a go cart. Ned was so excited he couldn't wait to take his first ride. I wasn't very happy because he was just six years old, too young to be on it. Sometimes his dad took chances, believing his son was capable of almost anything. I tried to convince him that Ned was just a little boy who needed to be treated like a child, but my words meant nothing.

Trips to the store were Ned's special treat. He could choose whatever he wanted. His special interests were tools, all kinds. He wanted to be like his dad. For every interest Norata insisted that his son was to have the real thing, no substitutes. He picked out a complete set of saws, planers, hammers, and whatever else one needed for building. He would beam with pleasure, watching the excitement on his son's face when his boy used the tools properly.

One Saturday, after making a delivery, I came home to a shocker. There was Ned on the kitchen floor surrounded by his tools. With a saw in his hands, he was busily sawing through my ladder-back chair leg. Norata sat nearby watching proudly and smiling. I was startled.

After scolding Ned, Norata's reaction was "Oh, leave him alone, he's just playing." I couldn't win. I had no control, I was being ignored. I walked out, disgusted.

Every night Norata looked forward to coming home to be with his son. He was so proud of his "buddy," as he called him.

Six years later I became pregnant again. My working days were threatened. The business was at its peak so the thought of having to give it up was a great disappointment. I held out, hoping I could work it through.

Nine months later, in February of 1955, our princess was born. Although Norata loved his daughter, he still favored his son, the apple of his eye.

My mom was thrilled when her wish was fulfilled. She longed for a granddaughter. She had three grandsons, and our promise to her was that the first girl born would be named Rebecca. She had seen the movie *Rebecca from Sunnybrook Farm* and was enchanted by the name. Norni, as my mom was called, was ecstatic.

Growing up, the rest of us called her Becca, but Mom insisted on calling her Rebecca. Mom looked forward to having Becca spend days with her. She wanted to care for her while I worked, and since my business was growing, having Mom to depend on was a godsend.

Becca was spry, full of vim and vigor, a real spitfire. She loved her brother, looked up to him, mimicking and following his every move. Ned was proud of his sister too, and gave her special attention. I was happy with their relationship, I admired their bond. There was never any sign of jealousy between them.

Since we lived rent-free, our money accumulated. We thought it was time to move on to a better location because our neighborhood was starting to go downhill.

Norata found a piece of land in a private setting adjacent to Neauticonicut Park and planned to build on it. The plan we chose was simple—three bedrooms, a living and dining room, and one-and-a-half baths. He subcontracted and did most of the work himself. I was impressed with the picture window that overlooked the beautiful park grounds. I was anxious to move in.

Norata explained that moving in would be a struggle since our savings were invested in the house. He thought it would be best to put it up for sale and make a profit.

After a month of advertising, the house was sold. The buyer had their home up for sale, so Norata wisely saw the opportunity to make an exchange and more profit.

"Their house, a three-family with seven rooms on each floor, a great investment," he told me. I was disappointed, but he promised to remodel the complete first floor to my liking. He assured me that living rent-free, with two extra rents coming in, would leave us comfortably secure. I agreed. I usually let him make all the decisions since he always seemed to make the right choices. We spent our nights remodeling and decorating.

Moving in was exciting, but then I realized that our front door exited out to the porch and on to the sidewalk. Most houses were built close together at that time, with walking space between them. The neighborhood children usually played in the street. I was always in fear and prayed for their safety.

I wondered if we had made the wrong decision. My fear became a reality. Ned, just seven years old, had spent the day with Norni and Poppy. It was early evening when Poppy drove him home.

Anxious to be home, he excitedly opened the car door before Poppy had come to a full stop. He rushed across the street without looking, and ran in front of a slow moving car. I panicked when I saw

71

the crowd gathering in the street.

Imagine my relief when I saw Ned standing with my dad, who was consoling him. I assumed he wasn't badly hurt. Clearly he was shaken up and extremely frightened. Norata, however, was so agitated that he refused to wait for the ambulance. He immediately put his son in our car and drove him to the nearby hospital. We weren't aware at the time that Ned had lost his two front teeth. I was sick at the thought of his losing his permanent teeth. How was he going to live the rest of his life with a front plate?

In spite of that set-back, I felt some relief that he wasn't severely hurt. Our dentist, Dr. Payne, explained that a fixed plate would do no good to a growing child. So he was fitted with a temporary and had to wait out the time until his mouth was ready for fixed dentures.

Norata was distraught that his son was afflicted. He vowed to please him even more in every way. Ned never complained. He was just too young to realize his loss. The father-and-son bond became even more intense after that tragic misfortune.

We enrolled Ned and Becca in the Assumption, a parochial school not far from our home. I proudly watched from my window every morning as the two of them walked down the street until they were out of sight. School buses were unheard of at that time. Not long after, however, a law was passed that all children of different race and color were to be integrated and bused to various schools.

Watching my children go off to school made me want to get involved in school activities. I suggested to Norata that I would like to join the PTA. In a jealous rage, he said, "Absolutely not!" He always had a streak of jealousy. I was disappointed and felt deprived.

Although the Assumption had a fine reputation for teaching, Ned, just twelve, was very unhappy. The nuns were exceptionally strict and showed little compassion. In the 1950s and 1960s teachers had the right to punish as they felt was needed. Children were exposed to correction by almost any means.

On a Monday in 1960 Ned walked in our door before the school session ended. I asked him why he was let out so early. He answered, "I'm not going back to that school again." I asked him why. I could see that his hands were red and hurting. He explained that during lunch he became unruly and was struck on his hands with a ruler by Sister Anne. He said he felt excruciating pain, and he had grabbed the ruler and snapped it in half over his leg.

With that, I immediately enrolled him in a public school, where he seemed much happier. Becca wasn't pleased with her brother's transfer since it meant that she had to walk alone to and from school every day.

One afternoon I received a call from Mother Superior that I was to come to school immediately.

It seemed that while playing in the schoolyard during recess Becca fell and accidentally pushed her hand through the window. I was frantic and rushed to the school. I was surprised that there was no metal protection covering the windows. The Mother Superior had already made arrangements with the doctor at St. Joseph's Hospital before I got there. She could see the emotional state I was in so she accompanied us to the hospital.

Becca's tendons in her wrist were severed and needed many stitches. I wanted to complain about the unprotected windows but the Mother Superior made a comment about the misfortune and I said nothing more. In due time, Becca recuperated and was back playing with the children in the schoolyard.

Mother Superior asked me if I had any knowledge about Becca supplying the children in her class with ice cream. I knew nothing about it, but I wasn't surprised. Becca was well mannered, unselfish, kind, and generous. However, I felt obliged and paid the school for a month's supply of ice cream for her entire class.

I explained to Becca that generosity was very nice but she must never be generous at other people's expense. Inwardly, I was proud of the fact that she was not a selfish child.

Ned was an introvert as he grew up. He had no real close friends and he kept his thoughts mostly to himself. He preferred to be inventive and creative, he spent time doing chores with his dad. They were

inseparable. They enjoyed the outdoors, hunting, fishing, and camping
out. They had target practice in the woods every Sunday.

He was a special kid, concerned chiefly with his own thoughts. For some unexplained reason he never brought any school friends home after school. Rather, he waited patiently for his dad to come home so they could resume their work together. He spent his time being productive. He loved using his tools.

Norata was energetic, not one to relax. There was always some chore to keep him busy. Like his dad, Ned anxiously looked forward to joining him. How proud I was to see them doing chores compatibly together.

Camping Out

August was a perfect time for traveling. After breakfast one Sunday, Norata thought for a moment, tapped Ned on his shoulder, and impulsively said, "Next week would be a good time to spend a few days camping in the White Mountains. How about it, should we do it?"

Ned quickly perked up and said, "I'm ready, Dad. Let's call my cousins (Greg and Ron) and make it a foursome."

The boys, all in their teens, were excited and anxious. They called constantly; they couldn't wait for the day to leave.

Norata was eager for a camping out experience too. He wasted no time preparing the necessary essentials—the sleeping bags, canned goods, eggs, toilet paper, matches, and warm clothing. The van was loaded and off they went, heading north.

They set up camp high on the mountain, next to a stream for convenience. They cooked over a campfire, walked the mountain with broken branches in hand, and explored the mountainside. It was a fun trip that kids remember forever.

The week had ended too quickly. The boys had such a great time. They asked their uncle how soon could they do it, again? They talked about that adventure long after.

Ned was ambitious. He liked to keep busy, to use his time productively.

He almost always walked home after school, carrying discarded pieces of lumber from the nearby lumber yard. He put every piece to use.

His workstation in the backyard was set up for his different projects. The tables and bowls he made were beautifully finished. He was extremely talented and of course we were so proud of his capabilities and skills.

Our house needed painting, but Norata thought that continuing painting the three-family building wasn't wise. He decided to cover it with aluminum siding to eliminate years of maintenance.

Ned, fourteen then, insisted that he work along with his dad after school. I would rather have seen him seeking new friends and becoming involved in teen sports but he wasn't interested. His only pleasure was working with his dad. He didn't need much guidance; he had confidence in himself and was able to follow quite well in whatever work was required.

It wasn't long before they had finished the entire siding. Norata was proud and praised his son for his involvement. He said he could never have completed the job without his help.

Ned loved the attention and took pleasure in pleasing his dad. But I was somewhat concerned as to why he had no schoolmates. It bothered me to see him being a loner.

He came home after school one day with his face red and clothes in disarray. I knew from the sight of him that something was wrong. I asked him what had happened to him. Did he get into a fight?

"Yes I did," he said. "I was jumped by two boys from school." I didn't know what to say. I knew this is what happens to teenagers but I didn't know how to respond. I just warned him to stay clear of those hoodlums and not let himself be bullied.

Norata always made time for our pleasure. Traveling with his family was his special enjoyment. He was a good father, always ready to please us. Often we packed our bags and spent weekends with the children up north.

January 1962 was bitter cold. Norata decided to escape the cold for one month, and since the children were doing well in school, he thought it would be an educational experience for them to travel across the country.

I made all the necessary arrangements. The teachers were very cooperative; the future lessons were prepared for me so that the children would not be missing any schoolwork.

Traveling by car made the journey real interesting.

We left Rhode Island's freezing temperature and kept traveling west, seeking a warmer climate. At that time there was segregation and discrimination was at a high level.

As we drove through the Mississippi countryside we stopped to take a close look at the cotton fields. There were rows and rows of magnificent beauty. African Americans were working in the hot sun with heavily loaded sacks of hand-picked cotton on their backs. Each bag was weighed and emptied into a truck. Their pay was measured by the pounds they picked. The children were extremely impressed watching them work the fields.

Ned was curious and tried to talk to them and ask questions, but the Negroes were hesitant when he approached. Their expression of fear was evident. My smile gave them the impression that we were friendly and sincere. I had instilled in my children that we are all God's children, in spite of our difference in color.

Ned controlled the movie camera and managed to take some movies while they were at work, picking the cotton with both hands and rushing to fill the sacks they carried. The children were confused by the segregation signs: BLACK and WHITE. We tried to explain segregation as best we could, hoping they understood.

We continued traveling west, visiting the special attractions in each town. We saw the swallows in Capistrano, the rows and rows of orange groves in San Diego, the flashing lights in Las Vegas, and the excitement and fun in Disneyland—a delight for both children. An experience they will always remember.

We looked for ways to keep busy while we were riding in the car. Besides doing their schoolwork, we would read the signs on the road and try to test each other with the spelling of the words. Norata was careful to keep the tedium of the constant driving to a minimum. He stopped often, and made sure we would bed down before dark.

He was interested in the culture and the growth of the communities. He avoided the highway and mostly drove through the small towns. "There's nothing to see on the highway," he'd say.

As we traveled, we once got caught in an unfortunate experience that had to be dealt with. It was beginning to get dark and we were on the lookout for a hotel. There was none in sight. Motels in that area were few and far between, and what we found were not to our satisfaction. We kept traveling far into the night. It was late, and we could no longer be choosy. We decided to take the next motel no matter what.

Luckily we found a motel, but it had very little lighting. Norata paid for the room and was handed the keys. Normally he would check the room first, but we had no choice. He was tired and we needed to sleep. It was just too late to be particular.

The room wasn't pleasant and we weren't satisfied with its cleanliness, but we had to overlook our concern. We had to make the best of it. As you can imagine, it was a dump. Norata refused to let us walk on the floor without shoes. He took the drawers out of the bureau for us to step in while undressing. That worked, and luckily, the beds had clean sheets. We did however, get a good night's sleep. The next morning the bath and shower weren't much better, so we wet a clean towel, gave ourselves a face wash, and left.

Norata promised that never again would we let that happen to us. Clean sleeping quarters were very important to him.

So, after that, we took no chances, he made sure we were prepared for the night before enjoying the town. Checking into the hotel became our first priority. It was a double pleasure when we could spend the night sleeping in comfort.

We left that town and stopped for breakfast. We still felt uncomfortable, needing a shower and a change of clothes. It was too soon to check into another hotel so we used the bathrooms to freshen up before having breakfast.

We continued our journey through Arizona, touring the Grand Canyon National Park and the surroundings. It was beautiful. That day ended too soon.

We had another bad experience. We always took advantage of the daylight hours, leaving the hotels early in the morning just to get a head start, avoiding the early morning traffic.

This one morning, as we approached our car in the hotel parking lot, we could see the trunk partially open. We had been robbed. The thieves had helped themselves to all our gifts and collectables. Our movie camera with the precious films of the cotton pickers was also taken.

Ned was especially disappointed because he was in charge of the camera and taking pictures of all special attractions. There was one good consolation, fortunately for us, the money Norata had hidden in the spare tire was overlooked.

After a month of traveling and our fun vacation over, we returned home to our normal everyday life.

Ned began to show little interest in school. I wondered, Could the month away from school have had a damaging effect on him? We were concerned and lectured him that since vacation time was over it was time to put all his effort into his studies. I kept reminding him that he must not fail his grades. He would always respond with "Don't worry, Mom, I will not fail."

We had instilled in him that education was to be his first priority.

He usually passed his classes with fairly good marks. He was capable to excel in whatever he chose to do, but he was self-centered, with a mind of his own. Although he was gifted in creating and being inventive, we stressed upon him that his talent would be useless without the education.

He was excited when he finally turned sixteen. He convinced his dad that having an automobile would be a more convenient traveling mode to and from school. He said he would be relieving me of the stress of having to drive him every day. Of course his dad obliged, with the stipulation that he must concentrate on his studies. I was somewhat relieved of the burden.

I will always remember that sorrowful day—November 22, 1963—while
waiting for Ned after school. The program I was listening to on the radio was suddenly interrupted with the announcement that President Kennedy had been shot.

I was struck—the news was shocking. I didn't believe what I was hearing. I felt extreme sorrow. I couldn't get home fast enough to watch the news. A very, very sad, unforgettable day.

Ned was proud as a peacock going to school in his new red sports car. Norata vowed to give his son all the luxuries he was denied, he sure kept his promise.

Some weeks later, I received a phone call from the school principal, Mr. Lionell, who was very concerned. He asked, "Are you aware that Ned has been missing school?" I was dumbfounded and speechless. What could I say? He left the house every day as usual, so we assumed he was going to

83

school.

He went on to say he was very disappointed in us for providing Ned with a car. A car at his age was the worst decision we could have made. I explained how Norata always acted impulsively on his son's desires. He was definitely right, but it was too late to reconsider.

The damage had been done. Ned was losing interest in school, failing in algebra and math. Our reprimanding him had no effect. We tried our best to convince him the importance of education but it didn't work.

Mr. Lionell helped us find a private tutor who worked with Ned at home. The special tutoring made no difference because he had no interest.

It brought to mind the regrets I had when I too chose a car above my education. Explaining that to me hadn't made any difference either. Ned finished the first semester of the eleventh grade, then dropped out of school. There was no convincing him how important it was to at least finish high school. The car obviously had a negative effect on him; it destroyed his will to continue.

Norata was disappointed, and insisted that he immediately find a job and get to work. It was the first time I heard him put demands on his precious son.

Ned found a job right away, working nights at a local

gas station. The job was cut short. After working three nights, he arrived home frightened and agitated. "I refuse to work in that place," he said. We asked what happened. "That place is infested with rats!" His dad of course sympathized and agreed. He too was terrified of rats.

He lectured Ned, "Let this be a lesson to you. Without an education, you will be facing this very experience all through your life." The lectures meant nothing.

Knowing him to be a super achiever, Norata, although disappointed, relished the fact that his son would be his partner in their future goals. They worked together building and remodeling. Ned was happy too. It was what he enjoyed most.

Every night after dinner there was continuous chatter about how and what their workday had consisted of. They were a compatible team.

November was hunting season. Father and son looked forward to spending two weeks in Maine each year with their hunting buddies, who were a great bunch of guys from our area.

Butch, the oldest guy in the group, was chosen to do the cooking. He had a history of cooking for parties, outings, and celebrations. Ned would brag about the delicious food and tasty apple pies Butch made. Ned was comfortable being in the company of adults.

I always had an uneasy feeling when they left,

packed with hunting gear and guns. Although Norata taught his son about safety and having respect for guns, I was afraid and always prayed for their safe return. How proud and excited they were when they brought home a deer that they strung from the loft for two weeks to cure.

Norata had no knowledge about butchery. After the curing time, when it was ready to be dressed, Bill, our cousin and a professional meat cutter, volunteered to dress and prepare the different cuts. Every piece was packaged, labeled, and distributed among our friends and family. Ned refused to eat any part of the deer.

Jamestown, a small island adjacent to Newport, was a summer resort where we spent most of our weekends. The island was approximately nine square miles of scarcely populated private land. The ocean was always in clear view when driving along the island's perimeter. Norata was impressed with the privacy and decided to make this our summer vacation retreat.

The little cottage he constructed was built with boards from an old abandoned pier under the Jamestown Bridge. We tore it apart, then made lots of trips hauling the boards to the site. The fireplace was built with huge rocks and boulders gathered from the island. The finished result, although crudely built, turned out to be a lovely cottage that was a short walking distance from the ocean. Our family and friends would visit frequently to spend time clamming and fishing.

Norata had a bad experience when he was a young boy. His friends played rough, holding his head below the water until he almost drowned. So he had a fear of the ocean and never cared to learn to swim. The children and I spent our days boating and enjoying the water. Ned was capable of handling the boat, but we cautioned him to be very careful especially when boating with friends.

Norata noticed that every weekend the gas gauge on his car seemed empty, even though he had always made it a point to keep the tank full. Ned confessed. He was siphoning the fuel for his boat motor. Dad laughed; he thought that was funny. Everything Ned did was acceptable in his dad's eyes.

We had recently liquidated the china business and considered the jewelry trade, since at that time Rhode Island was the jewelry capital of the world. I got my start working for my brother Pat who specialized in casting and manufacturing costume jewelry.

Pat was happy to introduce me to the business. I put every effort into learning all I could. Working with him for three months gave me the knowledge I needed. He was kind, unselfish, and always ready to help in every way. I was ready and eager to get started.

In 1967, when Ned had just turned eighteen, he shocked us with the news that he had joined the National Guard. We were surprised that he wanted to leave. He spent six months in the reserves, stationed in Oklahoma. We had no idea why he decided to join. I didn't ask, assuming it was his choice.

Two months into the service it was too much for him to bear. We detected his regret. The calls every night convinced us that he was extremely unhappy and homesick.

After supper one night the phone rang a second time. Each time he called we talked about everything and anything, to keep the conversation alive and tell him about the happenings at home. Norata was worried. He said, "Why would Ned call two times tonight? He must be homesick." He couldn't bear the thought that his son was lonely. He turned to me and said, "Mae, pack a bag, we are going to spend the weekend with him." Ned was of course happy to hear the news.

We immediately arranged a flight so we could be there for the weekend. That visit was a special time in our lives, particularly for Ned. He just glowed with contentment when he saw us. He was like a lost child who just found his lost parents. We tried to make every minute pleasurable for him since it would be the only visit we could make before his discharge.

Ned proudly introduced us to Larry, one of his buddies, who shared the same thoughts about returning home. Larry was impressed. He commented how very lucky Ned was to have such concerned parents.

Happily, the six months of guard duty ended. Father and son planned their coming projects together.

Excited at having his son home, Norata continued telling his constant tales without giving Ned a chance to be included in the one-sided conversations. I was frustrated and I gave him the cue by calling him a tick, as I usually did whenever he went on and on in any discussion.

It was the excitement of having his son home. I understood but, he didn't know when to let up. I always corrected him whenever he overtook a conversation.

He finally took the hint and gave Ned a chance to exchange views. Besides being a talker, Norata was always very opinionated. When he controlled a conversation correcting him had no effect.

Early Saturday morning, after I finished the wash, I put our clothes in the proper drawers. When I opened Ned's drawer I noticed a plastic bag that looked like tobacco. I was confused because he never had the desire to smoke. I had a strong suspicion so I immediately carried it out to our backyard and put a match to the bag. The smell was disgusting. Luckily, we lived in a private, secluded area.

Ned was furious when I confronted and chastised him about the tobacco. He said, "Mom, do you realize what you have done? That bag wasn't mine.

It was worth $500 and it didn't belong to me."I just ignored him. I refused to accept his explanation. I knew the old excuse, "It's not mine." I felt confident I had done the right thing. I closely observed his whereabouts and possessions thereafter, checking every possible lead. There never was another occurrence to my knowledge. I really believe he was coerced into that episode, the sound of a profit I'm sure, was convincing.

Jewelry Business

Norata, a workaholic, kept busy in his construction business, together with building our new home in Scituate and finding time to work with me arranging the shop. We worked very hard preparing for the jewelry business.

I was anxious setting up in a local store. We lined the walls with foot presses, benches, and machinery. Pat gave me some leads. I wasted no time and followed through on them. The business moved right along. It grew rapidly. Jewelry was in demand at that time. It was good news for economic success!

If you worked hard enough and made sacrifices, there was no end to the money you could make in the jewelry trade.

That work created a certain amount of inattention that I sometimes regret because I wasn't able to give my children my wholehearted attention. I relied mostly on my mom to care for them when I was flooded with orders. I've been reminded of that fact and I feel guilty.

There weren't enough hours in the day to complete the orders. The employees were working overtime to keep up with the demands. A constant flow of finished goods were delivered daily. The store soon became overcrowded with equipment. The workers were frustrated with the lack of space and I was forced to move to larger quarters.

We rented an old warehouse with more than adequate space. Each section was planned accordingly. For example, the soldering and plating ovens for baking painted finished goods were prepared for completion.

Brian, an ambitious nineteen-year-old, was a runner who kept the home workers supplied with their needs. He was conscientious; he made sure they were never without work. (It was customary for people to work at home in those days.) Many nights after work, Brian would refuse to leave. He was a lonely boy who was very unhappy at home. I wasn't pleased with him staying after work. I wanted him to take the time to rest.

One Tuesday morning we opened the shop and found him sleeping on one of the benches. We had worked far into the previous night to complete an order destined for shipment the next day. I felt sad and questioned him as to why he refused to leave. He gave no explanation. I gave him my house keys and insisted he get some rest.

Ned was resentful and was deeply affected by the close relationship we had with Brian. He was irritated to see the special treatment that Brian showed us. Brian was beginning to become attached, even calling me Mom and making comments about how happy he would be if he could live with us.

As much as I adored him, I had to consider my son's resentment. I also felt it was unfair to take him away from his family. It was a serious situation so I made a call to Brian's mom. I explained as best I could without hurting her feelings that he was unhappy at home. She was very concerned and convinced me that she loved her son very much. I felt somehow responsible for his attachment and convinced him that he belonged home with his family.

He continued to work with us and the subject was never brought up again.

I was thankful for our success with the jewelry business, and being unselfish, I encouraged my longtime friends Margo (I called her Maggie) and Tom to take advantage of the demand. They spent time helping out whenever we had a rush order. They also gained some of the knowledge they needed. I made every effort to introduce them to the organizing and manufacturing aspects of the business.

Setting up shop came easy for them. Six months was all it took for them to establish a growing business. Money was rolling in. Excited and anxious, they made plans to build a home.

Their apartment was elegantly furnished. Maggie had great taste, but the house needed repair and the surrounding environment was run down. She was so proud displaying the plans for the home they were ready to build. They had already purchased an acre of land in a lovely area nearby. Maggie was a wonderful mother whose every thought was centered around her two boys. She made every effort to prepare a better life for them while they were growing up.

Her plans were shattered. The pain she was having begun to worsen. After many doctor's visits and special treatments, she was diagnosed with an aggressive bone cancer. It made me sick. My dearest and truest friend, always there for me, did not deserve this. Tom was a loyal and devoted husband who had strong love and affection for her. The thought of losing her was causing him emotional suffering. It shattered all their plans and future.

I tried to visit often. I took advantage of every free time to be with her. I would always ask her, "What can I do for you, Maggie?" She always had a chore for me. She was fussy and proud. She kept up with the latest fashion and style until her last days.

One day during a visit she asked me to shave her legs, pluck her brows, and make some special dish for her boys and Tom. I tried to be as gentle as possible when shaving her but it seemed I always screwed up, nicking her. I never left her home without preparing a special dish for her boys.

After a year of suffering, my wonderful, thoughtful, and kind friend passed away at an early age of thirty-eight. I spent the last of her dying days trying to comfort her.

Tom suffered intense grief and had tremendous difficulty trying to accept her loss. He felt sad disposing of her clothes and the collection of antiques and mementos she cherished.

He refused to live in that same house without her. Tom asked me to take whatever pieces I wanted as mementos. I live with her memory every day. Norata kept abreast of things in Tom's life, trying to comfort him. "Maggie is gone," he told Tom. "You must get on with your life. You were a good husband. You should have no regrets." Those words were comforting to him. He lost interest in building but he continued to work at his business.

He never married but eventually he did keep company with a young lady who is an exact look-alike to Maggie.

Being a businesswoman and a mother was not easy for me. Many hours had to be devoted to completing and shipping the merchandise when promised. I was spending too much time away from home.

Norata's sisters Verna and Eve were working with me, devoting special time organizing and supervising the workers. I tried to fulfill my commitments at home as best I could, preparing the following day's meals and any other required necessities.

Becca was a junior in high school and I was very much afraid that I would not be home for her. Every day (except Monday) I felt compelled to leave at 2:30 and rush home before the bus dropped her off from school. We had a fear of her walking into an empty house. Winnie, our cleaning lady, never left the house on Monday until Becca came home. Our house had alarms throughout, but being secluded in a remote area, it didn't stop the break-ins. Our house was broken into several times.

It was just after the Christmas holiday when Norata, always finding an excuse to travel, decided to visit with his cousins in Montreal for a weekend. Before we left, we contacted the police to tell them we were leaving. They were aware of the previous break-ins and had asked to be informed whenever we left. Lieutenant Andison, our special friend on the force, was in possession of our house keys. We felt somewhat relieved because he could hear our alarm ringing from his home. We never left without informing him of our time away.

Our caution was never enough. We were unable to stop the culprits. We came home to an unexpected loss. We were robbed of all our Christmas gifts we had left under the tree; our collection of guns, liquor, a small jar of coins left in Becca's room; even the new microwave oven Norata bought was found in the woods nearby. It was evidently too heavy and was left in haste. There were many more incidentals also taken. Lieutenant Andison was shocked. He said

"How could this have happened without me knowing? I can hear the alarm from my home."

After checking for clues, we found that the hoodlums had bypassed the wires in the garage and cleverly turned off the alarm. It had happened before. We were in fear of what would await us whenever we returned home from vacation. We could not find a solution.

Although Verna and Eve were capable of handling the business, it was my responsibility to be there. Each day it was the same routine—leave at 2:30, rush home for Becca, settle her in, and rush back.

It was then that I decided the business was too much for me to handle alone. I was stressed out, so it became necessary for Norata to relieve me of the pressure and take over the operation. He was not happy giving up his business, however, he had no choice. The income from the jewelry business far exceeded the income from the construction trade. Working with him was not easy. We had differences of opinion of how to function. The many squabbles we had convinced me that there could only be one boss. So I then became the standby.

Hand painting on dress pins was our specialty. The ten- and twelve-caret gold-plated bracelets and accessories were unusual and of superior design. So pricing them was unlimited.

Our salesman, David Krass, had connections in most parts of Europe and Canada. He was considered top-notch in selling. The stores we opened previously, featuring our display of jewelry controlled by David, were showing little profit.

Norata was spoiled. His expectations were beyond reason. Comparing the same profit from the stores was impossible. He refused to continue and closed all the stores.

David was disappointed. He knew the potential. So he pressured and urged Norata to think seriously about what he was doing. "Listen to me. It would be a stupid mistake," he said. "You are anxiously foolish. Just give it time. I promise you they will show a substantial profit. You can't give up. You will be throwing away a fortune to the wind." But David's lecture was like talking to a child who wouldn't listen to reason. Norata was a bonehead. His stubbornness was one of his faults in many of his decisions.

The lecture had no effect. A stickler, careless, without reason, Norata refused to reconsider. David tried his best to encourage him, hoping he would change his mind. But it didn't happen. David couldn't convince him that time was needed to show a profit. He called him penny-wise and pound-foolish.

When Norata suspended the operation and closed all the stores, I was disappointed too. I had faith in David. He showed professionalism and his family was experienced in the sales field. There was every reason to trust him; listening to his theory made sense. Norata was impossible to convince. He refused to listen. With that, David, disappointed, left

without notice
Tension Release,

Nine years past, we decided it was time to stop paying rent and build our own plant to accommodate our growing needs. The land was purchased a short distance from our home. Norata thought of everything. He constructed it large enough to rent a second portion of the building for additional income. He included men's and women's bathrooms complete with built-in shower stalls in case we needed to shower before leaving the building.

Every day Norata would leave for work at seven a.m. to prepare for the workers. There was never a second thought about overworking himself. I continued to spend a few hours helping out, in spite of my having to leave early enough to be home for Becca. Ned had the responsibility of overseeing the building's construction.

One Friday Ned left around eight to open up for the plumber. I was at home preparing a dessert for Bob and Penny who had invited us for dinner on Saturday. Bob was our salesman who, together with Penny, was to surprise us with a Jewish dinner of matzo ball soup and gefelta fish.

I was just about finished when Mabel, one of our workers, called from the office, very agitated, "Mae, Ned has been hurt. Get over to the hospital immediately." My throat tightened; I began to tremble.

I asked, "What happened?"

All she could say was "I don't know."

I kept asking repeatedly, looking for an answer. "What happened? How bad is he?"

Again, she answered, "I don't know." I hung up the phone and rushed over to the hospital.

As I drove several thoughts ran through my mind. Did he fall? Did he have an accident? What kind of hurt? Every minute seemed like an hour. I walked right into the emergency room. Ned was calmly stretched out on a hospital bed with a bandage on his head. Norata stood nearby, prancing nervously. I felt somewhat relieved; it wasn't as bad as I thought.

The nurse noticed my concern, brought me a glass of water, and assured me that he was okay. She said, "We had to do some suturing to his head."

I asked, "What happened?"

Before she could answer, Ned said, "It's okay, Mom, I'm all right."

Norata was very disturbed. The anger in his face gave me the clue to let it go. Obviously he couldn't bear the thought that his son was hurt. At that moment I was agitated by not knowing what had taken place. Later I pieced it together.

Ned spent his time every day observing the workers construct the building while Norata worked at the office. Each day he would find some windows broken. He assumed that the children in the neighborhood were doing it, so he devised a plan to catch the culprits.

The following school day he waited in hiding. As he had guessed, a young boy, about twelve, got off the school bus and began throwing rocks, breaking the windows. Instead of calling the police, Ned followed the boy home in hopes of making a complaint to his parents. He got no response when he rang the doorbell.

When he returned to the building, he was surprised when he was confronted by three hoodlums with drawn guns. Without any explanation they began pistol-whipping him, then threatening him that should he call the police they would be back to finish the job.

Unfortunately, Ned was alone in the building at the time. The plumber and electrician were scheduled to work that day but other commitments kept them from arriving that early. We thought that, had they been there this savage attack might not have happened.
Frightened and dazed, Ned drove himself to the hospital.

Fearing for his life, Ned refused to call the police. Unfortunately, the boy was the son of a murderous gang leader and a member of the Italian mafia, though none of us knew it then.

Norata, terrified, rushed to the hospital to be with his son. Many stitches were required for his head wounds. Ned was never troublesome. He was always well behaved. He didn't deserve this violent treatment.

I was enraged. I made an attempt to call the police, but I had second thoughts. I feared aggression and retaliation. Norata was sick and full of contempt, blaming himself for allowing his son to supervise the construction. He wanted some satisfaction so he began by making inquiries at the mafia club hangout in Silver Lake.

He was advised to leave well enough alone. "Those hoods have no regard for human life," he was told.

I was unable to erase the thought from my mind that my son was innocently hurt by these vicious hoodlums. To think that they could do harm and get away with it haunted me.

I thought of taking revenge. Many different thoughts passed through my head. I desperately wanted some satisfaction. I drove past their house daily, looking for some way to retaliate. I had evil thoughts about how I could return the hurt they had caused.

I was becoming obsessed by this when I suddenly realized, what am I doing? Am I placing myself in their category? I have never been evil minded. I must stop this eye-for-an-eye feeling. I can only pray that one day they will be punished for their vicious wrongdoings.

A few days later, we received a surprise visit. The hoodlums sent a messenger to apologize! Evidently, they had reacted hastily without any knowledge of the situation.

Retribution wasn't long in coming. A few years later, the boy's father was found beaten to death in prison. I was pleased. Justice was served.

Moving into our new building was such a pleasure. The convenience of being close to home was a great relief. I welcomed the feeling of being able to leave whenever I felt the need to get away.

The jewelry business continued to grow rapidly, accumulating much wealth. We were living a happy, luxurious family lifestyle, never wanting for anything. Money was no object.

Although Ned's education was cut short, he was brilliant in his own way. He was a jack-of-all-trades, like his dad. Sometimes what he did simply overwhelmed me.

The new Jenn-Air stove we had purchased needed to be repaired. I was about to call the repairman when Ned, still a young boy, said, "Mom, I can fix it." I was aware of his capabilities, but I was unsure of his knowledge about electricity.

With that he got right to it. I asked, "How do you

know what to do?"

To my amazement, he answered, "I don't know, Mom. It seems that I've been here before. I know exactly what to do."

His response sent shivers up my spine. I thought, could he be thinking reincarnation? That made me fearful so I erased the thought from my mind and refused to question him any further. He did indeed repair the stove.

Ned was uninterested in the jewelry business but he loved skiing. He approached his dad with the proposal that he build a chalet up north. It seemed that while skiing he had found a tract of land adjoining Cranmore Mountain that was for sale. It didn't take much convincing. His dad was always ready to accommodate his son's desires.

Ned was excited. He immediately made the necessary contacts up north in preparation for the building. While I supervised the business, he and his dad worked together with a crew building the chalet. Norata returned whenever possible to keep tabs on our situation. A line of credit was set up for Ned to make charges to the jewelry business as needed. That was a mistake we regretted.

It took just three months for completion. Ned was excited and proud to have his very own chalet. He was anxious to show me how well he had chosen the furnishings on my first weekend visit. I was totally surprised; the chalet was lovely and nicely furnished.

He proudly gave me the grand tour. I complimented him on his good taste in decorating except for his bed frame that was covered with white rabbit fur!

As I looked at this beautiful chalet I thought how lucky he was. In his early twenties he had his very own furnished, mortgage-free chalet. Norata was so proud. He would stand and admire the completion of their work.

While Ned enjoyed his pad, he became a ski instructor and a good teacher. But not for long because he tired of things too easily. He was an adventurer who was always looking for more dealings.

On one weekend visit, he encouraged me and his dad to take to the slopes. We had never been on skis before, but I was willing to give it a try. We were fitted with skis at the ski shop, and off we went on the new adventure. After a few lessons, Ned suggested we try the intermediate run. I was a little skeptical. At forty-three, I wasn't interested in becoming courageous. He insisted and helped me on the lift. Surprisingly, I enjoyed the ride. The view of the snow covering the mountains was a beautiful sight. In fact, I truly enjoyed the whole experience.

Norata wasn't so lucky. His first experience on skis ended up with him in a hospital. He had fractured a finger when he skied into a tree.

After two years of pleasure, Ned tired of Cranmore. He began skiing Killington, which was primarily designed for professional skiers.

Always looking for new challenges and taking advantage of his dad's generosity, he constantly sought new adventures.

Consumed by the excitement and seeking a harder challenge, he thought that if he were to build a chalet to accommodate skiers, it would bring in a fine profit and still provide living quarters for himself.

"A good idea," his dad said, "earning an income and still enjoying your lifestyle." Just what he wanted to hear. Convincing his dad was never a problem. Again he played the confidence game. His dad was a pushover, vulnerable, eager to keep his son happy and encourage his new passion.

The chalet was put up for sale. It sold within a month. Over-anxious and still in control of the proceeds from the Cranmore sale and Cardin Jewelry, he went gung ho.

With the help of a realtor, Ned purchased land not far from the Killington slopes. The plans that were drawn were quite extravagant. Never considering cost, Ned chose to build a four-bedroom home, with a mudroom for storing skis.

The new quest seemed easy but the traveling distance to and from Killington was a hindrance. He needed to find a better way to make the necessary trips while they were building.

With little thought, Ned knew exactly what would solve the problem. Flying.

He admired a four-seat Cherokee that was up for sale at North Smithfield Airport, he convinced his dad that it was a necessity and it made sense. No problem. It was settled.

'The flying course will be easy,' he thought. Everything was easy to Ned as long as it satisfied his temptations.

He wasted no time applying and registering for flying lessons. There were different courses, short and long, depending on what type aircraft to be flown. The short course was the most convenient. It would also take less time. Determined and proud, he soon completed the necessary flying hours and was ready to show off his flying ability.

His dad was proud, He relished the fact that his son was a pilot. He agreed to the purchase.

The excitement of flying took effect before continuing with the building. Ned spent considerable time with his instructor, showing off his skill with his cousins. The chalet would have to wait until he got the flying pleasure out of his system.

Eager to show off his accomplishment, he convinced Dad and me to take a trip to New York to visit Cousin Dan who lived in Poughkeepsie. I was a little skeptical; I didn't think he had enough experience to travel that far. It seemed too soon for a long distance run.

Still, knowing Ned, nothing was impossible. Norata was excited at the prospect. He had complete trust in his son. He eagerly awaited the flight.

Before we boarded, I watched Ned as he walked around and checked the different parts of the plane. Everything seemed secure. After strapping us in and asking if we were comfortable, he took off.

Proud as a peacock, Norata praised his son for handling the plane with caution. He said, "You really know what you're doing. I'm impressed."

I was a bit nervous at first, focusing my eyes on the instrument panel. The tension soon eased as we admired the beautiful scenery below. I too had a feeling of contentment watching my son handle the plane so totally relaxed.

At that moment, I thought how Ned had the ability to accomplish anything that suited his liking. If only he had the same desire to continue his education, what a difference it would have made for his future.

Dan's home was situated on a hilltop among twenty acres of cleared land. It was easy for a small plane to fly in and out of the area. Ned always had confidence in himself, he seemed to know exactly what to do.

Dan was waiting for us as we made the approach. The proud smile on Norata's face was incredible when Dan praised Ned for his skill in landing the plane so smoothly. We were invited in for a quick drink, a toast to Ned's successful journey. Our stay was short since the visit was only to show off Ned's flying ability. Flying home was easier; we felt more relaxed.

Ned was becoming consumed by this carefree living. He was concentrating solely on flying and forgetting all about the chalet. Realizing that the long awaited project on hold was being neglected, Norata asked, "What's happening with Vermont?"

Ned replied, "Yes, Dad, I have to get to it."

The excitement of enjoying his plane had become his only desire. The chalet seemed unimportant; he seemed to have lost interest. But there was no way he could neglect that obligation. He had to commit himself to finishing what he started.

Finally, the time had come to prepare and focus on the chalet. Like his dad, he had the knowledge to do most of the plumbing and electricity himself. He needed construction help so he made a visit to the nearby prison. He arranged a meeting with the officials and was allowed to hire the work-release prisoners who were trustees.

Each day, the sheriff would drop off six or seven prisoners, all prepared to work for the day. Henry, twenty-five, was husky, rather short, and the most powerful of the group. He hungered for recognition. Trying hard to prove his strength, he chose the most difficult chores.

Catered food was brought in daily; it was a treat for them to enjoy their freedom and eat specially prepared foods. They were paid two dollars an hour, all that was allowed according to prison rules. The sheriff was prompt in picking the prisoners up at the end of the day.

Our jewelry business was being used to fund Ned's bill. Norata continued pouring money into the line of credit special account that Ned controlled. The transfer of funds from Cardin Jewelry allowed him to fulfill another one of his dreams. A log was set up to keep track of all expenses.

After three months of traveling and preparations, the chalet was completed and ready for occupancy. Skiers came from many parts of the country. Ned was relieved. He couldn't wait to get back to his flying. He spent little time at Killington with the excuse that his room was needed. Obviously, skiing was the last thing on his mind. He had completely lost interest.

In his early twenties, Ned was living a fine playboy lifestyle, traveling with his plane and new girlfriend. His trips back to Killington were only for necessities.

Norata, at that point, was concerned. Again he tried to convince him that it was time now to consider the jewelry business for his future, to bring him the same success it had brought us. But he had no interest and continued to seek new adventure.

In September of 1969, my Dad suffered a sudden, massive heart attack and passed away at the age of seventy-two, without a goodbye word. Mom was consumed with guilt. She regretted not being home at the time of his attack, she felt extreme sorrow.

Dad was money-conscious and had no confidence in banks. My Mom trusted him and never asked questions about finances. Her only concern was putting food on the table and pleasing her family. As a result, nobody knew the whereabouts of his money. We assumed he had a special hiding place somewhere in the house.

The bills were past due. Mathson Oil, supplier of the heating oil for all nine apartments, was overdue a year. The accumulated rent money was hidden somewhere, but where?

Mom showed no emotion for fear that we would make derogatory remarks against him. "After all, he was your father" is what she would say.

Unfortunately, after many days of scouring, the money was nowhere to be found. The collected rents that month from the apartments paid for the funeral expenses.

One night, Mom recalled, while in bed, she heard the cellar door squeaking even though it was kept locked at all times. Someone was trying to get in. Afraid to investigate, she passed it off until morning. It was evident someone had broken the lock because, in haste, they left the door ajar. It was then that she realized since Dad spent much of his time in the cellar, it was very possible he had his money hidden somewhere down there. We had our suspicions, but there was nothing we could do. Accusations would be meaningless.

Mom, the precious woman that she was, began selling off the property, item by item, in Maine, Florida, and the apartments—except the home she lived in. Then she generously shared the proceeds with her four children.

I was bitter at that point thinking that Dad could be so deceitful by not trusting Mom, who would have given her life for him. How could he be so cruel as to keep secret where he hid his money when it could have been left for Mom and his family to enjoy?

Mom never made any comments against him, in spite of the fact that he betrayed her. We were angry with her. She had let herself be duped. Although she missed him, she lived comfortably until she passed away six years later at the age of seventy-eight.

Becca was ready to graduate. I had planned a surprise party with some of her friends at our house. Upon learning of my plans, she made it understood that she wanted her senior prom to be celebrated at our favorite restaurant. I respected her wishes and booked a party five days later. We had visions of her pursuing a profession and hoped she would choose a college close to home. That's when we learned that she wanted to be a model.

Becca was very attractive, had a fine figure, and was obsessed with fashion. She enrolled in John Robert Powers Beauty Studio in Boston and completed the course with high honors.

After graduation, she planned to continue and advance her courses in New York. Norata and I were not happy with her living in New York and convinced her to give up the idea of advancement in that way. College at that time was out of the question for her too. She did, however, have interest in the jewelry business managing her own personal account, but soon, that became a bore. Trying to get her motivated wasn't easy.

Becca wanted her independence and refused to rely on us for support. We had to submit to her decisions and leave her future in her own hands.

She did have a business mind and seemed very capable, but she was looking for the one field that would make her rich quick. She was hasty in making decisions and prone to act on impulse. She never gave herself time to expand. Her expectations were beyond normal. She took one course after another— real estate, nail grooming, business management, sales, and more. All ventures were short-lived.

Norata wisely discouraged her from starting a ladies' shoe business. He had little faith in her decisions. He knew the amount of money that would be involved, and he also knew how easily she lost interest.

Her determination was firm. She answered an ad in our daily newspaper that read "Resale Shop, Going out of Business." She had finally found what suited her most. She bought the entire supply of used clothing, racks, and accessories at a very reasonable price and set up shop. She examined what she had bought and discarded what she thought was unsuitable for resale.

She placed a huge sign in front of the rented store to attract passersby. The exposure paid off. She encouraged the consignors to set reasonable prices for their items. Otherwise, besides taking up valuable space, the items would not sell. The pictures and paintings were attractively hung on the walls, the toys and baby furniture were set up in an adjoining room. It was a very pleasant setting.

Two years of responsibility was too much for Becca. The business was interfering with her social life, giving her too little time for pleasure. She decided to settle the accounts and distribute the assets. All remaining clothing was donated to the Salvation Army. She continued to seek new professions.

Norata continued his passion for traveling. His strongest desire was to visit all of Europe, or as many countries as possible. We'd go back to those he enjoyed most, he never let the business interfere with our pleasure.

We had enrolled in the Holiday International Travel Club of Boston. The tours were offered three times a year in all parts of Europe. We managed to join all of them. We felt confident leaving the business with Verna, Eve, and the employees. Verna knew the jewelry industry well and was capable of being in complete control.

When we returned from Paris, we received disturbing news: The Vermont police had called to inform us that the chalet had burned down. It had been occupied by six skiers from New York. Apparently a cigarette was left burning and ignited the bedding. The fire engines got to the site too late to save any part of the building.

Our first concern was for the skiers. "Was anybody hurt?" Norata asked.

"Luckily, no," we heard, with a sigh of relief.

The police asked questions that indicated a sense of suspicion. They were eager to speak with Ned. Norata was hesitant to call him, fearing the news would cause him to fly carelessly in his haste to rush home.

The police were somewhat persistent. Norata was worried. He was troubled and sensed a vague notion of wrongdoing. He immediately contacted our lawyer.

How sad it was. All the hard work, the expense, and the wasted money, all down the drain. It hurt financially.

We were somewhat lucky to have had insurance but

it wasn't enough to cover the entire loss. The news had some effect on Ned, who felt partially responsible, blaming himself for not being there to supervise, but the feeling soon wore off. Ned wasn't one to dwell on emotions. He had little compassion and could easily forget, which is what he did.

I was bitter with him, with his being so careless in his dealings. I mentioned that he was too occupied with his pleasures. His playboy lifestyle meant more to him than his chalet commitment. I was deeply troubled by the extravagance, but I am sure he felt, "what the hell, it didn't matter, money came easy for him."

Norata took everything in stride. He would never put his son down. I fumed, chastising him for always shielding and making excuses for his precious son. The police weren't through either. They made another visit, determined to speak to Ned. They didn't seem convinced about his account of what had happened. They had doubts, but without proof they couldn't support their suspicion.

Norata panicked, afraid of an accusation against his son. He made excuses to protect him in every way possible. He immediately had our lawyer investigate the problem. As it was, the situation was overstated and the police did not intend to pursue it further. Since the chalet had been left unattended and unsupervised, the police simply found it to be suspicious. The investigation was just a formality and nothing more came of it.

At that point Ned totally lost interest in chalets. He continued being a playboy, skiing and traveling with his plane to various resorts. He needed to be recognized. He was proud, always looking for a special something to keep him satisfied.

Norata, being a pushover, was like a genie, ready at all times to keep his son happy.

Transportation was needed to and from the airport. The spoiled kid with an expensive appetite decided that a Ferrari was much to his liking. I had no idea Norata would go that far with Ned's whims.

It didn't take much convincing. Father and son drove up in Ned's prized Ferrari.

I watched them like you watch children, going on and on, excitedly sharing their views. I was disgusted. Norata had gone too far feeding Ned's greed. I again stated that if he continues showering his son so lavishly, it will certainly ruin him. He will never be satisfied. It will destroy his ability to struggle in life.

Trying to convince him was like using twigs to hold back the tide. I was totally ignored, of course. He had complete trust in his son. "Ned will always be successful, he's a go-getter," Norata said. A go-getter indeed. "Go get all you can." Ned was fixated on luxury.

The time had finally come for Ned to prepare himself and face reality since he had to meet his own expenses. Living off his parents had gone too far. Fortunately, his developed skill in construction seemed to have paid off.

The following evening, while Norata was relaxing and watching television, Ned walked over to him and said, "Dad, I lined up two houses in Narragansett to remodel. Would you have time to help me?"

Norata was surprised. He perked up with excitement. "Sure, when will you be starting the job?"

"When I return from my trip."

We both asked, "Where are you going now?"

With his usual grin, he answered, "Aspen. I've planned a skiing trip with Thessa." He had to work in his last fling. He and Thessa were skiing partners who also spent most of their flying time together. Ned had made sure nothing was going to stand in his way of pleasure.

Thessa had recently moved from England and settled in Marblehead. She had established a dog grooming business but she never let work interfere with her pleasure. She was tall, very attractive, and wore no makeup—she was a natural beauty. Her personality was faultless. I was attracted to her immediately and I hoped that Ned would continue their relationship.

Once, in conversation, I mentioned how much I admired the exquisite window treatments that were popular in England when we were visiting there, I felt that every home was to be admired. I thought their décor was exceptional.

Before moving to the U.S. Thessa kept her promise to visit with her parents often. How sweet she was to remember that conversation. When she returned from England she surprised me with a beautiful, exquisite window curtain for our spacious picture window. It was a conversation piece. It was admired by my guests when visiting. She was special.

I was mad as hell at Ned's self-seeking, only-me attitude. He only cared for himself. He had no concern about the needs of our business, which supported his playboy lifestyle. To take Dad away from his responsibilities was going to put us in a stressful position. Remodeling two houses would take much time, and Dad was very much needed in our business. In fact, we couldn't manage without him. Norata wasn't thinking either. He was so excited that he completely forgot how important our business was.

I could see the concern in his eyes when I mentioned that his obligation to Cardin Jewelry was more important." Ned needs to find his own way to accomplish his commitments," I told him.

Norata made me a promise. "I will take whatever extra time is needed to be involved with the daily routine." He felt confident that the business would be in control with Verna and Eve assisting me, while he worked with Ned. I sensed the pleasure he was feeling, looking forward to doing what he loved best.

I reconsidered. I was not about to spoil a good thing, building was his lost love. I'm an easy mark, a weakling, always ready to please. The delight of pleasure he felt was indescribable. I refused to take that away from him.

Before the week ended, while relaxing, we were surprised to see Ned and Thessa walk in the door. They were back earlier than expected. I asked, "What happened, why are you back so soon?" Ned didn't answer, he simply walked to his room apparently, embarrassed and disappointed.

Thessa sat with us and told us what went wrong. She said, "Ned had a terrible experience, he felt capable of skiing the ninety-meter Olympic ski jump. I tried to convince him that it wasn't worth the risk," she said, "but he refused to take my advice. He insisted, there was no stopping him."

She went on. "Much to his surprise, the jump was more than he had bargained for. The frightful experience of lifting off the ground and finding himself in midair took every ounce of breath from his body. Luckily, he passed out and fell relaxed. I was afraid for him," she said, "my mind raced, how badly was he hurt? What should I do?"

She said, "The skiers gathered around him in fear.

As he got up, one young man asked Ned, 'Kid, what do you eat for breakfast? Nails?' He couldn't imagine Ned surviving that fall."

"Surprisingly, in spite of his aching body, he wasn't badly hurt," she continued. "We gathered his mangled bindings and prepared for our return trip home. He was very lucky to have survived that fall at all," she said. Thessa spent the night discussing future plans with him.

Now it was time for Ned to meet his obligations. He wasted no time preparing for his remodeling job. I was happy to think that he had finally realized that it was time to stop his carefree living. Each morning, he and his dad started out at six o'clock, working some nights until dark. Norata was happy being with his son, though I found it stressful at the shop without his help.

The weeks working with Ned were tiring for his dad. Each day, after leaving the job, Norata would rush over to our company to make certain all the jewelry orders were shipped on time. He felt my frustration, and as the building neared completion, he left the finishing touches to Ned. That was just about the extent of Ned's entire life's earnings.

Becca was included in most of Ned's plans. They both lived in one of our apartments, Becca on the first floor, Ned on the second. I felt very fortunate, having that brother-sister relationship and the love for each other. What a pleasure it gave me.

Ned was colorblind. He had difficulty matching colors. He trusted his sister to choose the clothes to wear whenever he had a special occasion to attend. He dressed simply, never putting much effort into his attire. Becca was always there to give her approval.

So many times I'd watch his plane take off and return to our field, it never occurred to me that he would have any failures until he and Becca talked about their near-miss occurrences. After that every-time they boarded the plane I remembered their conversations—and prayed.

One trip, flying south, was frightful, according to Becca. Cruising over Myrtle Beach, the plane had suddenly lost power. The pin in the throttle had let go, forcing an emergency landing. Ned was calm, showing no concern, Becca said. There was always a sense of confidence in him. He was headstrong but sure of himself. Better yet, he was unperturbed at every near-mishap.

Becca, on the other hand, was panicky, and terrified. She had to put trust in her brother. Luckily, they were nearing the airport and requested help. The only alternative was to glide the plane in. She felt somewhat relieved at the sight of the fire engines and ambulances waiting for them on the ground. Fortunately, the approach went smoothly.
Ned, she said, "kept his cool and seemed to have no fear." They continued talking about their past experiences. Overhearing their conversation made me shudder. I pretended to go about my chores while my ears were fixed on their chatter.

While flying up north, one cold and snowy day he again had to make an emergency landing because the plane's wings were taking on ice. My prayers were answered again, keeping them safe.

I lectured him many times to think safety and to take extra care in checking over the plane before flying. With his usual smile, he answered, as always, "Don't worry, Mom." He never took anything seriously. I patiently waited for the day when he would give up the plane and relieve me of worry.

Norata was an adventurer when buying and selling property. He was never able to pass up a bargain. I never knew what he was up to until closing time. I trusted his decisions since he always seemed to make the right choice. As the years passed we moved from one new home to another. He loved privacy.

The farm we purchased had been our last step in relocating. With the two homes, six apartments, and ten acres of beautiful green grassland privately surrounded by acres and acres of cleared land. A dream come true, and free of mortgage! Norata never believed in mortgaging.

Ned practiced landing his plane at the farm. Eventually, it was registered as Mystery Farm Airport, allowing him to fly in and out.

As weeks passed, I noticed his use of the plane had lessened. The pleasure he got from his toy soon wore off. He realized he had to do something more with his life.

Returning from his Florida vacation, Ned was intrigued with the thought of manufacturing suntan lotion. He turned to Norata and said, "I'm really serious, Dad. I think we can make a killing with suntan lotion. We can really make it work. Suntan lotion is always in demand at every resort. What do you think?"

Pleased with his son's idea and trusting him, Norata said "Sure, if that's what you want." The next few days were spent with Ned rushing into the preparations. He couldn't wait to get started. We thought this was his final calling. He seemed motivated to prepare for his future. At twenty-eight, he obviously realized that his playboy lifestyle had to end.

We went full throttle, wasting no time on research. We were overjoyed with his decision. It was exciting. We needed to move forward and make some inquiries. This new venture, although risky, must be a success. We had to have confidence since it would be his last costly business try.

We visited different plants to gain whatever information was possible. We were informed that Coppertone had special guided tours throughout their plant. This was a great opportunity. Immediately we made arrangements. Norata and I made the trip. The tour was very interesting.

It revealed the confidential information we needed, from the start of their production (a single barrel) to the complete automatic operation. Ned was impressed too. He couldn't wait to get started. We worked hard planning and preparing all the requirements.
The operation needed a great deal of space.

Chess Semiconductor, a well-established company, manufactured computer chips and occupied the second half of our building. They were moving forward and expanding rapidly. Luckily for us, they informed us they were moving their operation to larger quarters. It couldn't have come at a better time. Even better, some of their special unused equipment was left behind. Another blessing. It was just what was needed for our operation.

The special conveyors and large vats required an enormous amount of space. Boxes of all sizes were ordered for shipping the product. The bottles, chemicals, and equipment were ordered, machinery was set up for production, the special lab was prepared for FDA testing and approval, and the printing room was made ready. The preparations were finally completed. We were ready to go.

Rhode Island, in 1978, was no longer the jewelry capital of the world. Jewelry was becoming competitive, Japan was producing at a faster and much cheaper rate. That would have limited our production. Norata decided that being a young, fifty-five-year-old, financially set, living on the farm, surrounded by ten acres of land, three houses, six apartments, rent from the building, and a portfolio of stocks and bonds, he felt confident announcing his retirement.

I was not sure if being that young was a good idea, but it was his decision, and his excuse to concentrate on Ned's prosperity. His entire life was based on his son's welfare. It was time for Ned to realize how much his dad was sacrificing, retiring at a young age for the purpose of helping to motivate and prepare for his son's future.

I too was pleased that my son's carefree lifestyle had come to an end. I just hoped it would all be for the good.

The jewelry business was liquidated and sold. We saved a small portion of the building for Ned's friend, Angel, who needed a small place to continue with his jewelry business. Angel was a dear friend of Ned's.

Norata and I devoted the rest of our lives to working with our son, trying desperately to help and see him become successful. He was ready to make a life for himself. We continued to encourage him. We were confident, he had determination, so we were happy to fund the operation.

The suntan lotion business was very competitive. Norata realized it would take a great deal of money. In spite of the cost, he accepted the challenge with confidence, willing to take the risk.

Realizing the sacrifice, Ned felt obligated and

concerned. He eased his conscience of having to depend on us for financial support by being sure that this undertaking was going to be a success.

This was it, his final try. He felt compelled to take out a loan to relieve us of some of the financial burden. After many attempts and without credit, he was turned down. Desperate for funds, he asked if he could take out a $75,000 loan on our property just to get started. It was far-fetched. He had been a playboy all his life. How could he possibly pay for a loan? He never had any monetary responsibilities before.

Norata was against loans and instilled in his children that unless purchases were made with cash, there was no need for the purchase. However, I said, "Let's give him a chance to have some responsibility. Maybe we will be doing him justice." I felt we should give him a chance to prove himself. With that, I agreed to sign for the loan. I made it understood that he must be obligated to pay faithfully.

He assured me, "Don't worry Mom, I will make it." I trusted him.

We scheduled an appointment with Mr. Carlson, our bank manager, who seemed concerned. He turned to me and said, "Are you sure you know what you are doing?"

I answered somewhat reluctantly, "Yes." I could read his mind. He thought 'why would you trust Ned, just a young boy in his late twenties with no income, to pay off this loan?' How could I explain that the loan was to give him some responsibility and a self-start in life? We had to give him this one chance to prove his intentions.

I was convinced that the business had potential and would be a success. Also, because Ned put so much effort into trying to make it work, I trusted him. We had become a team, all working together.

The needed equipment was purchased and set up. He and his dad worked hard preparing, mixing, and storing the formula in the large vats. The machinery was purchased to automatically print the bottles and fill with oils as they rotated on the conveyor.

The silk screen room was ready for use to prepare the screens for printing. The ad in front of the building brought in many neighborhood workers.

Leon, Ned's right-hand man, was thirty-two, mechanically inclined, and quite brilliant. He was responsible for keeping the machinery in good working order and controlling the employees' specific jobs that were assigned to them.

A crackerjack, Leon had the knowledge to oversee and correct any defects the machinery developed. He was capable of taking complete control. But he had some difficulties. He was an alcoholic and usually went on weekend binges. Monday was the day when we held our breath wondering if he would show up for work. Ned was always prepared to open up on Monday.

Leon was a lonely man living with his only companion, his dog, Pal. With no family to guide him, he was careless about cleanliness, wearing the same clothes every day. Ned, with high regard for him, would occasionally, very discreetly, remind him to change his clothes. It was sad to see this talented young man living his life as an alcoholic. Despite his questionable hygiene, Leon was an asset to the company and very much needed.

The manufacturing part was completed, but now the product needed exposure. We called the product Colore D' Sole, meaning "color of the sun" in Italian.

We rented an office in Fort Lauderdale, Florida, and set up our operation for our salespeople. We advertised on radio, passed out samples, and placed printed circulars in every store window—we tried every possible exposure. Our van was completely painted with a colorful logo. The public benches along the road broadcast the Colore D' Sole product. We also posted pamphlets wherever possible.

We rented a condo for us not far from the Florida office. I spent the time alone, overseeing the salespeople and controlling the shipments as they were being delivered, while Ned and his dad worked at the plant producing the product.

I spent as much time as I could, offering small samples on the beach, at different golf courses, and at the malls. On the weekends Ned would fly his plane along the beach with the Colore D' Sole banner attached. Most of the retail stores accepted our goods on consignment. How could we lose?

With our bank account rapidly shrinking, I was filled with apprehension. We weren't showing any gain. Still, Norata felt confident. He assured me that in due time we will see a growing profit. We had to put trust in this operation. There was too much to lose.

Full of confidence, Ned took some careless chances. One Saturday he was preparing to fly the advertising banner along the beach. Ned's friend, Jack, who had taken flying lessons with him, decided to ride along during the flight.

When Ned made the approach to pick the banner up off the ground, the cord somehow got caught around the plane's wheel. If he should descend, he would surely flip over and they'd almost certainly crash. Time for some serious thinking.

They circled around wondering what procedure to take. Fortunately, Jack always had a pocketknife with him. They decided that their only choice was to try to cut the cord while they were in flight. It was a dangerous decision but the only one they could think of.

Jack took control of the plane while Ned got ready to release the cord. The only way he could do that was to secure the seat belt to his leg and hang from the open door while he cut the cord around the wheel.

Ned admitted this was the only time in his life he

was extremely frightened. It was a courageously daring stunt, but it was unavoidable. It worked just as planned! They were greatly relieved. Both admitted to have been terrified. I think God was watching over them.

We were spending an enormous amount of money advertising on radio. We were running ragged and hoping for some return. Ned was disappointed. After many, many struggling months we had exhausted all efforts. All for nothing. It was evident that the competition was too great. Coppertone controlled the suntan lotion market.

Ned was in despair. The failure left him in a state of depression. "I'm all done," he told us. He had lost all hope and confidence. It was a huge disappointment for the rest of us as well. The money and hard work, all down the drain.

Dad felt sad for Ned too. He assured him, "You're still young, you have a long life ahead of you. You're not a quitter. Never give up." Still, he was forced to give up his plane and Ferrari.

Tension Release

Norata and I needed some time to ourselves after working hard in the business.

We decided to rent an Oceanside condo on Hutchinson Island. We had rented that same suite one other time and we were familiar with the surrounding area. The condo was beautifully furnished and very spacious, easily accommodating six or more people comfortably.

The view from the sixth floor was thrilling. Every morning we would have our breakfast on the green-carpeted front patio overhang and enjoy the sights, the people walking the beach, men fishing, sailboats passing by, and the beautiful sunrise. Norata was preoccupied with his telescope, viewing people and watching for sharks and animals in the ocean.

Norata was always looking for adventure, anxious for something new. Before we left, we spread the word to our friends and family to come visit. A big pleasure during our marriage was entertaining and partying with our friends.

Saturday, while having breakfast, Norata said, "Let's take a ride to Homestead. I heard that's the one place we mustn't miss." I agreed with all the decisions he made. He knew how to make life enjoyable.

It was a lovely sunny day. We made an early start since it would take us at least three hours driving.

Norata was driving in the center lane when, out of nowhere, we were rear-ended by a nineteen-year-old woman who was speeding and drunk.

The impact pushed us off the road into a gully. It damaged the rear section of our car. Her car had a back seat full of beer bottles and front end damage. We were shook up but not really hurt. The police arrived soon after and insisted we get checked at the hospital.

We were treated and released. I later suffered severe headaches and was diagnosed with arthritis of the neck and shoulder. The only compensation we received was a check for $6,000 for the damage done to our car. The check was mailed to our home, but we never saw it. Believing in "what's yours is mine" philosophy, Ned, with his usual smile, confessed that he had received and cashed the check. He was always under the impression that our money was at his disposal to use as he wished. That belief was a gift from his dad.

We never got to see Homestead. The damage to our car had to be repaired. Since it was a new Cadillac, Norata felt it needed special work. He decided to drive it home, get it repaired, and return to the condo.

I suggested we terminate our stay and leave the island. "No way" he said. "Why would you want to forfeit our deposit? We're not leaving." He refused to end our vacation. He left early the next morning, promising to drive straight through. I suggested he take time to rest in between since it could be dangerous to drive the two-day distance without sleep.

It wouldn't have made any difference suggesting he stay the night at a motel. He wouldn't do it. Like David said, he's penny-wise and pound-foolish, though there were times when he would be cautious about spending money.

The unexpected happened. When he arrived home, Norata was full of confidence in himself since he was knowledgeable at handling most issues. But here he had the delusional idea that he could correct the car's woes—and also save some money.

He checked the car thoroughly, thinking there could be a short in the electrical system. He parked the car in front of the barn, which was isolated on our field with no one in sight. He hoped to lessen some of the damage before having to bring the car in for repairs.

As he climbed into the trunk, the hood slammed shut, trapping him inside. He panicked, kicking and kicking, desperately trying to release the locked trunk. The screams were to no avail; there was nobody around to hear them. He was terrified. In desperation, he began pulling the wires loose—and anything else he could find.

He fought and fought, while praying for a miracle. Then, miraculously, in what seemed like hours, the trunk popped open. Relieved, he couldn't forget how close he had come to death.

There's just so much you can do on an island. Norata doesn't swim and he refuses to wear a bathing suit, conscious about his legs being slightly bowed. So getting him to sunbathe is out of the question. With his open personality, he made friends with some of the men living in the hotel. He spent most of his time chatting with them. My pleasure was laying out in the sun reading a book.

Since we had invited our family and friends to join us, Cousin Pat and her husband Ben surprised us with a sudden visit. What a pleasure it was to have them with us. We pointed out the attractions and places of interest, they were impressed with the beautiful surroundings and scenery. We stopped to have lunch at the Ocean View Restaurant on the Dunes.

The menu was limited, mostly steaks and a variety of salads. Coconut is one of my favorite foods so when I saw coconut shrimp offered on the menu, I couldn't resist the temptation. That was the first time I had eaten that delicacy. What a treat!

We hadn't been vacationing long when Ned informed us that he had an opportunity to be a partner in the used car business. The expression on Norata's face, a slight grin, was an indication of approval.

I was objective. I wanted to put an end to Ned's whims. It was too easy for him to just take a chance with our money. Norata needed to stop agreeing every time. I had to make him realize what his son was doing to us.

I asked him, "Do you know how much money is needed in a car business? Do you really think our money will last? Think about this seriously. We've done enough for him already. He won't stop until he gets what he wants; he's headstrong and persistent. For once, why not let him find his own way?"

He gave his usual answer, "We have to give him an A for effort." I couldn't win. Norata was a complete fool.

That too, was a bad investment. Just a few months into the successful business, showing a profit, it came to a shrieking halt.

One car they sold had been tampered with. When a buyer had it inspected to be sure he was getting what he paid for, he found that the odometer had been turned back so the car showed fewer miles driven. The buyer pressed charges, however, they lucked out. The judge imposed a sentence of two months, with the privilege of leaving confinement every morning at six o'clock so they could conduct business. They had to be back at the facility by six o'clock at night.

With our vacation over; we left the island and returned home. Ned was content living in one of our apartments rent-free. He was a happy kid with no worries, thinking about new ventures, weighing which business risk he could take next.

He spent time remodeling his apartment to his liking. He was very exacting and had good taste in furnishings. He made his pad "very inviting," as he described it. Becca lived below him. She was thrilled at having her brother in the same house. They spent many nights together chatting and partying with friends.

In 1981, a family reunion was planned one Sunday, at one of the restaurants nearby. Everyone had fun dining and dancing.

I saw Ned sitting at the bar with a young lady. He noticed me looking at them, and motioned for me to come over. I was hesitant, not wanting to intrude, but he waved me over again. As I walked toward them, Ned stood up and greeted me with a hug and kiss, as he usually did.

I could see delight in his eyes when he introduced me to Jane, a plain yet rather attractive young lady. She was just a tad shorter than him. She had beautiful big eyes. Her long black hair covered her shoulders. She seemed shy and withdrawn.

She stood there silently, without emotion. She just answered, "Hi." I tried to make conversation, but she didn't respond. I assumed she was unfriendly, shy, or not pleased at being introduced. I did feel like I was intruding.

After exchanging a few words expressing my pleasure, I immediately walked away.

I'm usually a good judge of character. I wasn't happy at what had transpired. Nonetheless, their relationship continued as the months passed.

Becca was introduced to Jon at a party she attended for her friend Donna. She fell in love with him almost immediately. He was a pleasant gentleman, always ready to accommodate. They dated continuously. We loved him dearly and were very happy to accept him in our family.

On one date Jon noticed the scars on Becca's wrist. After Becca explained the accident in the schoolyard, he was amazed and remembered that very day. He had been playing in the same schoolyard and recalled the incident. He was surprised that after all those years he had fallen in love with his school chum.

I suggested to Norata that we include them in our next vacation, which was scheduled for the following month.

We presented Becca and Ned with an all-expense-paid trip to Italy and Greece. Becca was pleased when we invited Jon to join us. Jane, at the time, wasn't interested in any close family involvement, but I did mention that she was welcome to come along. I got no response. Jane kept her distance so I assumed she would never accept the invitation.

The connection between them was rather odd. Jane seemed uncertain and very serious. She lacked warmth. I wondered if she really loved Ned. Many times I was tempted to talk to my son about Jane's disposition, but I felt it wasn't my place to express my opinion. I felt in my heart that he was capable of making the right choice, but had he? I wanted my son to be happy with his choices, and of course I hoped he would find the right person to give him a pleasurable life.

Celebrating with my family was such a pleasure that our two weeks on vacation was truly an honor. Jon was fascinated. It was the first time he had traveled abroad. Being Irish he had trouble understanding Italian when we were in Italy, so we translated as best we could.

He was very impressed by the gondola ride through the streets of Venice. I was content knowing he was having a good time. It was his first vacation since his family business took most of his time. It required him to control the office and the truckers. The business was sand and gravel, to meet the city's needs.

At one point while Ned was driving the car, some minor incident reignited the emergence of Norata's Jekyll and Hide attitude. We just ignored him like we always did until he got over it. We had seen it happen many times. We don't know what triggers this sudden and offensive behavior.

Jon had never seen that part of Norata and was very surprised. I mentioned later, that part of him has to be ignored. It comes on suddenly but it leaves him just as quickly. Norata was too proud to consider it an issue.

The two weeks of fun finally came to an end.

Barry, who lived on the farm next to us, occupied the building and held bingo sessions every weekend.

When we returned from our trip, we were surprised with the news that his barn was suspiciously torched. It seems one of the mafia hoods, Footy, confessed, turning state's evidence against the mob about crime action in the organization. Flames from the fire were so intense they nearly ignited our second house nearby. The heat from the flames badly scorched the siding. Luckily, the house was saved from being destroyed.

The following night during dinner we were visited by the police. They gave no explanation as they told Norata that he was under arrest. I panicked. "What happened?" I asked. They completely ignored me, refusing to answer the why, or what.

We found out later in his confession, Footy had identified Norata as the one who paid to torch the barn. Norata was held overnight. I was in shock, not knowing what to do.

The following morning, I went to the police station looking for some answers. But that day, surprisingly, Norata was released. There was no evidence against him. His lawyer said that rather than go to trial to prove his innocence, he should pay a $25,000 fine and walk away. I was confused. I never could get the real or right answers.

Barry and Norata were friendly. There was no animosity between them, nor any reason for him to want the barn destroyed. Norata was saddened; he made Barry an offer of $35,000 to help him rebuild, but it was refused.

Soon after, Barry filed a lawsuit for $50,000 against me for what he thought Norata had done. The lawsuit, still binding, never went to trial. Why me? Why would he implicate me? I can only assume that it was because all of our property was in my name. We felt sorry about Barry's misfortune but we ignored the suit. Since we were not involved, we were certain there would be nothing further to support the claim.

Ned gave us the news that he and Jane had made plans to marry that following June. I was skeptical. He was not ready for marriage, he was penniless, and had nothing to offer. But that didn't seem to matter. Lack of money made no difference to him; it was always at his disposal. Why should he give it a second thought?

They planned an outdoor wedding—under a tent, held on our farm. He and his dad made all the necessary arrangements.

Jane put little effort in choosing the arrangements, other than ordering the flowers for the tables. The menu was catered. Chairs, tables, linens, and the white, large tent were rented and set up on the lawn in front of our home. I spent many weeks baking and planning for the occasion. We wanted the best for them. Expenses didn't matter.

Ned was pleased with whatever arrangements Jane made, and he acknowledged her plans to include her family. Ned very discreetly stipulated that his dad, being his best friend, was to be his best man. Norata was overjoyed and became emotional. It was the first time in my married life I saw him cry.

I was rather disappointed when Jane arrived. I expected to see the usual bride attire (a long train and veil) but she did look lovely. Her white plain ankle-length dress was simple but elegant. Her hair fell to her shoulders and was crowned with a tiny rosebud headpiece.

Before dinner was served, Norata made a toast, wishing them a happy and long life together. He then turned to Jane, with tears in his eyes, and welcomed her proudly in to our family.

The weather was in our favor; the portable band kept everyone motivated, dancing, eating, and having fun.

After spending their two-week honeymoon in the Bahamas, they returned, seemingly content.

Ned, now married, had to make another attempt to plan for his future. He and his dad, as always, exchanged opinions about business. Norata encouraged him to use what he had learned from the lotion business, since the equipment and machinery were available.

It sounded tempting, particularly since he was burden-free from all expenses related to the building. To further his study, Ned took a special course in packaging, and did some extensive research. Since he had the opportunity, and with no expense to him, he decided to take this one last chance.

Norata, admiring his son's confidence and abilities, again provided the funds needed with a line of credit, in complete control, he and his dad worked well together.

The machinery from the lotion business was being used again, in hopes that this venture would be his final attempt. At first, the packaging business was a struggle. The machinery and the conveyors had to be set up. Bottles of all sizes and shapes were ordered, and the lab was again prepared for storing formulas and chemicals as the orders rolled in.

To get a good start in production, help was needed in every spot. Since I had no commitments and Ned was now married and desperately needed to succeed, I offered to take part controlling the chemicals incubation periods and rotating the storage at intervals. Norata and I left at the same time every day to help with this venture.

FDA forms were filled and registered in preparation

for approval. Other employees were assigned to specific positions. Leon remained the supervisor. All preparations finally came to a close. We were ready to move forward. Like all businesses, time was needed for advancement.

Ned became a workaholic, trying hard to fulfill his dream. Making money meant everything to him, especially now that he had the responsibilities of a marriage.

Jane was a fine beautician and worked at the local college, but not for long—she became pregnant and gave up her position.

The thrill of becoming a grandmother overwhelmed me. I looked forward to the day when I would be called "Nana."

I strived for a good relationship with Jane. I wanted her to feel like my second daughter. One day in conversation I made a promise to her. I told her, "Jane, I want us to be a family. I will never interfere in your married life. If ever I should say or do something to displease or offend you in any unintentional way, please tell me."

She evidently never forgot those words since she confronted me with them many times. I tried hard to choose my words and live up to my promise but I never seemed to come across right. Jane would misconstrue anything I said or did. I had the feeling she resented the close bond I had with our son.

Ned seemed happy looking forward to being a dad. Although I noticed that their marriage was shaky. Many times Jane approached me complaining about Ned's behavior. She never gave me a why or what, just complaints. I really don't think she loved him. I concluded that the attraction between them came from his impression of wealth, from his plane and Ferrari.

It seemed that Jane wasn't happy living in Ned's small apartment. I understood how uncomfortable it could be raising a child in a one-bedroom apartment, but the thought of Ned having to pay rent was against his better judgment with his finances at that time.

With no resources to work with, just starting out and struggling was no time to take on added expenses. Businesses need time to catch on. Orders were coming in gradually. Still, Jane was persistent and Ned had to consider the alternative.

He desperately tried to ignore the threat, but she made the move without him. She rented a small apartment not far from the plant. Ned had no choice. He moved out and joined her soon afterward.

Their apartment was not much larger than the one they left behind, plus the fact that he now had to pay all the expenses. It was a bad time for him. He needed to concentrate on building the business. Jane and the move were inconsiderate.

I suspected that Jane's insistence on moving was to

distance him from his family. If so, she was in for a rude awakening. Ned had nothing to give. In his early thirties, he was still living off his parents and trying desperately to overcome his misfortunes. Without our monetary help, he would never be able to succeed in this business.

Copenhagen

Our travel group had our trip planned to visit Copenhagen before Jane was pregnant. Unfortunately, just before we were to leave, Jane had a miscarriage. It was too late to cancel our already-paid-for trip. How was I going to convince her that canceling would mean forfeiting our complete package?

I feared the reaction from her, and when we returned home I was right. Jane was angry. She let it be known that we were unconcerned. She made it clear how very important it was for us to be there for her at that sad time. My apologies meant nothing. But honestly, I felt that most of it was just an excuse. She took every opportunity to find a way to chastise me.

Business was slowly growing for Ned. He had a strong desire to make this work. He was determined and eager for success. He spent long hours at work and took too much time away from home.

Jane made several calls complaining about the long hours he spent at the plant. He sometimes arranged to leave work so they could spend dinnertime together. I tried to comfort her, explaining how sacrifices had to be made to succeed in business. I told her that I sympathized because I had experienced the same situation, but she wasn't convinced.

Jane always called me Mae, and once in conversation she said, "You know, Mae, I wish I had married a man with an eight-hour-a-day job." I did not respond but I thought, what would happen to this marriage if Jane has this attitude? Why wouldn't she consider working along with him in the business? She had the opportunity since she was now free after leaving her job at the college.

I sensed the troubled state they were in. Jane wasn't happy with their marriage. Norata and I felt the burden Ned was experiencing. We spent as much time as possible at the plant to try to relieve him of the pressure she was putting on him.

Two years later, Jane became pregnant again, Ned was hoping this time it would be a boy. In her eighth month, almost ready to deliver, she made a surprise visit at the plant. I was working the conveyor, dispensing bottles, when Jane walked in to show off the sonogram of her daughter to Ned.
I was excited. I passed the conveyor over to Betty, a coworker, and walked right over to Jane. I extended my hand and asked if I could see the picture. She stared at me for a second, and with a look of resentment, handed me the picture. I should have realized then that I had made the mistake of

intruding. It was the wrong gesture, without thinking.

If looks could kill, I would have died on the spot. Jane looked at me with hatred in her eyes. Why would she have so much animosity toward me? I tried hard to be nice to her.

I felt drained. It pulled the skids from under me. The resentment hurt. I was determined to hang in there and accept her as she was. I returned the picture and walked away. I spent the rest of the day wondering what it was I had said or done that she resented.

Three weeks later, 1985, Lianne was born a beautiful child. I was thrilled. I finally got my wish to be a Nana. But many disappointments were waiting for me.

My first sight of her through the glass window was not enough. I wanted desperately to hold and cuddle her. After four days, Jane was released from the hospital, starting her new role as a mother.

Ned was happy with his daughter and tried to spend as much time with her as possible, but his business still took up much of his time.

Jane's attitude had changed completely. She became very distant after Lianne was born. I hoped to have a close relationship with my granddaughter, but Jane was not about to give me that pleasure.

One day I felt a desperate urge to see Lianne. I called Jane and asked if I could come and visit to see my granddaughter. I was deeply hurt with her response. "You may come today," she said, "but I wouldn't want you to make it a habit every day."

My feelings were shattered; I felt so much hurt. I knew then that Lianne was going to be a stranger in my life. Jane knew that I wasn't one to impose. I was caught in a losing position, uncertain as to whether I should take a chance and make my visit or keep my distance and wait for an invite.

I wondered why she would deprive me of this one precious time in my life? I took the chance anyway. I didn't expect a warm welcome, but I overlooked my feelings and took the opportunity to see my granddaughter. I had an uneasy feeling as I walked up the stairs to the apartment. I kept thinking, why am I feeling this uncomfortable? Lianne belongs to my son too.

I wondered how Jane would react to my visit. I was relieved when Jane's mom, Marie, greeted me at the door. Jane seemed aggravated. Lianne was a colicky baby and cried excessively. Jane was busy walking, holding Lianne in her arms and trying to comfort her. The housekeeper was busy cleaning the apartment while Marie and I exchanged a few words. I felt uneasy and made my visit short. I never got to hold my granddaughter.

I kept silent, never discussing Jane's attitude with Ned. I refused to burden him. There would be no use anyway. He was a wimp; he'd never be able to stand up to her. My impression was that he feared her.

I was certain he was aware of her disagreeable behavior. He lived with her.

I didn't get to see Lianne very often. I offered to babysit whenever I was needed, which was very seldom and only when Jane was desperate for a sitter, However, it was offered, I welcomed the opportunity.

Lianne's long absence was hard for me. I hated myself for not being strong and accepting the fact that I was never going to be allowed the closeness I so badly wanted with her.

Lianne was six months old when I again had the desire to see her. Norata, feeling my pain, asked Jane if she would bring Lianne to see me. Cruelly, and without compassion she replied, "when Becca has a child, she can have her wish." It was almost like she found pleasure in hurting me.

Norata did not have the same feelings as I did. He showed no emotion and didn't care at all about her negative feelings.

I often wondered why Jane was so full of animosity. Despite her deplorable personality I tried to please her in every way. I considered myself a good mother-in-law, always ready to help, never refusing her. Finally, I convinced myself that I should be thankful, I can look forward to being with Lianne on her birthday and some holidays.

In April of 1986, I answered an ad to be a hospital volunteer. My goal was to work in the nursery caring for the babies. I loved children. I started as a patient representative, helping to improve the quality of their hospital stay. I really wanted the baby position, hoping to fulfill the feelings of loss and deprivation of not having my granddaughter in my life.

One special twenty-five-year-old impressed me the most. Debra, a pretty, light-skinned natural blonde with a million-dollar personality was blind and had just given birth to her first child. Each day Debra looked forward to my visit. She would squeeze my hand and talk about her happy life with her husband. She said there were times in her life when she was absolutely devastated with her affliction, until she met Bob who tries his best to make her happy. She said, "Our baby is God's blessing, and I praise him daily for our good fortune."

I visited Debra every day to deliver and read her mail. She became my special friend.

Being in the nursery somewhat offset the rejection I was feeling from the absence of Lianne. I had the pleasure of feeding and comforting babies whose mothers were unable to care for them.

There were days of sadness, seeing a baby with no arms, crack babies withdrawing from addiction, and babies born unwanted. It depressed me. Sometimes I looked at those beautiful unwanted babies and wished I could have taken them home. The hospital staff was pleased with my help. Every quarter they presented me with a gold pin for being efficient and caring.

The hospital waiting room needed to be wallpapered. I offered to take on the responsibility for doing the job. Mr. Spencer, the hospital manager, was amazed that I was capable of handling the project. It was a small conference room, just about eight or nine feet square. At the time I was gifted and talented in decorating. I wallpapered my bedrooms to correspond with the room's bedding. I took pride in my talent. Occasionally I would peek in the room to lift my sense of pride.

Ned had big dreams. He was unhappy with his apartment and wanted to build a home for his family. Approaching Dad was no problem. Norata encouraged him, as usual. Besides pleasing his son, he was always happy to resume his dormant love of building.

The land Ned chose was situated in a private community with elaborate, well groomed, exquisitely landscaped homes. That it was too exclusive for Ned didn't matter—money came easy. I assumed that Cardin Jewelry was taken advantage of as the source of this new luxury. He was so spoiled at using our funds that whenever he wished he took us for granted.

Money was no object. Oblivious to it, he chose plans for an elegant, seven-room home with an indoor adjoining pool, a Jacuzzi, a hot tub, a sauna, and a built-in fire pit. The pampered child, striving for recognition, had to have the very best. He was in no position to build elaborately. The business was growing slowly and he definitely had no funds of his own to work with.

I was concerned, I asked Norata, "Where is he getting the money to build this beautiful home? He's in no position for this extravagance. The business is showing little profit." I got no answer.

Norata never gave me answers when I asked questions about his son. He knew that I did not agree with Ned's expensive tastes. It was quite clear. The funds transferred from Cardin Jewelry to Ned's account were slowly ciminishing. Ned took advantage of his position as president, as well as being a junior. The fact that the account was continuously running in the red made it clear that he was draining the company for his lavish cravings. Norata was aware of his son's actions but he stood silently by, unconcerned.

I was kept in the dark about many things concerning the business. Only when I became inquisitive and asked were things explained to me. Norata buttered up the explanations to satisfy my concern. It was clear that Ned took advantage of our good benevolent nature with his extravagant spending.

Norata was excited at how the house progressed. His experience in carpentry and building homes in the past gave him the incentive needed to accomplish the task with his son. They worked hard running the business and building in their spare time. Leon too worked overtime supervising.

Money seemed to be no object for Ned. The rich kid's taste leaned toward grandeur—hardwood floors, hand-carved moldings, a mahogany fireplace, sliding glass doors into the heated pool area, heated skylights overhead—the luxuries of a millionaire.

Ned never gave a small offer of help or showed a small offer of kindness. He was becoming greedy. I had my assumptions. There was no way he could have accumulated any money in such short time.

Norata's philosophy all through life was, "Give to your children, watch them enjoy their inheritance while you are alive, you've lost that pleasure after you're gone." Those words were our destiny, and our destitution.

Whenever there was a lull at the plant, Norata's strong desire to travel kicked in. He made new plans. We always enjoyed shopping. With his son in mind, Norata enjoyed visiting stores that suited Ned's needs.

We went to Montreal and while walking through the wholesale district we came upon a lighting fixture establishment. Ned was not quite ready for fixtures but Norata couldn't wait. He was so anxious to please his son, he felt compelled to buy what he thought was suited for the new home. He had a controlling nature. He thought that by providing for his son he had the right to dominate.

I tried to discourage him about making any purchases where Ned was concerned because he was quite fussy about his furnishings.

As if that wasn't enough, Canada was well-known for their wrought iron. Norata had a special railing made for the second floor balcony overhang and shipped everything by freight. Ned was happy with the railing but unhappy with his choice of fixtures. They've been stored in our barn ever since, collecting dust.

Jane was not a happy person. She showed little emotion after moving into her beautiful home. Although she chose most of the furnishings, she seemed unimpressed and uncaring. I'm certain she was irritated with Norata for his trying so hard to please his son. It was both obvious and very clear that she envied the relationship between father and son.

At one point, frustrated and after many lectures, Jane turned to Norata and offensively said, "Why don't you cut the umbilical cord? Let your son stand on his own two feet. Let him be allowed to fend for himself."
Norata completely ignored her. He was immune to her remarks. I'm sure that she felt it wasn't Norata's place to choose which fixtures were suitable for their home.

She was right but those cutting words were meaningless to him. Ned needed his dad for support, and clearly,ax his dad could not survive without his precious son.

Jane apparently closed her eyes to the fact that her comfort was all due to our generosity. I suggested to Norata that since our money was beginning to dwindle, it was time to take her advice. He ignored me. He refused to cut that cord, his cherished son was his life.

Part of his thoughtless goal of retiring at fifty-five was to be an anchor, a buddy available for his son's needs. He beamed with joy at every burdensome task his son performed.

Ned continued to struggle in spite of the fact that he was keeping his head above water, or, so it seemed.

In August of 1989, we were approached and offered a sizeable sum for our building. It was an offer too tempting to refuse. It was an opportunity for our survival. It would be our nest egg, enough security to carry us living comfortably through our old age.

Ned was full of anger. He was determined not to let the sale happen.

Norata assured him that finding another building for his operation was not a problem. Convincing him otherwise was impossible. Ned kept pressuring, making excuses as to why his dad would be making a mistake. Ned knew how well situated he was, never having to pay rent or expenses on the building. That wasn't enough. He wanted it all.

He tried every angle and promise, upping the pressure, hoping to convince us that he would be able to buy the building. "I'm confident, Dad," he said, "that the business is growing. I will make it if you would consider my offer of $175,000."

After listening to his promises Norata continued trying to make him understand that he had no control because the building was in my name. That was the first time I heard Norata make an excuse against Ned's wishes. I was in no way fooled by my son's conniving. He kept at it, turning to me, looking for some way to convince us.

"If you give me the opportunity, Mom, with time payments I will be able to pay for it with the promise of $50,000 down and $2,000 a month."

Ridiculous. He was grasping for straws, without anything to convince us. The purchase offer for the building was three times his proposal. Why would we even want to consider his offer? I ignored him. I didn't answer him. This would be the one time he will be refused to feed his greed and selfishness. I listened as he continued trying to persuade me, but I gave him no satisfaction. Where could he possibly accumulate that sizeable sum, unless he planned to deceive us and continue to take whatever money is available? I loved my son but I didn't trust him.

There was no stopping him. Our spoiled son was determined to get what he wanted. He didn't give up trying.

Norata was weak. I could see his disappointment in having to refuse his son. I wondered how Ned would be able to make monetary promises with the position he was in.

The finishing touches on his house were left incomplete because he lacked funds. The landscaping was not in place, the shrubs still had to be planted, the patio leading into the pool area needed to be finished, and much more needed work.

He was spoiled because he had never been denied or refused anything; he just assumed his dad would continue to fulfill his dreams and desires without limit. But now his dad had no control. The building was in my name and I wasn't about to fall into his trap. Or, so I thought.

Ned had taken advantage of our generosity all his life. He knew nothing about returning kindness, just selfishly wanting what he chose.

I asked him, "Where could you possibly get that amount of money when your business is barely surviving and your loans are still outstanding?" I got no response. He was an introvert and words never came easily for him. He couldn't express himself or show emotion. So he had no answer to my question.

I suspected he was holding out on us somehow. Had our son been secretly stashing our funds for his own use? Could he have deceived us? He always felt assured and able to overcome any temptation. He was a taker, everything he had was taken from our accounts.

Norata never put his son down. He always buttered up every craving.

He suggested that this would be an opportunity for Ned to make good on his promises. "He's motivated to being a success. He will make it." Norata said.

Ned, I'm sure, made the suggestion and his dad bit. "Drawing up an on-demand promissory note will satisfy him," Norata said. "With that, you will have complete control."

I was hesitant. It sounded logical, but I wasn't sure because I didn't trust Ned. "Why worry?" Norata said. "If we have him sign a promissory agreement it will mean nothing unless it's paid." Again he said, "You will be in complete control."

Norata was trying to please me and his son. "Let him feel like he's being considered. He's struggling to make a life for his family. There's no way he can afford to pay for this building right now and as long as you continue to hold the note he can't have any control."

The pressuring continued, "We just have to give him some satisfaction." With the non-stop pressure I was beginning to weaken. I did feel secure with a promissory note. I was hesitant but thought that as long as I'm in control I have nothing to lose.

Ned took the opportunity in my uncertainty and arranged an appointment with Frank, our lawyer at the time, to draw up the note that would make the transaction legal.

I felt that was just a piece of paper, like Norata said, it meant nothing as long as I kept the unsigned note in my possession. It made no difference since the profitable opportunity we had, was lost. I doubted we would ever get another generous offer like that again.

The months came and went. Ned was making strenuous efforts to survive, struggling to make some progress. Still, the monthly loan payments on our properties were being ignored. Every time it was mentioned I got false promises.

More time passed. Ned complained all the time about his lack of funds and how hard he was working to keep his business operating. Norata sympathized with him—and believed him, even though he was spending enormous amounts of money buying equipment, time shares, and who knows what else. I felt that my son was toying with his dad. I resented his insincerity and manipulation.

Our travel group had scheduled a flight to Austria. I welcomed this particular trip. I had a purpose in mind. I needed some additional pieces of blue delft china to add to my collection that I had purchased on our previous visit.

Norata surprised me. He usually jumped at the

opportunity to travel. It was his greatest treat. But this time he refused. He wasn't happy about leaving because his son needed him right now.

I thought that this would be a good opportunity for Ned to realize how important his dad really was. I shared my thoughts with Norata. I told him to take this time to make your son appreciate you. Let him make decisions without your help. Let him think for himself. Let him realize how important you are to him. You need to do this.

It worked. He listened, and saw the wisdom of what I said. Sometimes I can persuade him to make the right choice. He's also an easy target when it comes to travel.

Norata always rented a car whenever we traveled. He was interested in the culture of the countries we visited. While we were enjoying a drive through the lovely countryside, we unexpectedly found ourselves at the Budapest border. We drove right into a nightmare.

Hungary at that time was a communist country. It was very unfriendly to outsiders, and movement inside of it was restricted to non-citizens. Certainly, this was not a place to visit.

But we were too far past the border to make a U-turn. Almost immediately, we were surrounded by heavily armed soldiers, some with their guns drawn. They made gestures for us to follow them. We were unaware of the danger we faced.

Speaking no English, they motioned for us to get out of the car, as they scoured the insides of the car looking for who knows what. They led us into a small, gloomy, run-down concrete block building with a huge solid steel door. We couldn't communicate. We were trapped and afraid.

When our passports were taken from us, I felt my body weaken. I wondered, what will they do with us? What if they refuse to return our passports? Did they think we were spies? How could we ever get home without our passports? We were definitely in trouble. We could never get out of here!

After their constant search they found nothing suspicious in the car, they motioned for us to sit down in this barely-furnished room—it had five chairs and a simple metal desk. The hallway was narrow with one door on each side. I assume they were leading us into private rooms. The floor was poured cement, painted grey, and somewhat pitted.

We tried to explain that we were on vacation and unintentionally found ourselves at the border. Since they didn't speak English, they didn't respond. The soldiers occasionally walked past us, in and out of the building. We just sat motionless, staring at each other, wondering what they were doing, what was going to happen next. I trembled with fear. Norata pretended to be calm, but I sensed the concern in him too.

After two frightening hours, our passports were finally returned to us and we were permitted to leave. We learned later how foolish we were to blindly stray with armed communists on guard, and how lucky we were to be released. A frightful experience.

Blueberry Season

July was blueberry season. It seemed like a perfect day for picking. Norata and I thought what a treat it would be for Lianne if she were with us picking berries. I took the chance and called Jane to ask if we could have her for the day. Much to my surprise, she said, yes.

What a pleasure it was to have her. She was only six, but she had the intelligence of a nine-year-old. I watched her proudly eating berries, dividing them up, one in her mouth, and one in her basket.

After an hour of picking and close to lunchtime, I noticed Lianne getting bored. I suggested we leave and have lunch at the Foster Country Club. Lianne was able to read quite well with our help, so she chose her lunch from the menu. She enjoyed being with us; we showered her with love.

After lunch, we gathered what was left from the bread basket and walked a short distance to a nearby pond to feed the ducks. Lianne was excited. It was a pleasure watching her throw scraps of bread to the gathering ducks. After our bread ran out, we decided to show her off to some of our relatives who had never seen her. We were so proud introducing her. Our visits with them were short since much of the day had gone by. It was late afternoon and time to take her home.

As we approached the front door, Jane was standing there, furious, with her hands on her hips. She let loose a blast of anger. "Where have you been?" she roundly reprimanded us. I had no idea why she was so disturbed. I guess we kept Lianne longer than was expected.

We were stunned and speechless. There had been no particular time for us to have her home. We assumed that in asking Jane if we could have her for the day meant just that. We were embarrassed and tongue-tied. Unpredictability with Jane was no surprise. All I could say was "I'm sorry."

Jane responded, "I want to know where my daughter

is at all times."

Didn't she realize that her daughter was in good hands and well cared for with her grandparents?

More than being surprised, we were especially hurt with Ned sitting there witnessing the outburst and saying nothing. He was obviously afraid of her. How could he allow his wife to talk to us so meanly? It was obvious that Jane was in control. This also affirmed that Ned was physically and morally weak, afraid of standing up to her—and not as loyal to us as we thought. That was the last time we ever had Lianne to ourselves.

Why had she refused to accept our family? What makes her so distant, I wondered, we had tried to overlook her unpleasant, disagreeable attitude—we pretended to ignore it, we so wanted family unity.

Becca and Jon were now married and living a wonderful life. They had their wedding on the farm same as Ned.

Becca was a beautiful bride. She planned her attire and ceremony to her liking. As usual, she looked stunning. Ned was best man for his sister. For whatever reason Jane was in denial and refused to attend the ceremony.

Becca was happy. She and Jon were compatible; they planned to build their home together. Jon told her to choose whatever plans she liked. Knowing Becca, with her expensive tastes, she chose an exclusive three-level exclusive home. Jon was a man of very few words with short conversations. He loved Becca and gave in to her every wish. His trademark comment was, "Anything to make her happy."

Our daughter, like her brother Ned, also had champagne tastes. She was fascinated by the special furniture available in Florida. She thought nothing of traveling there to pick and ship back what she wanted. Jon took delight in spoiling her. Luckily, he was able to afford her expensive tastes.

For eight years Becca tried desperately to conceive. She never gave up. Each month was exactly the same, waiting for a sign and receiving disappointment. Finally, after many more months of praying, the suspense came to an end. Becca was overjoyed. Her prayers were answered. She got her wish and was ready for her new arrival.

My world opened up too. I was very happy with the wonderful news. Unlike her brother, Becca didn't have a selfish bone in her body. She was kind, generous, and full of compassion. She was always trying to please. We were certain that her child would be a part of our lives.

I wished that my mom could have been here for the birth, sharing the joy with me. Becca loved her grandmother Norni very much. She spent most of her growing up days being with her. Norni had looked forward to the day when Becca would marry. She loved Jon and wanted so badly to see them walk down the aisle. Sadly, she never got her wish. She became very ill and passed away two months prior.

Norni was more than a grandmother to Becca, and the thought that she never got her wish made Becca very sad. She vowed to visit Norni in spirit. On her wedding day, after the church ceremony, she asked the driver to make a stop at the cemetery. There, she said a prayer and cried some. It was what she wanted to do on her wedding day.

Nine months later, August 28, was one of the happiest days of my life. Tayla was born, a beautiful healthy baby girl. She brought us so much happiness.

Becca was exhausted. Tayla had her days and nights reversed. I was thrilled when I was asked if I would spend a few nights with her so she could get some rest. What a treat to be with that beautiful child. I was happy being able to hold and bathe and cuddle her. I thanked God many times for bringing this pleasure of happiness to us. Every day was a blessing. As the days passed, she adjusted normally.

Tayla was three months old and needed to be christened. Becca's first thought of course, was to have her brother and Jane do the honors. Without hesitation, to our surprise, Jane accepted.

Since I had my new granddaughter to love and cherish, I gave up volunteering at the hospital and spent most of my days with her.

Saturday was Becca and Jon's night out. I was glad

for the opportunity to babysit. I was thankful for never being deprived the pleasure of enjoying Tayla. Becca felt the need for her to have a good relationship with her grandparents just as she once had.

Jane resented the fact that I was close to Tayla. She often told me to let Becca care for her own child. "You shouldn't be available at every whim," she would say. Why, I wondered, would she have so much resentment? Was it rivalry or opposition?

When I tried to explain that being with that bundle of joy brought us much happiness, she refused to understand. The tables had turned. Jane was full of animosity.
Two years later, just before Thanksgiving, Jane was pregnant again. Ned was overjoyed, hoping he would be blessed with a son. Jane was anything but overjoyed because she had no intention of having another child. She said it was a mistake. She was frustrated and unhappy. Ned, however, was eager for the coming, so sure was he that he was going to have a son.

The months passed, Jane was due. We were busy working when Ned got the call. In a flash he dropped what he was doing and left. Four hours later we got the expected call, "Mom, it's a boy." Norata was so happy for his son, congratulating him with kindness. The waiting was over. Ned was blessed with a handsome son—a healthy, beautiful baby boy.

We were both delighted to have a grandson. We

prayed that Jane would have a change of heart and let us be a part of his life.

Ned glowed with pride feeling the same love his dad had felt when Ned was born. It was true: like father, like son. Ned had the same expectations that his dad had for him.

The excitement kept him busy and bushed between his work schedule, the hospital visits, and checking in on Lianne who was staying with Jane's mom.

At that time, hospital stays were five to six days after delivery—too much for Ned. Norata and I usually waited up for him, expecting him to walk in the door after leaving the hospital. The extra twenty-minute drive home was too tiring for him.

Friday, at 11:30, after waiting patiently, Norata said, "Mae, let's get to bed. Ned isn't coming." Just then the doorbell rang. Surprisingly, it was him.

I asked, "What brings you here at this hour?"

"Jane is being discharged tomorrow morning," he said. "I had some unfinished work to tend to. I just left the building. I really don't feel like driving home. I'm staying the night."

Norata was delighted, hoping he and his son could enjoy some small talk. Not that night. I could see the stress in him. My first instinct was always the same, "Are you hungry? Would you like something to eat?" "No, Mom," he replied, "I've already eaten, I'm just tired. I'm going to be busy with Jane tomorrow." He wasted no time taking off his shoes. Without saying another word, he spread himself across the bed and in five minutes he was in deep sleep. I covered him with a blanket and left him to rest.

Our bedrooms were on opposite ends of our house. I awoke early and prepared a breakfast for him. I felt, like my mom, that food was very important. I feared that in his haste to get to the hospital he may go hungry.

After a while I wondered why he hadn't awakened. That made me curious. I walked into the room. He had already left.

I prayed that now Jane would let me be the grandmother I so wanted to be. Again I asked her to depend on me if I was ever needed. She seemed to be more understanding.

At one point in conversation she surprised me with, "I believe that children should have a good relationship with their grandparents." I was stunned. Could she be playing with my feelings? Until then I'd never heard such pleasant words from her mouth. I wondered if what she said was true. Had she really considered me to be involved with her children? If her intent was real, I thought, I would be happy. And maybe it was. Occasionally she depended on me when she needed a sitter.

Five more years passed. Tayla loved her cousin Lianne. She was a lonesome child and always sought other children to play with. She looked forward to spending occasional weekends at our house. Her first words when she visited were "Nana, will you take me to see Lianne?"

Although Tayla was her godchild, Jane somehow resented her. I wondered whether it was resentment that Jane felt, or envy of the pleasure we felt from having our grandchild with us.

Many times when I called and asked Jane if I could bring Tayla to visit I was given some excuse like, "Oh, we won't be home," or, "We were just leaving." she always sidestepped the question.

One Sunday morning I called Jane and asked if it would be all right to have Tayla spend an hour with Lianne while I went to church. She answered very arrogantly, "I won't babysit while your daughter is resting in bed."

I did not know how to respond, so I said, "Okay" and hung up without saying good-bye. I was crushed at having to make up excuses to that child why she couldn't visit with her cousin. Becca was unaware of the resentment Jane had for her. Why let it be known? I wanted family harmony.

Becca loved children and tried to have another child soon after Tayla's arrival. Nothing happened for a long time, but she never gave up. Five years later Maddy was born. Jon was hoping for a boy, but it made no difference. He loves his girls.

Maddy was born very fragile. She needed constant care. Her temperature would rise to 105°F or higher. Her hospital visits were frequent. The doctors performed numerous tests and could not detect the cause. We prayed, hoping to find an explanation and a cure. After three weeks in the hospital and many tests, the problem was found. It was Kawasaki disease, a rare disease about which little was known.

Becca had to be extremely careful trying to keep her physically healthy since her heart had been affected. She got special care; a recurrence was a constant fear. Fortunately, she outgrew the disease as the years passed.

I was so proud to have four beautiful grandchildren. I had visions of a close bonding relationship with them as they grow up.

Lianne, besides being a straight-A student, was also very talented. From a very young age Jane put all her effort into developing her abilities, especially ballet and piano. Each year I looked forward to seeing her perform at the college with the State Ballet.

Norata and I made it a point to buy our tickets early to be sure to sit directly in front of the stage with Lianne in full view. How proud we were watching her perform so gracefully.

Ned lacked nothing. His every whim was his command. He followed his desires completely. He built an indoor grille in the pool area for his personal enjoyment.

Many nights, after leaving the plant, he would head straight to the grill and prepare his favorite meals—hamburgers and steak. Jane was obsessed with Lianne becoming a star. Both devoted all of their time to ballet practice. Preparing meals was not one of Jane's choices.

One Wednesday about 4:30 Jane called me asking if I would bring some Tylenol for a slight headache she was experiencing. I hurriedly drove to her house. I took advantage and stayed a while to be with the children.

Ned came home shortly after I arrived. He was surprised and happy to see me. Jane prepared a lettuce salad with a clump of plain tuna and placed it on the table for him. Embarrassed, he said, "Jane, is this my supper?"

Jane arrogantly replied, "Oh, eat it and shut up." It broke my heart to see the abuse he had to face. Jane was evidently unconcerned about the effect it had on me, his mother. I supposed that she was trying to prove a point: she ruled, she was in control.

I wanted to spit out my anger right there, but I held back. I was disgusted with my son for ignoring her offensive behavior, for pretending not to see what she really is. What made her so cruel? She had everything to make her happy—a housekeeper to care for her home, a beautiful car, the freedom of doing as she wished, no responsibilities, never having to please her husband. What more could she possibly want?

She obviously was a good mother, devoting all her attention to making her kids good students. But a good wife? She was unconcerned. She had no idea.

In business, there were often times for Ned to make social commitments, but that would never happen, he could never offer an   invite. Our family often asked Ned how his home was progressing. They hoped to see the set-up in the pool area. In fact, Cousin Randy asked him directly, "When are you going to invite us over? Everyone is eager to see your home."

He was caught in a dilemma. In spite of Jane's resentment, he was proud of the beautiful home he built and was happy to show it off, so he answered, "Sure, come anytime."

Without giving him a chance to retract it, Randy asked, "Will tomorrow night be okay?"

He answered, "Of course."

The next night was rather cold, but everyone came anyway, bathing suits and all. They were having a great time using the whirlpool and sauna and taking pictures.

Suddenly Jane walked in the door to the unexpected surprise. She heard the laughter and chatter and walked into the pool area. She showed no emotion, just a quick hi and a quick exit. She clearly wasn't happy with the sudden get-together. Randy reacted to Jane's unpleasant attitude and decided that since everyone had enjoyed the three hours of fun, it was time to leave.

I wondered to myself, what will Ned face after everyone leaves? He'll surely catch hell. But, we'll never know.

Growing up was very special for Ned, our home always had a welcome atmosphere, friends and family gatherings were special, how disappointing it must be for Ned to be deprived of that pleasure.

I usually took advantage of the summer months to entertain. I got so much enjoyment planning occasional outdoor parties. Our home was set far back from the road with acres of beautifully cleared, well
groomed land, a perfect setting for open-air gatherings. Norata had a yen for barbecuing or roasting pig on a spit. We set up umbrella tables, a makeshift bar for liquor and drinks, and game necessities. An open invitation, Norata's three cousins and their families from New York were included. We partied until everyone decided to leave. Those were unforgettable, special times.

Ned yearned to be with his family of cousins. He was especially close to Cousin Dan who had much in common with him. They were motorcycle buddies. Their cycling day was always on Sunday.

Dan was interested in guns and anxious to see Ned's prized collection, which ranged from antiques to the latest design. Proud of his collection, Ned invited him to stop by and view it.

Dan took advantage of the invitation and brought his wife Loriann along with, thinking she would spend a short time with Jane.

Their visit was surprisingly short, Loriann was highly insulted at being treated so rudely.

After Jane greeted them at the door, she intentionally excused herself, without an explanation, and went directly upstairs to attend to her children. She ignored their visit, refusing to join them. They were humiliated and shocked by Jane's attitude. They couldn't wait to leave. They were so upset by Jane's rudeness they promised never to visit again.

It was plain to see that Ned was living in a state of embarrassment. I can imagine how he must have felt with her distasteful behavior.   Jane was irrationally jealous and extremely unpredictable. Her immediate family was all she cared about. They were her only concern, responding pleasantly with them.

Ned never said a word about Jane's rudeness, he was meek, a weakling, never able to fight back or spit out his ill feelings.

In his younger days I never remember him arguing or being negative in any dispute. He'd back off at any disagreement. He didn't seem able to show concern. It was unfortunate that Jane took advantage of his weak spot and good moral character. How sad to have pride in having built this beautiful home and not being able to offer an invite. I remember one particular day that I needed to bring some special paperwork that involved Jane to her home. To my surprise, her entire family was visiting for a special purpose, to take turns talking by phone to Jane's nephew Bob, who was in service and stationed overseas. Nobody seemed concerned about the cost of phoning and Jane couldn't have cared less.

Jared was very much affected by asthma; an inhaler was carried with him at all times. Jane, being overprotective, watched him very close. During her pregnancy, Jane was a heavy smoker. Although she was a caring and devoted mother, she evidently didn't realize the harm she was causing him.

I remember one time when she came to my home to pick up a document for Ned. I ran out to the car, excited to see Jared. When I opened the car door, the smoke poured out like a rolling cloud. My heart ached for him, still a tyke, breathing in all that smoke. I didn't dare say a word since Jane was not one to accept criticism. Today I have a heavy and unforgivable regret that I didn't reprimand her.

Holidays were very special to me. I especially looked forward to Christmas. It meant a time for all my family to be together. I took pleasure in preparing special foods, baking special desserts, and setting my table elegantly with fine china, crystal, and sterling silver. My table was always picture-perfect. I put all my effort into making it a pleasant day.

We would exchange and open our presents before dinner. How happy it made me to watch my grandchildren, full of excitement, anxiously tearing open the boxes. By late afternoon it was rest time. Everyone lounged around, fully contented, letting the food settle while the children played with their toys and games.

No matter how hard I tried to make Jane comfortable, she would always be anxious to leave. Jane soon informed me that they no longer would be spending Christmas Day at my home. She would, however, visit us on Christmas Eve. I was terribly disappointed, but of course, I had to accept her wishes.

After that, the holidays were spent with Becca and her family, usually at our favorite restaurant. We always made it a point to visit Jane and Ned after dinner, in spite of the hostile feelings inside me. The visits were always hurtful, sitting at her dining room table were her entire family, twenty-two to be exact. Uncles, cousins, nieces, and more. I guess there was no more room for my family of four.

The holidays following were always the same—Jane and her entire family. I could only look forward to Christmas Eve. I was compelled to visit so as not to give Jane an excuse to complain.

Pleasing her was very difficult, she was so hard to

understand. I had to accept her strange way of thinking, unfortunately, she was married to my son.

I was deeply hurt that we never got an invitation to spend a holiday with her family. It was always, "Stop by for dessert." I could never understand why we were excluded if you take into account that we helped make her affluent.

My son, being a weakling and a follower, closed his eyes to the fact. He avoided any verbal disagreement with her, evidently fearing her control.

Easter

Easter Sunday was to be celebrated in April. I desperately wanted to spend the holiday with my family. One month previous, I asked Jane if she and her family would like to join us at one of the fine restaurants we frequented. She was hesitant. I expected her to refuse, surprisingly she accepted, with, as usual, a nasty remark. "I will consider it, she said, but there must be no discussion concerning business in my presence." At that moment, I felt a desperate need to retaliate with words of contempt. I wanted to remind her how lucky she was to be a part of our family, and to be possessed with all the fine luxuries she was undeserving of, but I bit my tongue refusing to spoil our holiday. I can only assume that she takes unconscionable pleasure in hurting us.

Norata was agitated with her demands, he said bluntly, "Tell her to go to hell, we can do without her sarcasms, why should we cater to her selfishness?" I was afraid knowing that Norata might stop at nothing to put her in her place.

I begged him to "please make no comment for my sake; It will be a special day for me. I want it to be a happy occasion."

Norata was a challenge to Jane. He never took any BS from her; he wasn't like me at all. He would think nothing of retaliating in the same tone with a similar response. I noticed a sense of pleasure in her when she was challenged, since she showed a special liking for him. In spite of her demands, he kept his promise that Easter.

All through dinner, we conversed about the likes and dislikes with the children, Becca's everyday happenings, and newspaper articles. The only conversation between Ned and his dad was about their hunting experiences. It was evident Jane had also briefed Ned. In spite of the pressure, that was indeed one of my happiest days, no mention of business, and we had a pleasant day.

Business was slowly growing for Ned. He continued to spend as much time as possible working, but there was always that need for more financing.

Becca was financially prosperous and well set. She was always available with handouts for her brother. She played a hefty part in helping him. But payback time was always a struggle for him.

Jane was very unhappy. Every call she made to me was to complain about my son. I was positive that Jane married Ned for money. She was infatuated with the luxuries he possessed.

I listened but never took sides for fear of losing the in-law image. It wasn't easy for me to bite my tongue. I had to pick my words in order to avoid a confrontation, but it seemed I was never able to choose the right words.

Early Monday morning, I received another call. It was Jane again expressing discontent. She was fuming about the accumulated unpaid bills Ned always kept avoiding. I had the feeling that she was tormenting him, not accepting the fact that he was struggling in business.

To keep peace between them and to relieve the tension she was putting on Ned, I asked Norata to gather all their bills and bring them up to date. I didn't like to see my son so unhappy. Although Jane was resentful that we were always ready to oblige and available to satisfy Ned's needs, she was quick to hand over the bills, which made me wonder, why isn't he paying his bills, especially, since the expenses he is liable for in the building are still being billed to us.

Their marriage was falling apart. Ned was unhappy. I noticed him spending more hours than usual at the plant.

One Friday, at 9:30 p.m., Norata and I had just left the restaurant after having dinner. We noticed the lights were still on in the building. Concerned, he said, "I wonder what Ned's doing there at this hour? Why hasn't he left? He was ready to leave three hours ago."

When we walked in Ned was sitting at his desk, alone. He looked glum. Norata said, "What's wrong, why haven't you left? How come you're still here?" He made no comment. He never expressed how he felt.

I asked him, "Are you having problems at home?" As

usual, he managed a slight grin and said nothing. It hurt me to see my son so unhappy. He had many good qualities. What more could Jane want?
"Why don't you go home? You need some rest."

He answered, "This is my home."

That spelled trouble. "I don't want to pry," I said, "I know exactly what you're going through. Jane is one tough bird, not easy to get along with."

He answered, "As long as she takes good care of my children, that's all I really care about."

I was very concerned, I tried to talk to him about Jane's cruel attitude and his unhappy home life, but I couldn't put more pressure on him. I couldn't cause him added hurt. He never complained or put her down. I wished he had opened up to me.

That Sunday night Ned called me to come and care for the children. Jane had an asthma attack and needed to be taken to the hospital for an overnight stay. Her heavy smoking continued with no concern for her affliction. Ned frowned on smoking or drinking.

I didn't hesitate. I welcomed the stay. What a treat for me to be with Lianne and Jared. I selfishly hoped Jane would need to stay a few more days in the hospital so I'd have an opportunity to spend more precious time with my grandchildren. No such luck.

The following morning, after serving breakfast, Ned

drove Lianne to school. It was a nice day. I wanted to do something to amuse Jared. While the housekeeper did her chores, I took advantage. My first thought was to take a drive to the park. Roger Williams Park is fascinating, with animals of every kind. I knew Jared would be excited. We walked through the park taking time to view their habitats. After about two hours of entertainment, it was time to leave.

When we returned, I was taken by surprise. Ned was sitting at the kitchen table overly nervous. I asked him, "What are you doing home?"

He answered, "Jane's been released from the hospital. We just got home." I could sense something wrong. He said, "Jane is real mad."

I asked, "Why?" Before he could answer, Jane came in from the poolroom.

She looked at me, full of anger, her eyes cold and hard with contempt, and asked, "Where have you been?" scolding me like a child. I stood there dumbfounded, ignorant as to why she blasted me, again.

I said "Jane, what is your problem? Why are you so bitter? I try to please you in every way."

She put her hands on her hips, as usual, and sarcastically said, "And-- what would you like me to do, pay you?"

I said, "I don't believe this. I cannot understand you. My family is always here for you."

With deep hatred in her eyes, she answered, "I don't like your family." Not expecting such harsh words, I didn't know how to respond.

I turned away, very puzzled, and said, "I will never set foot in this house again."

As I walked toward the door, I heard her say "See what I mean? See what I mean?" What could she have possibly meant by "See what I mean?" Her evil mind played tricks on her.

Ned sat there embarrassed, with his usual grin, without saying a word. He tried to pass it off as a joke. The weakling was immune to her outbursts.

What did she want from me? Why couldn't I stand up to her? I had no guts defending myself. I wished I could have just opened up about her cruelty and selfishness, to put her in her place, but I didn't want to make it any harder for my son, knowing how contemptuous she was. It was sad enough that he was so timid, with no courage to stand up to her.

Ned never discussed the incident with me. He was never one to express his feelings, or argue. Very seldom did he become angry. When he was growing up he was rather shy and kept to himself. I can only assume that he's ashamed of her rudeness. I believe her anger was from not finding Jared at home when she returned from the hospital. That was no surprise.

Jane was a vicious person with no respect for anyone. She simply found pleasure in hurting me.

Ned was fortunate to bid on, and win a government contract to produce moisturizer for the army and navy. Unfortunately, all government orders must be completed before any money is paid.

It would have been impossible for him to accept the contract since he had no funds to work with. He was desperate. If he let this opportunity fall through it would be an irreplaceable loss. So again, he asked his dad for help.

Ned had a habit of borrowing from Peter to pay Paul, which his dad frowned on. But Norata could see that the completed order would bring in a substantial return. It would be pointless to refuse him, so he allowed Ned to borrow the necessary funds needed.

I wasn't pleased with the situation and I asked Norata to draw the line since Ned was still negligent on the loans he had on our property. I was completely ignored. My concern meant nothing.

To keep me satisfied, Norata promised that the profit from the order would easily take care of the loans. I believed him. I thought this order would solve the problem and clear Ned's debt.

Once more it seemed the right thing to do. I went along, to help. I spent as many hours as I possibly could helping eliminate some of the strain he and his dad faced. Help was needed since Jane preferred to be a stay-at-home mom and had no interest in the business. I was a runner for payroll and whatever else became necessary.

Ned had a habit of commanding instead of asking. He never used the word *please*. He always spoke with authority, giving the impression that his demands had to be met. "Mom, take the formulas to the lab for an analysis" or "Mom, you have to make a deposit to Merrill Lynch for payroll this week." He always appeared to be in control. I felt compelled to obey his command so, I too, am guilty and responsible for my son's behavior, although then it was unavoidable and necessary at the time. Completing that government order was the answer to solving all our obligations. We worked together, constantly trying to make the deadline for completion.

One Monday morning Leon didn't show up, and we needed him badly. Ned expected this to happen sometimes since the weekends were his time to binge. The calls were unanswered. Ned decided to pay a visit to his apartment and try to sober him up.

When there was no answer, Ned feared the worst. He asked the landlord to let him in. The shock when he walked in was sickening. Leon lay across the kitchen floor dead, with his dog Pal beside him. Ned was overcome with grief and sadness. It was a great loss. Leon was a true friend. He had respect for everyone. He was truly missed.

After months of hard work, the government contract was finally completed. Just as I expected, there was no mention of money afterward. Norata was a fool to think his son was going to meet his obligations.

Ned continued to neglect the loans with false promises. Again I made it understood that the loans on our property must be paid off. His answer was always the same, "Don't worry, Mom, I'll take care of it." I heard nothing more. Norata was unconcerned. He never approached him, fearing rejection from his son. The burden was mine to deal with.

The bank called, reminding us that the payments were delinquent. Since the loan was in my name, not to jeopardize our credit I had to make many payments. I then made a suggestion to the bank manager to forward the monthly statements to the office in hopes that my son would be more aware of his obligation.

I had to be more forceful. I approached Ned, angry and determined. I complained about his lack of concern and told him he was ruining our credit. In response, he assured me not to worry.

He promised again that he would not forget to make the payments. But he always did the same thing, he would pay the interest only, nothing on the principal. I was skeptical. My son was conniving, and pretending to be ignorant. It bothered me to think that he could be so uncaring. It was obvious that his overpowering desire for wealth was becoming an obsession.

Norata forgot the promise he had made to me. He failed to recognize the issue.

Spain 1987

In April of 1987 Norata and I were vacationing in Spain. As always, we left an itinerary for emergency purposes. After spending a wonderful day visiting the special attractions, historic palaces and cathedrals in Seville, we returned to our hotel to freshen up before dinner.

As we entered our room, I noticed our telephone message light blinking so I immediately called the desk. The clerk said that a long distance call had been received while we were out. I panicked; my mind was full of tragic thoughts. Why would anyone call us here in Spain unless it was urgent?

My hands were shaking with fear so I handed the phone to Norata, who had a much calmer nature. I think he suspected the call was from Ned, so he called him.

When he looked at me with a slight grin on his face, I sighed with relief. I asked him what was wrong. He hesitated, so I asked again, "What is it?"

He replied, "Ned is desperate and in need of $30,000 immediately for some much needed machinery."

That made me angry. "Can't you see what your son is doing? He's draining us. We have to stop. Enough is enough. This time we have to refuse him. We've carried him way beyond our reach. When will you realize what your son is doing to us? We are getting sucked in deeper and deeper into his grasp. Our financing him must stop."

Norata just listened as I continued spitting out my anger. He ignored me like he always did. Since he could never refuse his precious son, he again consented. He felt that refusing him at this point would mean all our efforts have failed, so he told him to call our broker, John Abatta, and draw the funds from our account—and also, imagine the audacity, he said that if more money was needed, the checkbook was at his disposal. I couldn't believe what I was hearing.

I was certain our son, knowing how vulnerable his father was, would continue taking whatever was available. I feared he would run us dry, that he wouldn't stop until we were penniless.

I was infuriated, spitting bullets, reminding Norata that our son is a taker, a selfish conniver who won't quit. I asked, "What happened to his promise to pay the loans after he got paid from his successful army and navy contract?" I never got an answer.

Norata was blind to the fact that he could easily be deceived by his son. I was afraid that Ned's selfishness would be endless. But my hands were tied. I could not convince him that his son would eventually ruin us.

Our discussions and bickering during our two-week stay was focused on this quandary. I was determined to make him realize that our son was money-hungry and was using us. That we couldn't let it continue. It was like talking to a blank wall that can't hear.

My concerns grew even more intense but I still couldn't convince him that Ned's needs are becoming a huge strain on our finances. I explained how money, like power, also corrupts.

We returned from our vacation mentally exhausted from all the bitterness and haggling. It was our worst trip, that ended in disaster.

When we entered the baggage claim, I was surprised to see Ned standing there waiting for us. I was suspicious. What now? I feared another encounter since it was unusual for him to take time out of his busy schedule to greet us. There must be some reason.

Norata beamed at the sight of his son. He quickly walked over to him and exchanged words while I waited for our luggage to come through the conveyor. Their conversation was cut short when I walked over to them. Ned greeted me with a peck on the cheek, a quick hug, and, "Hi, Mom."

The ride home was casual. Ned never liked to discuss business in my presence because I wasn't as submissive to his requests as his dad.

Norata was happy to be home, anxious to be back

working with his son. Ned continued to remind his dad that he would always take care of us. Norata actually believed him. I had my doubts. There was too much proof that Ned was making his usual empty promises.

Bedtime was my time to reminisce. I thought back to Ned's younger days. I never recalled him growing up to be generous. So many incidents came to mind that I wondered, could our generosity have spoiled him to the point of selfishness? Although he showered us with much love and affection, he never showed signs of generosity. I had never given it a thought or became suspicious at that time. Parents trust their children to grow up with morals.

I remembered the junior prom. Anne came calling almost nightly. She had a pleasant personality and was very sociable. A sweet kid. Her junior prom was very special to her and she asked Ned if he would be her date. He really wasn't interested, but I was excited and I told him it was an honor. Be kind, you really can't refuse her. Sometimes he could be easily convinced.

We were so proud taking pictures of them together. Anne looked beautiful. Before they left, Dad gave Ned thirty-five dollars to spend and said, "Have a good time." To our surprise, Ned came home with the thirty-five dollars.

I was humiliated. "Why haven't you spent any money?" I asked him. As usual, I didn't get an answer.

I thought at the time, he's just sixteen, he doesn't know how to respond. It was his first date. I guess I was looking for excuses. But still I talked to him about the incident. I never wanted my son to be labeled a cheapskate. The lecture didn't faze him.

The truth is, he was spoiled. Never deprived. If he wanted something all he had to do was ask. I'm certain that was his downfall. It was our fault. He just never learned how to respond.

I remember another incident. Our salesman Ray Dowley was impressed with Ned building his own chalet and having so many luxuries at his young age. Ray was a fine, well-educated salesman who had suffered a painful loss. His wife, in her late fifties, was battling cancer. Her days were numbered. Fearing for his only daughter having to go through life without a mother, he was looking out for her welfare, for something to keep her from being apprehensive if and when the tragedy should occur.

He had a liking for Ned. He thought how great it would be if he could get him and Shelly interested in each other. It would ease his mind since Ned was in a sound position financially, and that would mean a fine, secure future for Shelly.

Ray invited him over to his house saying he had a much needed repair to be done in his kitchen. Impressed with Shelly, Ned showed his talent. He tried to impress her by doing some special chores around the house. He was infatuated, and after three days of meeting her, he and Shelly went on their first date.

I was happy for him. But I forgot to brief him on how to impress her. I was hoping he had not forgotten our talk after the prom night. He had no interest in dating until he met Shelly.

His date with her wasn't in keeping with what was considered morally right then. Instead of taking her to a movie or dinner, he parked his car and spent the night chatting. I should have briefed him before he left, since he was ignorant about how to treat a date. Shelly refused to see him again.

Ned was deeply hurt because he had a real crush on her. He was withdrawn for days after that disappointment.

I sincerely feel that our son, being without friends during his growing up years, and with no real education, just never learned how to act socially.

Birthday

Norata's birthday on July 3 was a great disappointment. We waited and waited thinking that Ned and Jane would show at any moment. I couldn't imagine him forgetting his dad's birthday since his falls two days later. Becca and Jon never forgot. They had come early that afternoon with an ice cream cake for Dad. We were hoping that Ned would walk in to cut the cake. Wishful thinking. They never arrived.

Becca was disappointed with her brother's neglect. It wasn't like him. She was certain Jane had some power over his decision.

Norata was so disappointed he spent the rest of the day sulking and seriously thinking. I figured that Jane had been contrary, deliberately refusing to make the visit. The extreme hurt from his son was clear on Norata's face.

Two days later, July 5, was Ned's birthday. In mid-afternoon Ned and Jane came to visit. I guessed they thought the auspicious day would be recognized; that we would jump for joy and congratulate him on his big day. It didn't happen. Norata stayed in his room during their entire stay, refusing to acknowledge their visit.

I felt sad pretending not to notice that it was Ned's birthday, but it was necessary. He had to feel the same disappointment that his dad had felt. I didn't like playing the tit-for-tat game, but it was what I had to do to make him realize the wrong he had done. He needed to feel the same disappointment and to face the same reality. Our son really seemed to lack intelligence. He seemed unaware of right and wrong in life.

I again reminded Norata how spoiled our son really was, we must stop making it easy for him to depend on us.

"It has to stop." Feeling the pain, he finally agreed. This time he seemed sincere, with his son's deep hurt still heavy. But I could read his mind clearly: he will forgive and forget easily. His bitter resentment will only last for the moment.

There was always a need for equipment. Auction notices were received frequently; Norata and Ned enjoyed attending most of them.

An announcement came that a government building was scheduled to be auctioned off in Newport. Influenced, father and son both spent a full day at the building. They were totally impressed. Ned became anxious to present a bid, but he knew there was no way he could take the plunge. The two-story building was situated on twelve acres of land in a corporate park. It had forty offices in much needed repair. Each was expensively carpeted and paneled. The six bathrooms were tiled, with double stalls for both men and women.

At that time, I wasn't aware of Ned's determination, since I knew there was no way he could possibly afford to present a bid. On the other hand, knowing my son to be a persistent conniver, he would surely find a way. I noticed he and his dad constantly discussing what I assumed was business. In reality, the government building was their main topic.

Jane was aware of Ned's strong desire to bid on the building. She too knew there was no way possible for him to make the bid. She warned him to give up the thought. She felt the long distance to and from Newport would keep him from home longer than usual. She begged Norata to please discourage his son. Like always, she was ignored. Our son was obsessed and desperate for prestige, he was going to stop at nothing to get what he wanted, and he clung to his dream of being wealthy at our expense. As days passed, I wasn't aware of the scheming, I knew this was one time he will not succeed.

One early morning in March the phone rang. I was awake and about to prepare breakfast. Lori, my dear friend, spends her winters in Florida. She had decided to have a friendly get-together.

Her sisters were making the trip down from Michigan the next week. She wanted to do something special and asked me to join them. I felt privileged. Lori always included me in all her affairs. She insisted I hop a plane and fly down as soon as possible. Since I was never one to say no, I immediately got ready for the flight.

Lori and I were neighbors. Our relationship through the years grew almost like sisters. We confided and depended on each other for support. Many days when I was unable to make it home for Becca, Lori was there waiting at the bus stop. There were times when early in the morning I would receive a visitor at my front door. It was Lori's six-year-old daughter Sherri, who was beautiful, unusually friendly, and courageous, with a sweet, round face. She would take it upon herself to walk the short distance to our house, then head directly to Becca's room.

At the far corner of the room was Becca's dressing table, with makeup and cosmetics of every kind. Sherri would make herself comfortable and excitedly experiment with all the goodies. Becca would almost always have to correct the heavy glow on her face. Lori knew where her daughter was whenever she made a disappearing act. Sherri grew up to be a stunning beauty.

I went to see Norata at the office before I left for the flight. He and his son were discussing business as usual. Ned asked, "Mom, where are you going on such short notice?" I explained how Lori wanted me to visit.

He then said, "By the way, Mom, before you leave, run over to Frank's office and sign a notice for me." I had a habit of trusting and not asking questions so I assumed it was of little importance since Norata was standing next to him and made no comment.

So, without questioning him, based on the faith and trust I had in my son at that time, I just did what he asked. I quickly left, stopped at Frank's office without asking what the paper was about. I signed what Frank placed in front of me and left. I was never a suspicious person, never thinking my son would deliberately deceive me by trickery. That episode was the end of my beautiful life.

Two weeks went by fast, my pleasant stay with Lori was over, time to return home. Norata was waiting for me when I stepped from the plane. He looked glum, not very happy to see me. He didn't ask any questions, except did I want to have dinner?

Woman's intuition, I detected some trouble afoot. I asked if he was okay. He hesitated, and said "Yes." Then he told me about the new building Ned had purchased in Newport.

I was sick. It was then I learned that my deceitful, thieving son tricked me into signing the promissory note on my building over to him free and clear.

He had secretly planned this scam, then waited for the right moment to deceive me. Frank betrayed me too, not telling me what I was signing. I felt nauseous; the disappointment in my husband being an accessory destroyed me. His fear of disappointing his precious son came first. He had ruined our life.

I was devastated. Our building's value would have been our security and comfort for the rest of our lives. Ned had no conscience. The intensity of his greed for wealth had overpowered him. Nothing and nobody was going to stand in his way.

He was going to take it all, and, yes, he did. I was crushed. I felt betrayed by both my son and my husband, to think they could be so deceitful.

I was certain now that Norata, afraid of losing his son, had collaborated with Ned's plan and had allowed him to betray me. How blind he was to let his own son manipulate him that way. The cruel deceit made me sick.

I had no one to blame but myself. I was so convinced that as long as I held the promissory note there was nothing to fear, that our building was in my name only. In haste, I asked no questions at Frank's office.
I could not wait to confront my son, we immediately drove to the office and, with violent anger, and intense rage, I screamed at my son, "You tricked me. How could you do this to me? What are you made of?" I fumed, "How could you be so deceitful? You actually stole my building right from under me."

As usual he just listened, showing no remorse. His explanation was simple: "Mom, this will be my inheritance. This is all I will ask for. Just take care of Becca now, I'm all set."

I was spitting bullets. "Inheritance? You just cleaned us out of our life savings and everything we owned, you didn't stop until it was all gone. There's nothing left for Becca. Where's her inheritance?"

Ned said nothing more. No guilt. The damage was done. What more could he say that would deny the truth? It was clear now that my son would go to any extreme to satisfy his selfish greed.

Jane was also angry with Norata for encouraging Ned. She knew that he would be spending more time away from home. It made no difference what anyone thought, what Ned wanted was all that mattered. He was in love with power and he would go to any extreme to get it.

Norata, still completely devoted to his son, cowered in the shadows for fear of losing him while I became the aggressor. I felt that I alone was in the struggle, my son's resentment of me was escalating since I refused to agree with his dad's going to battle to win his love.

My husband now became my enemy too. I lost all feelings for him. I couldn't accept his betrayal.

Whatever I felt, Norata spent his days cleaning, renovating, and preparing the forty offices to rent. My hurt burned. I was losing control. We were not on speaking terms; we were two strangers living under the same roof. But I was curious as to where Ned was getting the resources to renovate.

Norata refused to discuss any dealings he had with Ned. We had no contact. But the mystery was solved when I received my bank statement for that month. I was stunned. It had a *ZERO* balance. $50,000, gone. My son had finally cleaned us out of all our hard earned possessions.

I took fright. I couldn't believe what I saw. I immediately called Norata and asked why I had a zero balance. He hesitated, then said, "Ned needed the money for the transactions and renovations. He asked to borrow our savings with the promise to replace it in two weeks."

I was fit to be tied. I was so angry I could hardly say, "How could you do this? Why would you continue to jeopardize our life savings? Do you really think he intends to replace that money? You are a fool. Your son has conned you into thinking we will be well taken care of. We can just forget that."

There was a long pause, with no response. What was he thinking? Ned had taken control of our entire life earnings and all our possessions without any offer of repayment! How naïve was he to trust him after all Ned's lies and deceitful promises? My husband was as conniving as my son. I screamed obscenities at him and hung up the phone.

My rage was so intense that I immediately packed his clothes, ready for his moving out. I hated myself for being so careless and unobservant of this scheming and trickery. I realized then that my husband was totally consumed with his son and that I, his wife, meant nothing.

Norata and I separated after fifty years of marriage. It would have been impossible for me to live with him under those conditions.

Ned had no intentions of replacing our funds. Seeing

my bank statement wiped out made me sick. Extremely stressed, full of hostility, in a huge fit of anger, I called and castigated him for ruining us financially and causing our breakup. There was no response or apology. No emotion. It was like scolding a little boy who wouldn't listen to one word I said. He had literally stolen our life and everything we worked hard for, without shame, regret, or guilt.

Now Ned was in complete control. He found an apartment for his dad a few blocks from the building, scarcely furnished, small, comfortably suited for one person—and very conveniently located. All to his advantage. It meant that his dad, being his caretaker, could spend more time at the plant and could do his bidding. It was just what Ned wanted, having his dad under his control with no interference from me.

Despite the fact that my anger had scarcely diminished, Norata and I still had mutual commitments. I had always relied on him to handle the finances even though he was careless. Now I found the load on my shoulders very heavy. There was so much unfinished business. I was left carrying the major responsibilities. I suffered many sleepless nights.

Bitterness was eating at me, hatred was tormenting me. I wanted so badly to become estranged from my husband and forget that he existed, but that was impossible. I needed his support. The burden of responsibilities was becoming too much for me to ignore. "Where do I begin?" I had to bear the loss alone.

The months that followed were hard for Norata as well. He was unhappy, totally lost, and suffering from intense grief. He had never had to perform any household chores. I had spent my married life catering to his every need.

Since this tragedy of having to choose between me and his son, he became withdrawn, then he slid into a state of deep depression.

Although I could never restore the faith I once had in him or forgive his actions, I felt a small amount of sadness for him. His weak mind controlled him. He was unhappy, caught in a bind between us. Though I was still angry at him, in some small way I also pitied him. I knew he was suffering inwardly by avoiding any confrontation. His weakness consumed him. He felt needed and wanted by his son.

As the months passed, I suffered from the physical stress. There was so much responsibility on my shoulders, I couldn't handle it. My visits were few, but I still felt obligated to do his laundry and clean his apartment. A part of me felt sad to see him in this predicament; nonetheless, if anything, I grew angrier at the thought of him deceiving me.

I knew how important Italian food was to him, so I prepared his favorite dishes, which he took back with him on his weekend visits.

The complex where he lived housed many seniors.

Most were widows desperate for a male companion. Being an extrovert, a talker, and very friendly, he enjoyed conversing with people. He spent most of his evenings in the community room where everyone would congregate.

The room was very spacious with overstuffed chairs, lovely tables, a large screen television, and a completely equipped kitchen with all the appliances for their convenience.

In the far corner of the room was a large table with a 500-piece puzzle, partly assembled for anyone interested in taking part. Through my visits there, I was introduced to many of the neighbors. They were lonely old women who conversed like children who were still looking for a relationship.

June, a neighbor who lived in the apartment directly across from Norata, would somehow sense my presence and greet me whenever I visited. She tried her best to be my friend, but I was fully aware of her intentions. She made every effort to please Norata with food and goodies.

Over the ensuing months, I noticed Norata's weekend home visits were inconsistent, and of course I became suspicious. I decided to drive out to see him one Saturday evening.

I invited Sue and her husband Elmo to take the ride with me. When we arrived, I noticed that Norata's car was not in his assigned parking place. I assumed he had gone out to get something to eat, so we decided to drive around town and enjoy some of the lovely sights.

Newport, the summer retreat for America's wealthiest families, had their lovely mansions, the International Tennis Hall of Fame, and a spectacular view of the Atlantic Ocean. It was very impressive.

We got carried away by the beauty as I drove around. Suddenly I realized I was here for a purpose and I immediately drove back to the apartment.

About an hour later, just as I parked my car, Norata drove up the driveway. He was startled to see me waiting there. In the passenger seat was an attractive lady. I casually walked up to the car and smiled.

The guilt on Norata's face was frightful. His companion was terrified. As they stepped out of the car, Norata hesitated and was lost for words. To my surprise, I felt no animosity toward the lady. I extended my hand and introduced myself as Norata's wife. She responded nervously with "Barbara," said good-bye, and hurriedly left.

I felt some anger, but I was not going to let it irritate me. We proceeded to Norata's apartment. As we approached the community room, some of his friends were gathered around the table working on the puzzle.

One of the ladies motioned for us to come in, but I was in no mood to converse at that time, so I made a gesture and said, "Not right now."

We took the elevator to the second floor. As we approached the apartment door, June came out to greet us and began to make conversation. I became frustrated with the interruption and let myself into the apartment with just a quick hello.

I was startled at what I saw. The apartment was in disarray and needed cleaning—a sink full of dirty dishes, a frying pan on the stove with crusty oil, papers strewn about. It was totally disgusting. Usually when I visited I would normally get right to cleaning, but that night I was enraged. I refused even to make an attempt.

Norata was extremely nervous, trying hard to hide his guilt with kind offers. I waited for some explanation, but like his son, he never could express himself.

Although I felt humiliated, I was somewhat sympathetic. It was plain to see that he was unhappy, that he needed companionship to fill the void in his life. He made no explanation as to why he was out with Barbara. It was obvious that he was just a lonely seventy-two-year-old man looking for company.

I made a gesture to leave but Elmo was sympathetic, feeling sad for Norata. He felt the need to make the visit more comfortable. He tried making conversation just to ease the tension, but it went nowhere. It was one sided. I'm sure Norata was embarrassed having

Sue and Elmo observe his infidelity, something he'd never done before.

Our stay was short. I was disturbed at the sight of the cluttered apartment. I couldn't wait to leave. With nothing more to say, we left.

Ten years earlier Norata had been stricken with bladder cancer. Through the years, with medication and many treatments, the cancer was in remission. As a result, he became impotent. His sexual desires had been lost for many years. It was highly unlikely there could have been any involvement with Barbara other than just companionship.

The months away were taking effect. Living alone was devastating. Norata was losing weight and becoming careless about his attire. The apartment was untidy and lacked attention.

My conscience bothered me finding him in that condition. Even though my hostility lingered, I decided it was time for him to come home.

We posted a card on the bulletin board and donated what little possessions he had. Having to say good-bye to his neighbors saddened him, but he felt relieved. He was contented living back home but he continued to drive to Newport every day to work with his son.

Fridays after work were a special time for Norata and Ned to discuss business over dinner at the nearby pub. He always came home anxious to fill me in on their daily routine. I pretended not to be interested, but I was curious as to what was happening with the much needed repairs.

I gathered that they constantly worked toward getting the offices rented.

Nine years had passed since the barn fire, which was the beginning of my continued, sorrowful life. Barry became uneasy and started proceedings. It was one last try before the ten-year statute of limitations went in effect.

Lennie, his lawyer, started the action. I feared the thought of appearing in court for a mere $50,000. I wanted desperately to put this behind us. Norata was dragging his feet, hoping for some miracle that would make it go away.

Lennie was getting nervous. Since the ten-year statute was almost expired, outside the courtroom he took Norata aside and said, "Norata, you're known to have lots of money, pay my client the $50,000."

Norata responded, "I have nothing, my son owns everything."

Lennie replied, "You own the building and lots of property. You can well afford it."

I finally realized we were in a financial bind. Ned never repaid any of his obligations, putting us in a regretful predicament. With our bank funds gone, we had no choice but to take out a loan on our farm.

That was the first time in our life we had to take out a loan.

I made an appointment with our bank manager and explained the situation. Much to my surprise, we were refused.

Ned's loans on our property were still outstanding. The bank manager expressed sorrow for us and explained how forceful he had to be with Ned each month to make his payments to them—interest only. Therefore, our loan request was turned down.

I was frantic and tried another bank. Although we had two houses on the farm with six apartments and acres of land, it made no difference. The loans were delinquent and we were refused credit.

Norata left me with this burden. He showed no concern about it, nor did he make any effort to resolve the issue. It was like he didn't care what happened anymore. He had lost interest. We were wiped out.

I hadn't spoken to Ned since I'd received my zero bank statement. In desperation, I swallowed my pride and called him. I asked him, "Why have you refused to meet the payments. Do you realize you've ruined us completely?"

In his usual non-response, he just listened, refusing to recognize what I was saying as I scolded him. There was no mistaking his cruelty. He had no intention of paying off the loans. His greed had consumed his conscience. The pressure was mounting. We were called into court many times. Our lawyer at the time was not a fighter. He put little effort into our case.

Leaving me with this responsibility, I continued to search for a loan since the suit now was for $100,000. Norata was in despair, caught between me and his son, willing to give in to whatever demands that were handed to us. He didn't care. He had lost interest.

We were surprised by a visitor who came to appraise the property. Evidently, Lennie had started proceedings to have the property auctioned off. Now, I was desperate.

I found a bank that was happy to give us the loan at a whopping eleven percent interest. It was a ridiculous rate but I had no choice. Mr. Mason, the lawyer who handled the loans for his company, was surprised that we did not pursue our case more diligently. He felt that our obligation could have been reduced to a fraction of what it had escalated to. I explained how Norata was weak, with no tolerance for pressure. He would agree to anything to relieve the burden.

We agreed to pay Barry the $100,000 and $15,000 in lawyer's fees after our house sold. Each month the loan payments were becoming harder and harder to meet.

Since Ned's loans also had to be paid off, we were

forced to sell our second home to defray the cost of the loan.

The home was lovely. It had greater value because it had a second apartment plus an acre of land. The pressure was too hard to bear without support. I needed relief.

From that point on, I was confused and troubled. I suffered a collapse.

We were left with our home, the adjoining ten acres of land, and mortgages that Ned refused to recognize. Our safe deposit box, which had contained many valuables, was empty. Our son left us in poverty.

Norata, in his seventies and bewildered between me and his precious son, had lost interest. I asked myself, 'Why did he leave me with this burden? Why was I put in this predicament? Why didn't he see how greedy his son was? Why was he ignoring the trouble we were in?' So many unanswered questions. He seemed like a zombie, uncaring about the consequences.

He also lost interest in maintaining the property. It was disgusting to see the uncut grass and neglect. His only interest was leaving every day for Newport to work with his son.

He constantly pressured me to downsize, to take the easy way out. "Let's relieve ourselves of the responsibility of caring for the property. With the proceeds we could spend the few years we have left traveling, without commitments."

"Traveling?" I screamed, "All you ever cared about was traveling. It was your only foolish, stupid concern." He painted a rosy picture, like always. I had to believe him.

I was a fool, naïve, and misled. My distressed mind was a blank.
I had no idea what it would be like living under imposing rules. I had visions of living in a lavish condo or an apartment with the same luxury I was used to. That wasn't going to happen.

I had built up a tremendous amount of grief and sorrow that haunted me long after.

My home had been my castle that I deeply cherished. Now the pleasure I got from watching my grandchildren play and enjoy the farm would all be taken away. I wondered, do I really need to do this? Is there no possible way I can keep my home? How am I going to walk away and leave my life behind? Just thinking about it made me sick with sorrow.

Ned kept his distance, out of touch. He had gotten what he wanted. He didn't care what happened to us. His craving for wealth had been met.

I talked to myself every day asking why I hadn't seen years earlier how selfish and grasping our son really was.

It brought me back to one day, while we were at the office, when I questioned his character. I wondered why he never showed any signs of returning kindness. I went up to him and bluntly said, "Ned, have you ever thought of giving me, or Dad, a twenty-dollar bill and saying, 'Mom (or Dad), have lunch on me.'" His answer was always the same when directly confronted or corrected: a grin and silence. Everything I said was taken as a joke, never seriously. We spoiled him from a very young age. The fault lies with us.

Ned made no effort to call or visit for fear we would ask him to repay his loans. If ever we needed him, it was then, at that special time in our life. He could have guided and directed us to make the right decisions.

Whether it was pride, or shame, he completely avoided us, turning his back and leaving us to boil in our own stew.

Jane too had become distant. We were seeing less and less of Lianne and Jared. I was in fear of losing my grandchildren, so I tried to keep in touch as often as I could.

I called Jane several times, hoping she would influence Ned into helping us financially. She was well aware that he had taken everything we owned and put us in this predicament. As expected, she was no help.

I was looking for some consolation or even advice. I

asked her, "What are we going to do? We have to do something."

Her answer was cruelly arrogant. "Do whatever you have to do, we have no money."

What a fool I was to think she would have compassion for me. She hated us from day one. I knew right then from the hostility in her voice that we were about to lose her and the children.

Becca, feeling our pain, offered to help us in so many ways. I refused to involve her in our misfortune. She never interfered or gave her opinion. She loved her brother in spite of his unscrupulous, devious disregard for his parents. There was nothing she could do. We had put ourselves in this tragic position.

Josh

Jane's Uncle Josh, whom she idolized, had suddenly passed away. We were obligated to show respect and make the visit. I immediately called Becca and made arrangements to visit the funeral home. It was a necessary commitment and what was expected of us. Becca was elegantly dressed, as always.

As we approached the entrance, we were greeted by Jane's sister Ellie, who unlike Jane is sweet and very cordial.

She kissed us both and commented with, "Becca, you look beautiful."
Becca, smiled, thanked her, and gave her a hug.

The room was quite full with Jane's family and relatives.
We both kneeled at the casket and paid our respects to Josh with a prayer.

Jane was seated directly across from the casket, with Ned at her side. Becca was first to shake hands with Jane and expressed her sorrow.

As I left after kissing Jane and relating my sorrow, I heard her, with a thrust of anger, turn to Ned and say, "Get her out of here." I was startled and could not believe what I was hearing. I thought at first she was referring to me, but it was obvious, her anger was directed at Becca.

With that, Ned being a disgusting ignorant, unscrupulous wimp, with no respect for his sister, and under Jane's dominating control, hesitated, walked over to Becca, held her under arm and said, "Come on, Becca," and cowardly escorted her out the door.

I was torn with rage, my disgusting illiterate son, I'm so ashamed of, again disgraced my family.

How could he treat his sister so shamefully after all the many generous offers of money she gave him that were never returned?

That encounter tore me up inside. I wasn't sure if, at that moment, I felt intense hatred for my son, or for the loathsome, ill-mannered woman he married.

Becca was humiliated and kept silent during our ride home. I'm sure the real hurt was from the brother that she idolized all her life. How could he again allow Jane to treat us so badly? With his lack of education, he was illiterate, and never knew right from wrong.

After spending a restless night thinking, there could be no rest until I confronted Jane and demanded an explanation for her devious act.

The next day, I was anxious and called Jane. On the surface, I was calm, but the anger in me was intense.

My first words were "Jane, how in God's name could you do such a terrible thing to a person who came to pay their respects?"
There was a moment of silence. I wondered, could she have found a little remorse for her cruelty?

She answered, "Well, he was like a father to me." Whatever she meant by that stupid remark had me baffled. Jane never had an explanation for the hurt she caused. It was clear, she had no other way to express her hostility toward Becca.

Becca was deeply hurt and unaware of the resentment Jane had for her, that is, not until that terrible incident, Jane made every effort to let it be known.

Becca was obsessed with the latest fashions and always made a special appearance. She was often complimented with the expression, "You've just stepped out of vogue." There seemed to be no other explanation for Jane's animosity toward her, other than pure envy.

I bit my tongue many times, trying my best to keep family peace.
There could never be peace; Jane held too much hatred.

The months following were hell. I was physically and mentally exhausted. Ned stepped out of our life completely; he had become a complete stranger. I found myself sulking and depressed. I asked myself repeatedly, why were we so naive, so blind, to let this happen to us? We spent our entire life sacrificing, helping him to become successful, how could he hurt us this way?

Norata, unconcerned and, uncaring was confused. He continued to lose interest in the property. To see the neglect made me realize that I should take his advice and downsize. The thought was haunting me. I spent many sleepless nights with a number of thoughts passing through my mind.
To give up my lovely home was sickening, but we had no choice, with nothing left, It had to be the right decision; there was no way we could afford to stay.

Our lovely home was put up for sale. I placed a 'For Sale' ad in our local paper and had an open house. The response was unbelievable.
We sold most of our possessions—my beautiful mahogany bedroom that I cherished for fifty years, Limoges china, silver, antiques, and anything we could do without. I was sick to think I had to lose the beautiful paintings and antique relics I treasured from the Quine's estate.

It was heartbreaking to lose my collector's items I brought back from the different countries we visited, but I could not let my feelings control me; we were unhappy, devastated, in a state of psychological depression, and anxious to put this burden behind us.

Our house, land, and properties once valued at almost a million dollars, were now down to a mere fraction. The proceeds from the sale of our house was not as I expected. Many discrepancies were involved. The buyer wanted a new roof, our lawyer took five percent for his transaction fee, and the realtor took her six percent. As a result, we were no better off. I admitted to making a terrible mistake.

I found it to be one of the worst moves we have ever made in my entire life. The days passing were uptight for me.

I was suffering a living hell. I realized then how much of our life had been greedily taken from us.

The proceeds from the sale, our stocks and bonds, and what we held in securities had to be carefully considered since this was all we had left to carry us for the rest of our lives. Our taxable land was a heavy strain. Our only alternative was to put what was left from the sale into a mutual fund and draw a monthly check.

We tallied our expenses and drew exactly what was needed.
Norata always felt that since the jewelry business was profitable, accumulating a fortune, plus the income from the building and apartments bringing in a fine sum, there was no need for insurance.
How very wrong he was.

The fact that he retired at an early age, to help his son, resulted in a minimum of social security benefits. We finally concluded that we were in a poverty situation. Our son brought us down to our knees without remorse. It wasn't going to be as easy as we thought.

After giving up his apartment, Norata had continued to work for Ned, for a salary of $125.00 a week. I considered it an insult but a little extra income was helpful.

The move to a condo was an experience for me since it was the first time in my life having to pay rent.

Although it was nice, it was a great expense. To continue to live there would deplete our funds drastically, so we waited until our lease ran out and moved to a smaller apartment, paying less rent.

At that point, I could not find happiness. It was a far cry from what I was used to. I was impressed with the cleanliness of the new apartment, believing it would be of some consolation. However, at that time, I had not considered the second flight of stairs, the loss of privacy, or the lack of washing facilities. It was what we could afford, my new life of disappointments.

I felt so degraded, ashamed to have left behind a part of my life that can never be restored.

While living there, I had a suspicion that someone was entering my apartment while I was away. I sensed it to be the landlady, but I had to be sure before approaching her. I decided to set a trap by folding a small piece of paper and placing it between the door and the doorframe. Opening the door would release the paper and it would fall to the floor.

As I suspected, after returning home, I noticed the folded paper on the floor. I immediately called my landlady and asked why she had to enter my apartment without my permission? Of course, she denied the accusation. I asked her to inform me in the future, if ever she needed to get into the apartment. I wanted to be on friendly terms with her since we lived in the same house together. Out of embarrassment, she tried her best to avoid me. Living under that pressure was stressful.

Clinging to his dream of being a success, Ned ventured into the pharmaceutical business with the help of a chemist. He was showing progress. The building, with the forty offices renovated, was completed and rented. The income from the offices, plus the proceeds from his business, were bringing in a substantial profit, $45,000 monthly, according to Norata. He finally succeeded in maintaining the prestige and power he selfishly created.

He and his family were living in luxury—expensive cars, traveling, and living a healthy lifestyle—while we were struggling to survive. I was desperate.

This, I thought, would be an ideal time to approach him. I swallowed my pride, and hoped to regain some of the benefits that he received from us through the years.

I discussed with Norata the probability that perhaps I should confront Ned with the proofs and canceled checks; it may remind him of our abundant money supply that brought him to this level of success. Perhaps he might have a little compassion and realize it's time to repay us in a much-needed way, relieving us of the financial burden we are suffering.

Norata showed no emotional response. I could tell he knew his son was a monster of greed, but again, he was hesitant and afraid of the outcome.

I asked him to gather all the necessary records we accumulated through the years relating to Ned's chalets and businesses since he had control of all the past records. I was surprised at the amount tallied— well over three million dollars. I thought, why would he refuse us?

I made double copies, assuming some could be misplaced. At 9:30 Monday morning, I drove to Newport with a feeling of unrest.

As I approached his office, I feared the reaction he might have since he is very proud and not one to acknowledge the effort we put into his accomplishment.

His office, on the second floor of the building, was elaborately designed with mahogany-paneled walls, a display of antique guns, an oriental rug, overstuffed chairs, and a lovely mahogany desk.

The view from the picture window overlooking the

ocean was a beautiful sight. The spoiled kid with champagne taste needed to be showered with luxury at any expense.

As I walked up the stairs to his second floor office, I had a feeling of regret that I should be put in this predicament.

Although I felt resentment and hatred for my son's actions, a proud feeling came over me to see the accomplishment.

Ned was sitting at his desk, surprised to see me, and greeted me warmly, but not as he usually did in the past with a hug and kiss. I sensed a cold, unsympathetic feeling in him. I assumed he felt a little suspicious about my sudden visit. Norata stood nervously by, his arms folded, worried about the reaction from our son.

I sat across from Ned and nervously placed the copies on his desk. I reminded him how hard we worked for him to become successful.

I mentioned the fact that we were having financial difficulties, and since our money created his wealth, it was time he offer his much needed help.

My son looked at me for a second, with an expression I can only describe as extreme hatred. His face flushed with anger, his eyes bulging, I never saw this other side of him until that very moment.

Like a lightning bolt, he jumped up from his chair in

a fit of rage, without saying a word, he violently threw the copies in my face.

I was startled, frightened, and quickly jumped up from my chair, fearing he was going to attack me. I ran hurriedly down the stairs, with him in pursuit, continuously throwing the copies at me.

I could not believe this was happening to me. Was this my son turned monster? He was like a complete stranger seeking revenge. How can one explain such cold heartless hurt from the son you loved? My car parked in front of the building felt like a two block distance. I could not stop trembling. I was confused and fearful. The sick feeling I was having made me want to throw up. Deeply hurt, I ran with tears falling down from my face. What have we created? Could he be the son of a devil, atrociously wicked, cruel, and ill tempered? He truly believed he was here before, he probably was.

Norata's easily deceived mind stood silently mute throughout this painful ordeal. I felt betrayed by my husband standing there watching the cruelty toward me, without saying a word. I didn't expect any consolation from him; to stand up for me might put his friendship with his son in jeopardy and the fear of rejection might give him the feeling of being unloved. I sat in my car thinking, what have we done to deserve such punishment? Is he so blinded by power that nothing or no one else matters? I cannot deny the truth, it was clear that greed and selfishness had consumed him.

This cannot be my son. The loving sweet kid who

always showered me with love and affection, the happy kid who always came home with a smile on his face, picked me up in his arms, and hugged me tightly.

I knew at that moment, all our sacrifices, hard work, and intentions were lost.

The days passed with every hope that Ned would come to his senses, regret what he had done, and show some sign of apology, but I was sadly mistaken. He's become diabolic, not the proud son we cherished.

Never shall I forget that painful day. I was suffering emotionally. In a state of depression, I began to avoid contact with my friends and relatives. I was ashamed of my devastation, of being brought down to this level of poverty.

There was a feeling of coldness when I confronted Norata about his uncaring attitude. To avoid the situation, he made no mention of his son's cruelty. We were two different people living in the same house, I felt betrayed, but I was aware of the fact that he would make any sacrifice to keep close ties with his son.

I vowed one day he will realize what his son really is and the day will come when his son will turn on him the same as me.

I felt a tremendous amount of grief and sorrow that haunted me long after. From that day following, I had many sleepless nights. The feeling of resentment from the son whom I loved haunted me. I felt a hurt that cannot be described. My son, so unbearably cruel.

I comforted myself being fortunate and thankful for at least having a wonderful daughter who helped me through this terrible ordeal. Becca never showed signs of envy observing her brothers greed. She never took sides or made any defamed remark against her brother.

The differences in character between them were far, so unlike each other. Becca avoided any confrontation in fear of family conflict. She, however, felt some grief at her brother's treatment toward us; her support was always there to fill the void in my heart.

Several weeks passed, I needed to talk to somebody, hoping to relieve some of the tension I was experiencing.

Becca's friend Jan worked for Sam Perlan, a fine attorney. Jan was like a second daughter to me, she often called with her pleasant voice, "Hi, Mae, what's for dinner?" It was always a pleasure having her over after work sharing our Italian meals.

Many days, while passing by her office, I would stop at Dunkin' Donuts and surprise her with coffee and doughnuts, sometimes bringing an extra for Sam, a special person who felt some compassion and introduced us to a financial advisor. Sam was aware of my heartache and offered his help, assisting and guiding us with our finances. He introduced Norata and me to an advisor who handled our remaining funds.

Sam, understanding our misfortune, was very disturbed with the fact that Ned refused to help with our needs. He asked Norata to set up an appointment in hopes that just maybe he can make Ned aware of the help we need financially.

Sam's mother lived in Newport, not very far from the plant, so he thought it would be a good time to visit with her after the meeting.

Norata was hesitant, he did not want to be put in that go between, frightful position. Fearing the reaction from his son, and having no choice, he was forced to agree. Norata, made no mention of the meeting to Ned, taking the chance that it will happen without him being involved. It was an unfavorable calamity for both Sam and Ned.
Without warning, they were put in an unpleasant position. Sam was angry and embarrassed, he felt deceived by Norata, and expressed his disappointment for being a weakling.

I explained how Norata's obsession with his son would make him hide in the shadows while conspiring with us. It brings to mind an old Italian phrase "Mane la prethea e' scona la mana" (throwing the stone and hiding the hand).

After the meeting, Ned was furious with his dad,

chastising him for not informing him about the unexpected visit. I assumed from what I gathered that Ned turned on his dad same as he did me. Full of anger and with many harsh words, he bluntly told him to leave. Norata, saddened, immediately left the building a broken man and never returned. Our cruel son turned demonic and destroyed his dad. It was the beginning of his physical derangement.

Although I felt bad that Ned hurt his father, I felt some contentment in returning the insincerity Norata felt for me.

How sad to have spent our entire life caring, sacrificing, and providing for our son financially, only to find that after he became successful and independent he turned his back, threw us into poverty, and completely forgot our generosity.

Norata was hurting, devastated, never expecting to be treated so badly by the son he cherished.

I was anxious to find out what had transpired between them. Waiting to hear some good news, I called Sam, he refrained, and with an expression of disgust said, "Your son is despicable. I would be ashamed to call him my son."

A cold feeling of disgrace came over me. Sam refused to go any further, I assumed to prevent from causing me added pain.
Ned also made it understood that his children wanted nothing more to do with us. What happened to this evil minded, vicious, corrupt son we cherished

all our life? Could he really have been possessed?

Sam advised us that we should not make any contact with them. Those words tore at me like a broken branch. To take my grandchildren away from me was torture. They were my life, and above all else, Ned managed to take that pleasure away from us too.

Why? I ask, repeatedly, what could we have possibly done to turn our son into this demon?

I was determined to find out. It was not long in my inquiries that I found, at one time without my knowledge, he had found my will (before he took possession of my building). It states that he had already received his share of our estate and was not entitled to any part of the remaining property. Becca, who never asked for anything, was to inherit what little was left.

I thought, could he possibly be that greedy? Did he forget his words before he took control of our building? "This will be my inheritance. Take care of Becca now, I'm all set." The thought of his rummaging through my personal files was sickening. Our spoiled son was a taker and never knew how to give. Money at his disposal was so forthcoming that I guess he truly believed that our well would never run dry.

We realized now that all our efforts had failed. Sam suggested our only alternative was to force Ned to at least pay the $175,000 signed promissory note, eleven percent interest, nine years past due. Also, the portfolio of loans and funds, yielding an enormous sum, would most certainly relieve us of the financial burden. However, it would be detrimental, knowing we could hurt him financially. I loved my cruel despicable son as a mother in spite of the aching void in my heart.

I was hesitant. How hard it was for me to even think of taking my pitiless son to court. In my mind I thought, parents cherish their children and cannot hurt them in any way, no matter how cruel they become.

In spite of his uncaring and disastrous hurt causing us mental pain, I was in denial. How could I possibly live with myself after bringing my son to court? What would people think? I would be disgraced. My family meant the world to me. I always felt that family was a bond of love shared unconditionally.

Sam was concerned, pressuring me to file the motion. I asked him to please make one more try, hoping to avoid a court battle. I asked him to speak to Victor, Ned's lawyer, an old friend of our family. The meeting took place at his office with Norata and I present.

Sam showed proof of and the breakdown of over $2,000,000 to Ned's business ventures.

Since he has never replaced the fifty thousand dollars he literally took from our savings, plus the fact that he left us with unpaid mortgages on our property, it most certainly would be his duty to compensate.

We were in need and would be happy to agree on a $30,000. settlement and $500.00 a month salary, which he could well afford.

Victor thought it to be very fair; however, as I expected, Ned's obsession controlled him, so he declined.

He was certain and knew in his heart that we would never bring him into court.

With a burst of anger, Sam tried desperately to convince me to proceed with the injunction, he was certain the judge would throw the book at Ned for his devious record.

I realized this was our only alternative, but again, I feared the humiliation and asked him to please give me a little more time before making my decision.

Norata was hurting very badly. He became frustrated, irritable, in a bad state of deep depression. He was physically and morally destroyed. His outlook on life went from one extreme to another. The separation from his son was bringing him down. Every day that goes by gets harder and harder living with him.

His belittling and negative attitude toward me and everyone else was escalating. He had become arrogant and intolerable to people around him. I knew how much he missed his son. It was taking a toll on his health. I tried my best to cope, in spite of the fact that he put us in this predicament.

I was concerned about his emotional condition. He was lost and under great strain. I considered leaving, but because of his failing health, and our financial state, it was impossible. The chest pains and poor circulation in his legs were becoming more frequent; his refusal to be checked gave me the impression he was giving up. I convinced him, after a week of constant pain, to see our family doctor.

The examination showed a damaged heart and he was immediately prepared for surgery. Many complications developed after the triple bypass; as a result, he spent four weeks in the hospital.

I spent as much time as I could with him to keep his spirits up, but he was unhappy, taking his frustrations out on me. I am sure in some way he blamed me for the breakup of his son.

Cousin Dan was socializing with Ned and disapproved of his behavior, he shamed him into paying a visit to his sick dad.

However, I assumed out of embarrassment, Ned did indeed make a surprise short visit to see him after visiting hours. Norata, excited, called me after Ned left. I could sense the joy in his voice. He thought that quick visit would result in a happy ending, but there was no other contact from Ned thereafter, not even a phone call.

Norata was pleased to be home after his hospital stay; however, his legs were weak and painful. The stairs were becoming more difficult to climb. He couldn't go on living there. He was determined to find a first-floor apartment. Each day he would search the daily newspaper, desperately seeking a first-floor unit.

I was contented to remain here in my apartment since my rent was rather reasonable, although the trip to the laundromat every two days was hectic. I found it strange to have to do my wash at a facility, when we furnished our tenants with washing facilities. It was difficult finding a decent place to live. Rents were out of reach, and Norata was getting restless.

I decided to make one more attempt to Ned's lawyer. I didn't think it would make any difference, however, I thought, being desperate and with nothing more to lose, it was worth a try.

Victor was very sympathetic. He assured me he would talk to Ned and try to convince him to buy us a house (was how he put it). He promised to call me back. I waited patiently each day hoping to hear from him; however, that return call never came. I assumed our son with no mercy had declined.

Trailer

To deepen our wounds, Norata received a strange telephone call. The man was very disturbed and said, "You sold me a trailer that didn't belong to you, and I demand my money back." Norata was speechless. Ned and his dad frequented many auctions in the past for equipment needed at the plant. At one particular auction, Ned bid on a trailer equipped with elegant furniture that was used for corporate executive meetings. Impressed with the furniture, he won the bid. His purpose to purchase the trailer was for the contents only.

After emptying the trailer, he turned to his dad and said, "Dad, do whatever you want with the trailer. I have no use for it." With that, Norata suggested perhaps moving it to the farm for storing garden equipment would be a great idea; however, after reviewing the wheel- less stationary trailer, it was not worth moving. Eventually, he sold it for one thousand dollars.

Norata, recalling the incident, turned to the caller and said, "If you talk
to my son, he will explain it clearly."

With that, the caller said, "Your son is right here. He wants to donate the trailer to the school." Our despicable son, so consumed with an inordinate desire to possess wealth without remorse, was ready to take our last dollar. How much more could he take from us? Wasn't it enough he put us in poverty? Did he have no concern at all whether we lived or died?

It was hard to accept the fact that our cruel son could be so devious and without remorse to continue to hurt us this way. I thought, what could possibly have possessed him to do this terrible thing to his parents at a time when we were troubled and in need? How deceitful could he be to continue to hurt us? Has he really no feelings?

I had the suspicion that Jane, having close ties with the school, insisted on the donation. Knowing Ned's fear and under her control, pursuing her every command, he was bound.

Feeling hurt and betrayed, Norata apologized to the caller and returned the one thousand dollars. It hurt so bad to think my son, knowing how financially desperate we were, would make us return the one thousand dollars.

After constant searching, Norata found a one-bedroom apartment in a newly built elderly complex in subsidized housing and made the move.

I somehow felt relieved knowing the bickering and quarreling had finally ended, but it was inevitable, at his age, and in poor health, he was not capable of caring for himself. I was not ready at that time to leave my apartment, so we lived separately.

There was no doubt maintaining two apartments would be a struggle; his social security was considered enough for his living expenses only. Somehow, I convinced myself there is nothing I cannot handle. We will be much happier.

After I helped him get situated, I decided to find a part-time job. I was a healthy seventy-two-year-old woman, still active, and not about to let my age get the better of me. The extra money would help with expenses.

The separation was working out quite well for me at the time; however, Norata's attitude had not changed. Every visit I made was hell. There was always something said to spark his short fuse.

With self-control, I would overlook his remarks and walk out, giving him no chance to continue arguing.

I found a job—packing sausage. Although I felt fortunate to be hired at my age, standing on my feet all day was tiresome. Being the oldest person in the plant, I was treated extra special by everyone.

After work, my daily visits to Norata's apartment were constant. I would check in on him, prepare his meal, and tidy up the apartment.

The hustle and bustle of caring for two apartments and working at the same time was becoming a strain. I was trying to burn the candle at both ends. It was not working out. The extra money wasn't helping any. The funds we were living on were slowly diminishing.

I suddenly realized I had to relieve myself of this pressure and give up my apartment.

Becca, considerate and very thoughtful of others, had opened her   home to us several times. I have always considered myself strong and able to maintain my independence. I fear being a burden. I consider it unhealthy for two women to live in the same house together. My daughter is my best friend. I would never want to spoil the wonderful relationship I have with her.

I lost many hours of sleep trying to find a solution to this distressful burden. I constantly thought how incredible it was I had everything in life I could possibly want. How my life has changed from one extreme to another, Did I ever think my life would end this way? Did I ever think that I would be deprived of the wonderful life we had— securities, properties, new cars, all the luxuries money could buy?
The turmoil haunted me.

My son, hungered for power, let nothing stand in his way. How sad how much greed can destroy a once happy family.

I think back to the happy times when Becca and Ned would accompany us on all our family gatherings, trips abroad, and related discussions. The many times Lori and Bob would knock on our door waking us from a deep sleep in the wee hours of the morning with our next-door-neighbors Marie and Jack, just for a surprise laugh.
Marie became my special friend while we were building our home next to her, thirty-eight years

earlier.

She and I were drawn together by the same common interests, she always admired Ned with the hopes that he and her daughter Paulette would eventually become attracted to each other. I wished it had, but the attraction never came to light.

I remember the blizzard of 1978 when the streets were closed to traffic, people stranded in their homes for days, our neighbors congregating in our home eating pasta, drinking wine, and enjoying each other's company. Our home was always open. The happiness I shared with my family and friends will never return.

My thoughts lingered, how wonderful it would have been if Robert were alive to have shared our love will stay with me forever.

Becca and Jon's marriage was doomed to fail. Becca was determined on purchasing oceanfront property. Her search soon ended after finding a lovely home directly across from Old Silver Beach in Falmouth.

she was so overwhelmed with being across from the ocean she completely distanced herself from her home in Rehoboth. Jon was obligated to the family business and found it impossible to live at the Cape. His weekend visits were becoming less and less since much of his business was indebted to weekends. Eventually, their separation caused their divorce. We were heartsick. Jon was like a son to us. In spite of their divorce, we continued to include him in our family gatherings.

The years passed with Jon failing in child support. He became an alcoholic and suffered an addiction to drugs. Becca was forced to sell her oceanfront home and move back to Rhode Island, close to the family. Jon is living alone in his beautiful home that Becca forfeited through their divorce. Becca had regrets, being unhappy since leaving the Cape, but vowed eventually to return. Having her nearby has made my life a lot easier to cope with, since I see her and the children often.

My Sibling

My dear sister Sue and I have been a twosome all through our lives. Seven years older than me, she had the spunk of a forty-year-old. Her home had a welcome atmosphere with food always ready for whomever walks in. Her wonderful husband, Elmo, treated me like a loving sister; he took pride in welcoming people to his dinner table. His generosity was too much for Sue to bear. He often took it upon himself to invite friends and neighbors to visit without notice, leaving her unprepared.

Their three children, whom I love dearly, are warm, full of compassion, and especially devoted to each other. Sue was concerned and aware of my financial status and unhappy life. Concerned, she and Elmo insisted I move in with them. Their spacious home was large enough for anyone to have the privacy needed. I knew I would always feel comfortable being with them, but I was confused, troubled, and needed time to consider. They refused to take no for an answer, so I packed my car with some clothes and necessities, and moved in with the promise to make my stay short lived in preparing to get my life in order. Sue was happy with my being there. It meant spending our days together shopping and going to the casino bingo.

Their youngest son (we call him Junior), still living at home, insisted I take his room since it was the largest room in the house with a private bath. I was honored and felt special. He showed concern for me and tried his utmost to make me comfortable. I was included in all his plans, trying desperately to help me overcome my emotional state.

I was especially concerned for Junior, a thirty-eight-year-old with a terrible habit of smoking two or more packs a day—a chain smoker. Each time he lit up, I felt a gnaw in my stomach. I tried to stress the fact that smoking is a killer. Every time I scolded him, he would give me a beautiful smile and say, "You are right, Auntie." It was useless, he played on deaf ears. Junior replaced the son I lost.

Living with Sue and Elmo was comforting. They treated me like royalty, but I needed to find some closure in my life.

I felt like a nomad, deeply depressed, not knowing what to do. Living out of my car, I was sulking, my depression was progressing. I always thought I was strong and could handle any obstacle, but I became a confused weakling. This downfall had a profound effect on my life. I felt alone, disgusted, and nothing seemed right. I was desperate to let this go away.

Nighttime, the worst part of the day, I cried continuously; I hated the thought of going to bed, my thoughts of the beautiful life I once had haunted me.

My life had become meaningless with no purpose in living. I was giving up. This was not the life I envisioned for myself. I cannot go on living this nomad lifestyle, it hurts so bad, how hard it was for me to accept, to have lived a luxurious lifestyle to a dejected downcast, pauper's life.

I was close to suicide. My depression came to a point that I lost my will to live and could not go on. While driving, I suddenly came upon the ledge. I lived across from the ledge in my young days; it was remembered as bat haven, a shelter for bats. The fall, equivalent to three stories down, meant no survival, I was tempted. I wanted so badly to relieve myself of this misery. The pressure was too great for me to bear.

I attempted to continue over the embankment but some undetermined notion stopped me. Deep in thought, I considered Becca and the children. The hurt I would have caused them would be unfair. I had to reconsider. I just prayed for a miracle.

Monday morning, just before five, the phone rang. I quickly answered for fear it would wake everyone. It was Norata. He was hysterical. He said, "Mae, the fire alarm is ringing here in the building, and I cannot get out of bed. Please hurry." I immediately dressed and drove out to see what was wrong.

Sure enough, the alarm was sounding. Evidently, one of the tenants forgot some food on the stove and set off the fire alarm. Norata's legs were frozen, unable to move. After rubbing them a few minutes, he was able to dangle them off the bed.

His face was white as a sheet, petrified. He begged me to come live with him. I was doubtful, but how could he possibly live alone? He was aging drastically. He was having difficulty dressing and unable to put on his shoes and socks. How am I going to tolerate his unpleasant attitude? I realized then, he obviously needed help, but I dreaded going back to that unhappy life with him. The taste of being free from his control was somewhat gratifying. However, after spending two months with Sue and Elmo, I felt it was time I ease my conscience and move in with him.

I packed what little clothes I had and prepared for my moving out. I was somewhat relieved. I expressed my gratitude to Sue and the family, promising never to forget the kindness they have shown me.

It was a time to be specific, a time to make it understood with Norata that, since we are going to live together again, we must come to a mutual agreement. I stressed upon him that he must accept the fact that he has lost his merciless son. We must live our lives independently. I promised to prepare his meals, keep his clothes clean, and take care of his needs. In return, I demanded respect at all times and he must change his negative attitude toward me and everyone around him. The lecture was short lived. This troubled man was afflicted with hostility. He hated the world.

I sacrificed living with him. I had to organize this one-bedroom apartment to accommodate for two. The closet was jammed with clothes and stored records. The living area, a thirteen-by fifteen-foot room, was confined with two love seats, a television, a table, and two chairs.

The pantry was small enough for one person to work in. I was devastated, terribly unhappy living under those conditions, but I had no choice. I had a duty to fulfill, in spite of the fact that he was undeserving of my care.

We both had some counseling, which made very little difference in our relationship.

The first few weeks were working out fairly well, with me ignoring his mental state and living in what I called his "two-room hut."

I really tried to stay on good terms. Occasionally, he would become unruly, but I overlooked his mental attitude and paid little attention.
In some way, I truly sympathized and felt pity for him. It was sad to see the change in him. The rejection from his son destroyed him completely.

We were living just above poverty level and accepting life as it comes. Our golden years were the worst years of our lives. I can only pray that one day Ned will realize he put us in poverty, in exchange for wealth and power. His wealth will pacify, but will never make him totally happy.

Being a veteran, Norata was entitled to medical help. A true blessing, since there was no way we could afford to pay for his medical bills. His failing health was getting worse, I was making constant trips to the hospital, and his body was breaking down with so many complications.

I dream my life somehow will turn for the better. So often I regret the carelessness of our once happy marriage and wealthy fortune, how gullible we were, watching it flow into the hands of our disloyal son.

Norata's cousin and dear friend Paul suddenly passed away. Norata wasn't feeling his best but he had an obligation, so we made the visit to the funeral parlor. We were sitting directly in front of the far corner of the entrance. Suddenly, we were surprised to see Ned walk in; it had been years since we last saw him. I was impressed, how slim and impeccably dressed he was. After he made his entrance, he walked over to us with, "Hi Mom, Dad." With a smile, pretending to be happy to see us, he bent down to kiss us both; it was quick and to the point. All an act, I surmised.

I could see the contentment on Norata's face; he lit

up like a Christmas tree. I, however, felt intense animosity. Never could I forgive the cruelty my son put upon us.

Six years had passed with no contact from Ned or his family. It's been six years too long. Norata was overcome with the desire to speak to his son. My phone bill stated two calls made to Ned's office. So as not to embarrass him I pretended not to notice. I am not aware of Ned returning any calls. I cannot imagine how or why Norata could so easily forget what his son's ruthlessness did to us. How could he not care?

Lianne is fifteen years old, and Jared, eleven. I miss them terribly. In my travels, I would constantly look about, hoping to see them somewhere—in a store, a mall, or a movie theatre. All I hoped for was a glimpse of them.

I wrote a letter to Lianne, expressing my love for them and how much I missed them. I made it clear that they will always be in my heart. Jane recognized my handwriting and returned the letter unopened.

I was determined to get that letter to Lianne, in spite of the fact that Jane denied me having any contact with them.

I disguised my handwriting and made a second attempt. I was confident the letter was delivered. I received no acknowledgement from Lianne, however, I did understand. The fact that I was able to express my feelings toward them gave me the satisfaction I needed.

They will have to know how much I truly love them.

I shed many tears thinking about them. I'd go to bed at night with both children on my mind, hoping that one day I'll be able to put my arms around and hug them.

The neighborhood carnival was a gathering place for most children. I had a feeling that perhaps if I scoured the area I would be lucky to find Jared and Lianne roaming about.

While watching for the sight of them, I was approached by Ellen, one of Jane's friends. She proceeded to tell me that Jane had divorced Ned three years prior. She mentioned that he was living in Newport, quite lavishly, in a mansion by the ocean. I was taken by surprise. My stomach ached to the point of wanting to throw up. To hear that he was living a millionaire's lifestyle with the hard-earned money Norata and I worked so hard for in our business made me sick. His need for possessing great wealth was his life's desire; he succeeded.

I refused to give up. I had to relieve my longing. I made another attempt. After breakfast, I had a sudden urge to take my chances and wait for Jared after school.

I hadn't realized the pain I had caused myself. It's been too many long years, I remembered his beautiful smiling face, the kind you just want to grab, hold, and kiss. He was six when I last saw him.

I wondered if he would recognize me, or I, him. Six years can make a drastic change in a child's life.

As I entered his private school, I inquired at the office as to what room Jared was in. I didn't want to miss him, so I waited in the hallway. He was in clear view, sitting in the front row of the class. There was no mistaking him. His face was a carbon copy of his dad. It was like looking at Ned sitting there.

I knew at a glance that he certainly was Jared. My eyes filled with tears as I looked at him.

One of the children, returning to the classroom, noticed me standing against the wall and asked who was I waiting for. I responded with, "Jared." I assumed she made mention of the fact. With that, his teacher noticed me and came out to ask who I was waiting for. I said, "My grandson Jared."

Her response was, "Jared does not know you." I suddenly felt an extreme hurt.

I wondered, did he really not know me, or was he following Jane's instructions? I left the school with tears streaming down my face, disappointed and extremely hurt. I later felt some little comfort. I, at least, got to see my Jared.

Jane evidently was notified about my being at the school.

The very next day, I received a call from the school principal who was extremely arrogant. She said,

"Who am I speaking to?" I, of course, gave her my name. She said very boldly, "If you should ever come anywhere near this school again, the police will be called, and you will most certainly be arrested."

She gave me no chance to explain, so I apologized and assured her it will never happen again. I cannot express the hurt and extreme pain I felt. I was devastated, humiliated, and felt like a criminal. I didn't deserve this unkind treatment. How much more hurt could they put us through? I always put my needs last where Jane was concerned.
Why is there so much animosity? Could she have taken her failed marriage out on me? I thought; never will she allow me to see the children again.

Jane had also made a complaint to Sam. The next day, Sam called me with a distasteful attitude. He said, "What were you thinking? Do you realize Jane has a restraining order against you? Never try to make contact with the children again."

I asked myself, why is she hurting me in this cruel way? What could I have done to make her so resentful toward me? I could not imagine Jane being so malicious and spiteful, since the issue here is with our son's wrongdoing toward us.

I was hurting; the weeks following had a devastating effect on my life. I had never had anything of this nature happen to me.

Why have we been treated so cruelly? We gave them our life and everything we had. We were good, loving parents, always ready to accommodate their desires. Our reward was devastation and a broken heart. I encouraged myself with the feeling of being somewhat fortunate to have our granddaughters, Tayla and Maddy, who love us dearly.

On April 24, Arna suddenly suffered a heart attack and passed away. She was my big sister, always ready to lead me in the right direction. Her death was sudden, and a complete surprise.

As I watched her lifeless body, I thought how quickly life could end. Sue and I visited and had lunch with her the day before she had the attack. We three sisters were close, confiding, and depending on each other always for support.

We had spent a pleasant afternoon together the day before, discussing our daily routines. What a blessing, I thanked God; it was as if fate had brought us together for the last time.

While I sat in mourn at the funeral parlor, I was suddenly surprised.
I felt someone place a hand on my shoulder. As I looked up, I was startled to see Jane standing there. She gave me a hug, kissed my cheek, and said, "Mae, I just want you to know, I always loved you." Tears filled my eyes. I was suddenly lost for words. I forgot for a moment the anguish and misery she caused.

Without a second thought, I thanked her and

immediately asked how the children were. They were my only concern at that moment. She said, "They're fine." After a few brief words, she wished me well and walked away. I was only interested in the children. I was happy knowing this would bring me in close contact with Lianne and Jared.

It did not matter now. I surmised a trick to prepare me to be on her good side, I knew there was a reason for Jane to make the sudden visit at the wake, she had a plan.

I was on cloud nine, a long awaited time for me to be with Lianne and Jared.

Assuming we were still stupid and gullible, knowing how Ned destroyed us, she evidently thought in her mind that we would be favoring her in her dispute. How very wrong she was.

After the funeral, I couldn't wait; I knew this would be my opportunity to see Lianne and Jared. I called Jane to express my appreciation for coming to the wake and approaching me. It was an opportunity long awaited. I so desperately looked forward to this day when I would finally get to see my grandchildren. My first instinct was to ask if I could see the children. She then arranged for me to meet at the Newport Creamery the next day. I was so excited and anxious for the time to pass.

As I walked into the creamery, Jared was in plain view directly in front of me. I was consumed with joy. I cannot describe the wonderful feeling I felt being with my grandchildren. Jared had grown tall, very handsome, with a beautiful smile. I put my arms around him, forgetting to let go.

Lianne, a raving beauty, greeted me warmly with "Hi, Nana." and kissed me as if there was no loss of time between us. I asked Jared if he had forgotten me. I was happy to hear him say "No." We conversed about everyday activities over lunch. Jane made no mention of Ned or their divorce.

After being together for that short period of time, Jane made gestures about leaving. Being with my grandkids after those lost years was heaven, one of the happiest days of my life. I enjoyed every minute with them.

Again, I wondered why Jane was suddenly so kind to me after those hurtful years, unless she had a need for something. I grew even more curious. Our correspondence became almost daily. Her first call was to fill me in on the problems she was having with Ned. Then she told me that she and Ned were divorced and were involved in a bitter three-year financial battle.

She specified that the settlement he offered was not acceptable to her. She was seeking one million dollars, her home, all expenses paid, and a weekly salary. How cunning and so undeserved. She never loved Ned; she obviously married him for financial gain. I never remember her ever making a kind jester toward him. She continued asking questions, seeking information about the past. So I was careful not to disclose any past dealings. If Jane was looking for some consolation, there was no way she would get it from me. I could never erase the malicious treatment I got from her.

She kept in close touch thinking I was vulnerable because Ned and I weren't on speaking terms. The building was an important factor in her dispute. She needed for me to tell her about the true dealings with Ned about the building he had deliberately stolen from me.

I refused to let myself become involved in her fight. I just listened as she continued to try to get me to answer. She needed information but I pretended she never asked any questions. I still had feelings for my cruel and deceitful son.

Her disappointment in my refusing to divulge information annoyed her. She straight-out asked me, "By the way, Mae, was the building a gift to Ned or did he buy it from you?" That was the million-dollar information she so needed from me.

When I ignored the question again she realized that I was not going to yield to her interrogation. Agitated at not getting me to reply, she said, with fury, "I will break him, no matter what." Luckily, she went no further. She knew that Ned had destroyed us and she somehow hoped I would consider testifying in court against him. I guess that was her plan!

Jane's lawyers continued to leave messages on my answering machine to return their calls. I was already frantic. My life had been a living hell. I couldn't survive another tragedy. I wanted no part of their battle.

I begged Jane to please not involve us. When she became convinced that I wasn't about to reveal any information, she promised that she wouldn't subpoena me in court. But her lawyers, unable to get to me, tried several times to talk to Norata. He too refused to answer their calls.

It brought back to mind how I had begged Jane to help us when we were having financial difficulties. I clearly remember her response, "Do what you have to do, we have no money." The shoe was now on the other foot.

About a week later, I got a surprise call. Jane was having a surprise homecoming party for Lianne. I was totally shocked at her kind invitation, one that very rarely was received. I was hesitant but I had no choice, I needed to honor my granddaughter. As I walked in the door after Lianne greeted me, I was surprised, the rooms were filed with Jane's relatives and friends. I felt uncomfortable wondering what everyone was thinking, I'm sure they were well aware of our family conflict. My visit was short, I could not wait to leave.

Marriott Newport

Susan was a banquet server at the Marriott Hotel in Newport. Our family planned a get-together to celebrate the holiday. After dinner we were lounging with a cocktail when I was surprised to see Ned walk in with a well-dressed, lovely young lady. They were carrying their Louis Vuitton luggage. I assume they were returning from a vacation.

Not having contact with my son for those lost years and suddenly seeing him walk in, gave me some deep emotional pleasure.

I know that my family are peace-loving, sympathetic people always ready to help in any situation. They felt the depths of my compassion and tried their best to ease my suffering.

I assumed that Ned and his girlfriend were invited to sit at the bar with them, but, I wanted no part of that reunion, so Sue and I left the room.

Obviously, Ned had been informed that Jane and I were corresponding. I'm sure he now feared that I would be taking her side.

A few days later, during dinner, we received a surprise phone call. I soon realized it was Ned. I wondered why, after those lost years, he would be contacting us. And, what could he want unless it was for some profitable gain.

I could hear Norata's joy when he made

arrangements to meet. I was suspicious—there had to be some method to this madness. Ned was playing again with his father's feelings. I was totally disgusted. All the hurt came back to mind. How much of our lives had been taken and thrown to the wolves?

I suspected he was in fear, because of Jane's sudden correspondence. I wondered why this sudden contact? Does he plan to use us again for some fraudulent scheme? We never knew with our deceitful son.

I asked, "What was that all about?"

With a smile of contentment Norata excitedly replied, "Ned wants to take us out to dinner." I watched his transformation from one extreme to another in that short time while he spoke, it was almost like he died and went to heaven.

"Dinner? Have you forgotten what your son's cruelty did to us? You've obviously forgotten the harm, putting us into a pauper's life. You forgive him? Are you blind? Can't you see what's happening to us? Doesn't it bother you?"

I went on and on reminding him of the hurt Ned put us through. Remember what Sam said? "I would be ashamed to call him my son."

He just listened. He knew I was right but it never mattered to him. He could never put his son down—ever.

I could feel the deception. why would Ned want to contact us after those lost years? Could the reunion with our family make an impression, something he missed out on? Could he be afraid of Jane's contact knowing we could hurt him in court? There had to be something behind this sudden correspondence. Ned didn't know that whatever happened with their court battle, we would have no part in it.

Our son doesn't know how to be nice unless there's a plan of deceit awaiting.

But, I wasn't about to spoil a good thing for Norata. He never forgave his son. I was reluctant. I had carried the pain for so long it was not easy for me to suddenly forget the past. The hurt will always haunt me.

The plan was to pick us up the following evening at six o'clock. I didn't say anything. Norata was so blinded by pleasure he had no clue as to how I felt. He waited patiently for Ned's arrival. His son's return had finally come true.

At 5:45 Ned called and asked if we were ready. Norata anxiously said, "Yes, I'm waiting downstairs in the lobby."

"Isn't Mom coming?"

Norata didn't explain, he just said, "No." I was disgusted at his erasing the past so easily. Didn't he realize that his son stole our life? I couldn't allow myself to take part in this act of hypocrisy. My fearsome son was again trying to use us, afraid that we might take Jane's side and hurt him. I refused to give him the satisfaction of forgiveness.

I had butterflies in my stomach as I watched Ned from my window, helping his dad into his lovely white Cadillac Escalade. They drove off with me wondering how Norata could so easily forget what his son was. How could he forget the day his son literally threw him out of the building like a dog and how that episode caused him to have a heart attack? Was he so blind that he couldn't understand his son's insincerity?

I was bitter but curious as to how they would communicate and what they would talk about. I couldn't help wondering what Ned wanted.

Becca was a good person. There were times when she'd get angry and blow off steam, unintentionally hurting, but she would easily forget and never hold a grudge. She held no remorse for her brother's wrongdoing. The fact that he had stolen her inheritance made no difference, in spite of her living moderately.

Happy with the sudden invitation, she said, "Mom, I finally have my brother back. I want us to forget the past. We only have each other. Please accept Ned's invitation, let bygones be bygones, let's have our family again." I never realized how much she missed her brother until this sudden reunion. The intense love she had for him was evident. It didn't matter how hurtful he was to her, she loved him.

I mentioned, "There's been too much hurt, Becca. I'm still suffering emotional scars. How can I accept his invitation? He's done so much harm. I'm not ready to forgive him. I live every day with the shame and disgrace he caused us. He destroyed us completely, with no conscience. Why would I welcome his sudden social visit?"

Without listening to a word I said, she answered, "I know, Mom, but please try to forgive him."

At nine o'clock, Norata, fatigued, came struggling in the door. The two hours away was too much for him. His weak legs were throbbing. He said, "I can't wait to lie down."

After settling himself, I waited for him to fill me in on their conversation, but instead he harshly said, "Why wouldn't you come with us? Ned was disappointed."

"Oh, you fool, disappointed?" I said. "How could you be so naïve? Our lives were taken away and thrown to the wolves by your precious son. How could I suddenly forget? Do you really think he cares? Your son hasn't changed. He's still the same manipulator. There's got to be a reason for this sudden attachment."

He listened as I continued chastising him. He didn't comment because he knew there was truth in what I was saying, but he would never give me the satisfaction of degrading his son.

I waited for him to continue. I was eager to find out what they talked about, but he completely avoided the questioning.

When I asked, "What did you talk about?"

He replied, "Oh, we only discussed business." He was too tired to continue. He ignored me and went directly to bed.

The next morning, I wanted information, asking what transpired in the two hours of their dinnertime. My questions were unanswered. Norata had a deep feeling of guilt and refused to talk about it.

After that, Ned kept in constant touch. He called almost nightly. I wouldn't answer the phone since I felt that was Norata's delight, not mine. I had no reason to talk to my son, nor did I want to. So many thoughts entered my mind. Obviously, Ned was aware of Jane's correspondence, and I assume he was in fear of the outcome.
I thought of so many reasons why Ned made this drastic change.

Ironically, Norata's birthday and Ned's, the third and fifth of July, were approaching. I guess he finally remembered his dad's birthday. He called and suggested that as a family we celebrate both birthdays together at Custy's Restaurant that following Saturday. Norata was so happy, his attitude completely changed.

I had not recovered from the agony I suffered. Why would I subject myself to this hypocrisy? I refused to sit at the same table with him. How could I put all the hurt behind me? The six years of hurt seemed like yesterday.

Norata resented my refusing to accept the invitation. He longed for this reunion; he lived for this special day. Being with his son after those lost years made him feel like a new person, like he had gained time. Inwardly he knew that I had a right to be angry. The calls continued and Norata happily accepted them.

Becca's longing for her brother, however, was hurting me. I felt her pain, and her strong desire to be reunited with Ned would make her happy.
   I thought seriously and wondered if maybe this reunion would be better for her. By accepting the invitation, I would be doing her justice. I remembered how sad I was at her describing how much she missed her brother and the effect it had on me.

I gave it a lot of thought. I convinced myself that I must try to put aside my ill will and consider her feelings. I felt obligated to make this happen for her. In my heart I wanted her to be happy. I wanted her hurt to go away even though I felt like a pretender.

Very uncomfortably I accepted the invitation. It was a hard decision for me. On the third of July Ned called his dad asking for us to be ready by five o'clock. Norata was so excited, patiently waiting for the time to pass. When it was time to leave, Becca refused to join us. She said that we should have that special time together.

I was disappointed since I agreed to the invitation to please her. She then mentioned that Ned and Jared had already been visiting her. She had evidently planned for our family to be reunited again. I realized then that this family bond had to happen for her sake.

Ned greeted us very warmly, with a hug and kiss. I was still in denial—his hugs and kisses could never erase the devastation he caused us.

Norata was very relaxed, like there had never been any animosity between them. I sat in the back seat of the car feeling uneasy and thinking of all the trickery, his draining us of our possessions, and all the other disgraceful happenings.

How could our son mask his deceptive character? How could he pretend to be caring? I sat there thinking how cruel he had been, without ever feeling a bit of remorse.

Before we drove off, Ned turned to me with his phone camera and said, "Smile, Mom." Surprisingly, he took my picture. I wondered why he would even want to take a picture of me.

During their talks over dinner, he would direct his attention to me, saying "Mom" occasionally to make certain I was included in their conversation.

The two hours we spent together was like regaining the lost years—the steady conversation about business, the failure of his marriage, and the costly court battle. By the end of the night the tension I was feeling seemed to have lessened some.

Tossing and turning, I couldn't get to sleep that night. I was surprised at the sudden change in him. It was like he actually longed for the reunion. Or, was he playing the good son fearing Jane's sudden correspondence hoping we would not get involved in his divorce battle? I wondered about many things; so much went through my mind. But I still had suspicions. Ned could never be trusted in my eyes.

I wondered, what could he be feeling finding us in this depressed condition while he is living in a Newport mansion by the ocean? Could it have had some effect on him? Had he realized his hunger for wealth had put us here? Could he actually be feeling some remorse?

I will never know. He's my son but I don't know him.

The next week Ned and Jared came to visit. I was so happy to see my grandson that all thoughts of anger were gone. I had longed for the day when I would see him walk in my door.

After that, he and Jared visited weekly and we were becoming attached. I looked forward to my grandson's visits, his embrace, his arms around me with a hug and a kiss. It helped ease my feelings of contempt.

It was plain to see that Jared was happy with our reunion. He wanted to visit often. He especially appreciated the discussions and pleasing conversations with his grandfather. Poppy kept him interested with stories of his dad's adventures in the early days.

Becca was delighted to have her brother back in her life too. The visits almost always ended with Ned and Jared staying overnight. Becca refused to have them drive to Newport late at night.

The fact that we were accepting Ned made Jane furious. Her calls were anything but friendly. I purposely mentioned that Norata was happy with their reunion. He looked forward to that special day when he would be reunited with his son.

Jane, I assumed, wasn't pleased at hearing the news because her calls were becoming less and less.

It is said, "What goes around comes around." Five years of court hostility had not stopped. The ongoing battle of Jane's promise to break Ned continued.

The divorce was becoming more and more costly. The courts, according to Ned, took control of all their assets—the business, the building, and their beautiful home included.

The advertised assets were sold and the proceeds were divided sixty-forty. Not enough for Jane. Now she insisted on a complete settlement of two million dollars.

It was said that Jane's lawyers had personal, friendly ties with the judge, who ordered Ned to pay Jane $1.5 million or be incarcerated. He chose incarceration—for just one week.

Jane's battle of charges and countercharges were bitter, her greed between them was going nowhere, except that their lawyers were reaping the harvest and draining their finances.

Jane's selfish desire for wealth was underserved. She contributed nothing to her marriage other than being a good mother. She had no concern or consideration to Ned's business failures, refusing to listen or take part in his difficult decisions, just living her life of freedom and luxury with no desire to please her husband in any way or allow him to make decisions as to whom or where he could socialize.

She hired a housekeeper to take complete control of all household duties and never spent a day at the business no matter how desperate Ned was to fill orders. She refused to listen to any business discussions. She was a good, caring mother to her children but malicious and abusive to her husband.

Jane was unaware that, through a series of loans and manipulations, Ned had bought back the house and building. There was no way he was going to forfeit the possessions he so diligently acquired from his parents.

The daily court appearances and anguish caused the business to suffer. However, Ned was making a tremendous effort to regain the money he had lost. His success in these efforts angered Jane to the extreme. She became even more determined to crush him in any and every way possible. Full of hostility, she now refused to accept her sixty percent as a final settlement. She appealed and took the suit further two million dollars, which wouldn't be heard for another year.

It was obvious, Jane was out for blood. Her extreme hatred for Ned was to bring him down to pity. Why I thought, so much animosity? She had a life of contentment. Her calls were fewer. Ned said that he was not concerned since his possessions are indebted and beyond control. Jane refuses to accept the fact that he has nothing more to give. She refuses to end the fight because she believes he has hidden money. She is grasping for straws, hiring one lawyer after another, all of whom make promises (as they fatten their bank accounts). She has declined all offers and is flat-out seeking complete revenge.

Ned ordered her to vacate the home and gave her ample time to relocate. He is feeling the financial drain and is borrowing again, as he says, from Peter to pay Paul. He's confident he will eventually regain his losses.

How sad to have this woman, who married for security and never offered or contributed help in all the years of their business, have the right to break him as she promised. She literally destroyed my family life as well since almost everything Ned acquired from us has been awarded to her.

Ned was given full custody of Jared, though the boy spends some of his weekends with his mom. I see the same father-son attachment, the same closeness that once existed between Norata and Ned.

Lianne, majoring in business finance, attends Boston College. She's not totally affected by her parents' divorce. We rarely get to see her, except during spring break and on holidays. I wait patiently for her occasional calls. Our conversation is usually about her school activities and her future plans. She always ends our conversation with a plea to help get her mom and dad back together. I eased her mind with "I'll try," but I know there is no possible way that could happen.

Come September, she will continue her studies at the University of Florence in Tuscany, Italy. It's comforting to know that she's being spared the turmoil her parents are going through.

The Reunion

Not a day goes by that Ned doesn't phone. It was easy to see that either he missed the family or that he feels alone in his present troubled state. I wonder which. It's hard to judge his actions. He is my son, but as I said, I do not know him now. He's a puzzle, a two-sided image.

I accept the compassion as a mother but the hurt lingers. I cannot comprehend what has turned him around to being the loving son we once had, unless he feels alone and needs family guidance. I have wanted to trust him but there is no mistaking, you are what you are, people don't change. I will always have doubt.

My grandson's bond, however, has helped me moderate my feelings and overlook my son's hypocrisy.

The unhappy memories were beginning to fade. I was trying desperately to resolve the hostility and anger I felt toward my son. His frequent visits were becoming habitual and showing signs of caring and concern. He asked questions about our unhappy living conditions, my frequent overnight stays with Becca, and the disagreements between Norata and me.

I wonder how he feels finding us living a pauper's life as opposed to our once wealthy lifestyle? Does he really feel some concern or compassion? Or was he pretending to show that he cared and was just seeking some consolation, hoping to relieve his hypocritical conscience knowing he caused us this downfall?

Or, having fulfilled his dream of wealth, does he now recognize our desperation and fate?

He's done so much harm there is no way that he could be concerned. These puzzling thoughts continue to boggle my mind.

One time when he and I were alone, he surprised me. He questioned me about the state I was in. I gave him all the reasons why I was unhappy—losing all the finer things in life that I once had, losing my beautiful home and our luxurious living, and having a contented marriage collapse. How could I possibly be happy with the change from wealth to poverty, having to live in a tiny apartment in a low-class area with nosy neighbors and Norata's uncontrollable temper?
I was shamed and destroyed. He just listened without emotion.

Since he came back into our life, Norata had become a new husband. He was pleasant, caring, and sympathetic. His longing for his precious son had finally come to an end, which pleased him most.

Ned was showing an abundance of care. Suspiciously, I was not quite sure if he felt indebted to us, concerned, or perhaps needed a shoulder to lean on. He made no offer to help us financially which we most needed. I was confused. My mind would stray wondering why the kindness versus our much needed help. Then again, he may have had a fear of Jane's sudden desire to be my friend. So many whys, so confusing. I just didn't know.

Friday, after supper, Ned turned to me with a genuine offer. "Mom, I'm working hard, trying my best to keep my home comfortable for me and Jared, but walking into an empty house isn't very pleasant.

My home is large enough for all of us to live in with all the privacy we need. As long as I'm living there, you and Dad should come live with us."

I was flabbergasted. Really, I was overcome with shock. Was this my son talking? The effect it had on me was almost too much. I could hardly speak. To think that he would want us to share his home was very surprising.

I was lost for words. I didn't respond, I just listened, my head whirling with so much to consider. I wondered if he felt some guilt at seeing our living conditions. Could he have suddenly realized he had let this happen to us? Or was this all part of a plan with some other purpose?

I thought seriously about his offer. I was so unhappy, avoiding people and making excuses to my friends why I wasn't inviting them to visit. I was shamed, I was so influenced by what I'd had in the past.

The more I thought, the more the chance to relive a part of my lost past sounded good to me. Taking me away from this environment would make me happy. It was a very tempting offer. I would be relieved of the anguish I am living under. Once again I would have the special home life I longed for.

In spite of the lingering resentment toward my son, I also felt some gratitude. Would his offer be better for me?

Besides being handicapped and dependent on oxygen, Norata felt very comfortable in his small apartment. He had made it clear that under no circumstances would he ever leave. The excessive heat he requires (sometimes over 80 degrees) is too much for me to bear. The chance for a better life would be a blessing to me.

Becca was saddened by our unhappy life and had begged me to come live with her. Though I couldn't be any happier than living with my daughter, I know how uncomfortable it would have been for the children. Becca's house is lovely with just enough comfort for her family. To share Maddy's bedroom would be unfair. Her closet space is barely enough for one.

Feeling my discomfort, Norata persuaded me to accept Ned's offer. He said, "Mae, I'm getting old and I'm quite sure I will pass away before you. It will be comforting for me to know that you have a decent place to live after I'm gone."

Hearing those words made me emotional. I had to wipe the tears from my eyes. It was pleasing to know he still had so much concern for me after our unhappy aging years together.

I had trouble controlling my tears. "I don't know if I can do that. I feel like a hypocrite. I still have the vivid memories of the pain and suffering he caused us. I can't dismiss my inner feelings of contempt for Ned. I'm struggling to clear that negative state of mind. It's hard to erase the past."

Norata responded, "Don't be stupid. Take his offer. You will be much happier." I wondered how much of that hurtful past would haunt me.

We spent the next week discussing what was best for us both. I finally made the decision that changed my life completely.

Living with Ned has been great. He has been happy with me caring for him and Jared. I've had the privacy I've needed. He reminded me often that his home is mine, and I should feel free to do whatever I wanted. It's like old times, with expressions of love and the hugs he shared in his youth. Whether they were sincere or not, I had felt a sense of security.

Every day he discussed his daily routine, always leaving the house with a hug and "I'll be back soon." The affection, I thought, was truly sincere, though in the back of my mind I couldn't fully trust my son.

How nice it was to be able to invite my friends and family to visit. The pool parties in the dead of winter, the weekly dinner parties, a new sense of excitement for everyone. That was what was missing in my life.

In spite of the sudden contentment, I felt a deep, unexpected loss. Elmo suffered a stroke.

Our family stayed by his bedside until his passing. As I looked at his frail body, I thought of the kindness he showed me while I was living with him. I stood next to him as he spent his last minutes. He took my hand, kissed it, and whispered, "I love you." This wonderful, special man, loved by everyone, expressed his love in his dying state. The tears flowed from all while his family stood beside him.

To the very end, this precious man gave his love. The loss especially affected Sue. She was feeling guilt, confessing that she had taken him for granted. She said, "I haven't done enough to show my appreciation for him." It wasn't until he had gone that she realized how much she loved him.

Although Sue was kind and giving, she was easily hurt and not one to quickly forgive. Fifteen year's prior, Elmo made an unfortunate mistake by saying a trivial sexual insult toward her. It was without malicious intent yet because of that statement she had harbored a deep and strong resentment toward him. The effect of it had kept her alienated, and from sleeping with him their remaining years.

Many times I scolded her for holding that grudge, but she refused to forgive him. Close to his bedside she became emotional. She showed her true love for him. I prayed she would be forgiven and that her guilt would be absolved. Elmo loved her dearly.

Jared was happy with our living together. He would always greet me in the morning with a smiling "Good morning, Nan." How special he made me feel. It was what I longed for all those lost years.

Jane was fuming mad that I had chosen to live in the house she had been forced to vacate. "Ignore her,"

Ned said. "She has no say in the matter. This is your home now, Mom. I want you to be happy."

Could I be dreaming? His kindness was mind-boggling. I couldn't believe the change in him. Could he really be sincere? I was having a hard time believing his kindness toward me. There was never a feeling of sorrow or pity toward us, so how could he suddenly show such compassion? Was there some invisible purpose or a scheme awaiting?

I needed to put some trust in my feelings and overcome the embarrassment. I was happy with my new living conditions; why should I have any doubts? I felt no guilt either that Jane felt resentment. She had to consider that our hard-earned money built this home.

God knows that I was happy with my privacy and being able to entertain. That was what I missed the most.

Norata knew he would not be neglected. I tried to make my visits daily to make sure he was well and comfortable.

My life had been a turnaround, complete contentment with a new abundance of energy. I kept busy doing all the things I had missed, plus my daily routine of house cleaning, doing laundry, and caring for Jared. It felt good to prepare meals again and to be able to sit down at the dinner table at night. It was what I longed for.

Ned was spending most of his weekends away from home. I soon learned he was involved with the young lady he was seeing at the Marriott. Thanksgiving he mentioned that he made reservations in Boston for us to celebrate the holiday with his new girlfriend and her two young daughters. I figured there was some reason for Ned's sudden transformation.

The dinner reservation was elaborately planned at the Hilton Hotel, top floor, overlooking the city of Boston. Very impressive.

What was his purpose for this new friend? I saw the glow in his eyes when he proudly introduced Mona. I wondered if he needed to prove he's a great son with a strong family bond. I hadn't eliminated my suspicions. I still had a hard time totally trusting him.

Mona was absolutely beautiful. A fine figure, a faultless body almost like a Hollywood model, and a very pleasing personality. We felt very comfortable being with her and her well-mannered children.

As the months passed Mona and the children became a part of our family. They were happy to be involved in our life. She was everything that Jane was not. Her kindness to me was special. Every time she visited she brought gifts, love, and affection. Every call ended in "We love you." She was fourteen years younger than Ned but that didn't seem to matter. They were happy together. He was madly in love.

One day when we were talking, Mona and I became intimate, sharing our family life and her meeting with Ned. She described how her life had changed after their first meeting. She questioned him and asked about his family. "He always avoided the question," she said. "He always changed the subject."

Their first contact had taken place at the building. She had been working on a project with her brother and she approached Ned to talk about purchasing some product that she needed. Ned's first sight of her sent him into a whirling spin!

Impressed with her good looks, the selfish, spoiled kid was determined to win her over at any cost. The fact that she was happily married made no difference. He had no scruples. His wants and needs, like always, consumed him. He stopped at nothing to satisfy his cravings.

She lived in New Hampshire. Apparently the three-hour distance between them was unimportant. He spent many nights stalking her, waiting in front of her house hoping to see her.

In due time, with promises and lavish spending, he won her over. With no regard for breaking up a fine family, his determination got him what he wanted.

Mona was impressionable and easily influenced. The temptation of wealth was too great, and the intimacy between them continued. Her husband, Ben, was distressed. He loved his children; his family meant everything to him. But he lost his struggle to keep from losing them. Mona had made her decision.

Yasha, Mona's mom, a lovely lady who cherished her close family of five, including Ben, said in wonderment, "What will happen to our devoted family?" They lived side by side, supporting each other with love and affection. Yasha promised to do whatever she could to prevent the breakup.
She and Ben kept in close contact with Jane, hoping for some consolation. But it didn't work. Attempts to prove to Mona how foolishly inspired she was by Ned's wealth were lost on deaf ears.

Ben continued corresponding with Jane, looking for answers. In spite of his frequent visits, he could do nothing, Mona filed for divorce.

"Who was this man who came from nowhere to suddenly break up our loving family?" Yasha asked. Lost and without an answer, she gave up as well. Mona had chosen a better life for her and her children.

Ned finally found happiness with someone who gave him the love he desperately needed. Her children were so impressed by the extravagance and by Ned's expressions of love, the loss of their dad had no effect on them. Maggy and Missy, nine and ten years old, developed a loving father relationship with Ned, who bathed them in luxury. Clearly they made a fine foursome; they were very happy together.

I thought Mona was a special person. She was very easy to get along with, full of compassion, and understanding. I never witnessed her ever raising her voice or getting angry.

We hit it off immediately. She treated me like her second mom, she included me in all their fun times together. Sometimes I felt that I did not belong, but she never took no for an answer. She always made me feel special.

We had many discussions. Some were personal, others not so. She questioned me why Ned had been estranged from our family. I held nothing back. I told her exactly like it was. It all came back to haunt me when I relived the heartache describing our downfall.

I mentioned how hard Norata and I worked in our businesses to lift us to a luxurious, wealthy lifestyle. How vulnerable Norata was never able to refuse his son. How he met Ned's every whim and want, without any concern or cost. About Ned's dependence on us to meet his every craving. How he never tried to earn money. How until he decided to marry, money was readily available just for the taking. Then how, after his marriage, he felt an obligation to think hard at what he had to do to become a breadwinner. And how that was the beginning of our destruction.

I got carried away, blurting out my own mental anguish. I told her how, "He tried different paths, business after business, squandering our money for all his failures. Nothing was successful. He earned just enough to satisfy his needs."

"That's when he became desperate to take whatever he could. His demands for survival had to be met, and in the process he created an insatiable hunger for wealth. I don't know if he planned it or it just happened. He had our building at his disposal without any responsibilities, no debts or payments to maintain the building. He just continued to take advantage of our kind, benevolent nature. He never knew responsibility; he was ignorant about right and wrong. Everything came too easy for him. He learned nothing from living a playboy lifestyle off his parents."

"He was possessed with power and he underhandedly took everything he possibly could, without compassion or remorse. He literately cleaned us out, completely. He caused us to lose our properties and he secretly drained our savings until there was nothing more to take. He was totally absorbed by his selfish greed."

I was in an emotional state, spitting out my past and spelling out my heartache. I so wanted to put it all behind me but it all came back as I blurted away my hurt.

Mona listened carefully, making no comment about Ned. "I was inquisitive," she said. "I asked him about his family, but he ignored the question. He never gave me a clue."

After our discussion it all became clear why Ned had suddenly appeared in our lives. He had to play the good son and prove that he too had a binding relationship with his family.

I'm sure that she had much to do with his decision to include us. She had the power to make him do anything. Our discussion ended there. Ned had no notion that she and I had discussed his past.

Mona had created a special family unity of her own, until Ned appeared and displayed his wealth. She had been a stay-at-home mom who had put much effort into teaching her children discipline. She was a very devout Orthodox Greek churchgoer. She had an open relationship with the priest and his family, taking part in all the functions at the church.
Mona took a liking to me almost immediately she asked me to visit often. Although the long ride was tedious I took advantage of her invitations. I liked her too. She made me feel special.

One weekend, while visiting, I attended mass with the family. It was quite different from my Catholic Eucharist celebration, but I did enjoy the service. Mona introduced me to Malia, the priest's wife, a friendly and pleasant person, who began to discuss the preparations of a certain dish to feature at the bazaar planned for the following weekend.

Mona once told her about one of my exceptional Italian dishes made with pasta and cheese. Malia asked me if I would mind giving her my pasta recipe? "I love pasta," she confided. "It's one of my favorites!"

"Of course," I told her. "Mona will have it for you."

She thanked me, smiling as she spoke. I could hear the sincerity in her voice. She had a kind and sympathetic attitude toward everyone. She was a good-natured person. I decided to make the special dish for the occasion along with the recipe. Malia was very grateful.

In spite of the fact that Ned spent some of his boyhood days in a convent and parochial school, he never followed the laws of the church. Mona changed all of that. Although he remained a Catholic, he became devoted and followed her religion. She turned him into believing that Sunday was a special day for attending church services. She taught him well.

Ned was spending most of his time with Mona, trying desperately to impress her. The home she lived in was an old country Victorian very much in need of repair. He kept busy remodeling and reconstructing it.

He came home occasionally, just long enough to catch up with his commitments. It was always done quickly to get back to be with her. Good fortune for Jared that I was there to fill his needs.

Weekends together, sometimes at our house, were always the same. Mona was a gourmet cook and she would prepare a lovely dinner, we would play cards, or take a ride to the mall. Extravagant shopping is what Mona liked best. Ned was rather laid back, sort of a stay-at-home TV watcher. Other than hunting and skiing, he was never interested in sports. Still, he kept the family satisfied. He would do almost anything to please them.

The girls had never been on skis, or even wanted to be. Ned inspired them to try it. Since it had been some time since his skiing days, he was eager to do it again. They spent a day shopping for the proper attire and off they went for a weekend of skiing pleasure. The extravagance of it all impressed the girls. They were experiencing a new life of pleasure.

I made the mistake of introducing Mona to the casino nearby. It was a calling card she found irresistible. Once there, it was hard to get her to leave. That was easily understandable because up to then, she had lived a rather peaceful life with little excitement.

Ned was very much against gambling and he frowned on her interest. He would never deny her, however. He had to keep her happy.

Their town up north was rather dull. The main street was lined with cabins and rentals. The beach activity and people enjoying the ocean were all they could look forward to.

In April, before school closed, Ned and Mona planned some time away. They booked a trip to the Bahamas. I offered to care for the children since Yasha was not well. It was fun for me. I liked playing the role of making breakfast, sending them off to school, and waiting for them to walk in the door.

We repeated that routine many times thereafter. It

was like family fun time for me, and Yasha was readily available when I sent invitations to join us.

Holidays were special for us. Mona delighted in helping prepare special dinners and group gatherings for our family and friends. She was very affectionate. Everyone accepted her lovingly.

I remember our first Christmas together, when Mona's passion for shopping fit right in. She and Ned spent most of their time gift buying for the holiday. Money was no object. Mona had extravagant taste— and she made all the decisions.

After dinner, everyone gathered around the living room waiting for the moment to exchange Christmas gifts. Our family was programmed that every Christmas we exchanged one gift to each other, so nobody was offended if they couldn't afford more. I had no idea what to expect this Christmas.
I felt humbled, in fact totally embarrassed, at the outcome of our gift exchange. Mona excitedly showered me with a profusion of gifts, one after another after another, all of them lavishly expensive. I probably spent at least a full hour opening gifts. It was like Christmas for me only. I had never experienced such attention. Her passion for buying seemed limitless.

I was humiliated and shamed because I had given just one gift each to her and her children. She evidently didn't realize the position she put me in. My funds were limited. I couldn't afford to splurge.

Ned was probably oblivious, or at least he never thought to warn me, about what was about to take place. Unfortunately, the girls were very disappointed. They sulked at the letdown of me having given them one gift each. That embarrassment stayed with me long after, it hadn't bothered Mona, her generosity didn't end there. Her shopping passion continued. Money was no object. Ned did everything to keep her happy.

Incarceration

I was beginning to feel comfortable with my life when fate took a sudden turn. It was Friday night about 12:30 when I exited the highway and came upon a roadblock, with fire engines, ambulances, and police everywhere. It felt too close to home. I felt a fleeting premonition: could Becca somehow be involved? Could it be related to her usual Friday night out with Jan? I tried to erase the thought. Where had that come from?

I got out of my car and tried to get past the neon-yellow caution tape that the police were guarding. I was turned back but my suspicion kept me from leaving. I continued to make my way through the caution tape, asking questions. I began to panic when the officer described the car involved as a Jeep Cherokee with Becca's plate number. I begged him, please let me in, my daughter may be hurt.

He walked away, assuring me that Becca was not hurt. But the small Kia involved was heavily damaged. Both occupants inside were injured. They were trapped and waiting for the "jaws of life" to release them. I waited nervously until the ambulance left the scene.

Becca was intoxicated. Her alcohol level was above the limit and she was cited for DUI. She remembered drinking two glasses of wine at the club, not enough to lose her mental control. The fact that she wasn't hurt and remembered nothing about the accident or driving home made us suspect that someone had spiked her drink. She was found unhurt and sitting by the curb with no shoes on. She was completely disoriented.

The two people in the small car were hospitalized, and luckily, survived. I followed the ambulance as Becca was taken to the hospital. She felt compassion for the two people hurt and prayed they would forgive her.

Bert Murrey was said to be one of the best DUI attorneys in the state. His first words regarding the case were, "My fee of $45,000 will cover this, whether or not we go to trial." He assured Becca that the judge would impose a sentence no harsher than home confinement or six month's jail time. Becca relied on his promise of six months.

Every day was a problem. With her license suspended, she had to rely on her friends to drive her to and from work. Fortunately, she worked within walking distance from her home.

Becca worked for two doctors as a coordinator. After two years of constant court appearances and postponements, the state prosecutor became agitated and demanded closure. Becca felt frustrated with losing her license and having to rely on others to drive her around. She felt that she was a burden to everyone. "I'm tired," she said, "I want to put this behind me. I'll accept the six month's incarceration rather than fight my case in court."

Bert was confident she would get home confinement. But her final appearance before the judge was a shocking disappointment. He imposed a sentence of five years to serve, plus ten years' probation.

Becca was in tears and panicky. Her confidence in Bert was destroyed. "Why was I deceived by his false promises? Why did it cost me a mortgage on my house for his fee, putting me in this position? What has he done for me?" she cried.

The thought of my daughter—a good mother to her children, kind and considerate, never hurtful—being led away in handcuffs was embarrassing and sickening. Bert seemed somewhat surprised at the sentencing too. Feeling compassion, he promised to make good on his promise of getting her out in six months.

Becca had no concept of prison life. We waited patiently for her first phone call. At seven o'clock that evening the long awaited call finally came. My heart was pounding. Becca was crying hysterically, in dread, begging, "Please, Mom, get me out of here.

Sell my house, do whatever you have to do, but please get me out." I cried for her but there was nothing I could do.

I called Bert early the next morning and every day thereafter, leaving messages. He either refused to answer my calls or he had given up all efforts. I lost confidence in him too, thinking he was doing nothing to help the situation. Still, in spite of my feelings, he was our only salvation.

My last message to him was a reminder that for $45,000 we deserved at least some courtesy on his part.

One week of torment was all Becca suffered. I realized then that we had underestimated Bert. We simply hadn't given him a chance to use his own means to keep his promise and exert his influence.

Becca was released from strict incarceration. She was fortunate to be housed privately in an apartment-like facility, on work release, which meant she could keep her job, wear her own clothes, live comfortably with all the amenities of home, including a washer, dryer, refrigerator, and her own bedroom. She was very lucky be able to live in comfort.

Her job as a medical coordinator was still open to her. She was quite reliable and extremely devoted. Becca was well liked by the patients and both doctors. Doctors Maxim and Bortle were loyal and caring all through her work release. Their compassion helped her get through her daily confinement routine.

Every day, taking time out of his busy schedule, Dr. Maxim would faithfully pick her up from the facility, and at the end of the workday, bring her back. If at any time he had a conflict, he would make other arrangements with Kate, the nurse. How very special he was.

One third of Becca's pay was forfeited to the prison for her fine. She was not allowed to carry any money except for bus fare to and from the DUI sessions, plus fifty dollars for grocery shopping, which was scheduled on Sunday. Whatever money remained was deposited in the prison commissary account for necessities she may need. I was surprised at how frugal Becca became, cutting out food coupons from the newspaper and magazines to save what money she could. She found out that fifty dollars did not go very far.

We were allowed evening visits. We could bring food and enjoy suppertime together as a family.

We suddenly realized we had a decision to make. Ned suggested we close up Becca's house for the winter and have the children move in with us to cut expenses. It was a wise decision, but it wasn't going to be easy on me living two miles away from their home, traveling to school, baseball practice, school functions, and various appointments. A grind on my aging eighty-year-old body.

Tayla, fifteen, was not happy with the arrangement.

She preferred to live in her own home. Her friends were pulling away. We tried every effort to please her and keep up with her commitments. I tried to explain how difficult it was for all of us. My lectures always closed with the famous cliché, "All things come to an end." It seemed to ease the emotional stress we were all experiencing.

On February 12, Maddy's twelfth birthday, I made plans to have a special surprise party. The word got out and Maddy wasn't happy about the plan. She said "Nan, please, no party. I don't want to have to answer to my friends when they ask 'where is your mother?'" My heart ached because I was saddened by that remark.

I simply said, "It was just an unfortunate accident, your mom is sad and very remorseful. She is hurting and we have to forgive her." Maddy just listened as I tried to get through to her, but instead, I made a reservation at Bugaboo Creek Restaurant where the staff puts on a brief display and sings "Happy Birthday."

Maddy is an exceptional child, modest, very proud, and easily embarrassed. I noticed a slight resentment for her mother whenever we visited. She found it hard to put her arms around her and she was unable to say "I love you" as she had always done in the past. I reminded her often that her mom had made a terrible mistake, one that could happen to anyone.

Six months passed and it was time for Becca to

appear before the parole board. Bert had one of his lawyers attend the hearing. It probably made no difference. She was denied parole the first time up. They felt she had not been punished enough for her crime.

Becca was very disappointed and it was a hard blow to the family. We had to look forward to yet another hearing in six months. Becca remained remorseful for the two people she had hurt, sending letters of apology. Fortunately, they accepted the insurance settlement and did not sue. We continued to make our daily visits while we all waited for another parole hearing.

Ten months passed. It was just before the Christmas holiday that the hearing was due. Once more the children sent letters begging for their mother's release. I called Bert daily trying desperately to talk to him. I was determined to get him to promise to appear before the board this time. As usual, he never answered my calls. I was beginning to lose faith again, but I was persistent.

The next Monday, I drove to his office at nine a.m., knowing he arrived by ten. I made my presence known to the staff, and I demanded to speak to him. I sat in the waiting room for hours. The office associates occasionally made offers of water and mentioned that Bert would be in court all day. I made it clear that there was no way I would leave without seeing him.

Howard, one of the attorneys, came out and tried to

convince me that Bert would attend the hearing. He said, "Go home and rest. I will personally talk to him, I promise. He will call you."

I specified how important it was for him to be there to advocate for my daughter. With that, he handed me a citation, from the office of George Fox, Speaker of the House, praising me and congratulating me on my eighty years of good health.

But my mind was focused on my daughter's freedom. Nothing else would replace my bitterness. I wasn't impressed with the citation. As a matter of fact, I refused to accept it. I was suffering for Becca. "Just send my daughter home," I said. "I don't need any praise at this time."

I wanted closure and Becca needed to be home with her children. Not only that, my responsibilities were strenuous and it was wearing me down at my old age. My mind was full of disturbing thoughts: What if she was denied parole again? What would happen to the girls if my old body should fail? What if I pass away, who would care for them? These thoughts continued to haunt me during my sleepless nights before the meeting with the board.

The following morning, I again made a call to the office and talked to Donna, his secretary. She felt the concern in my voice. "Please don't worry," she said, "everything will be all right. I promise you, Bert will be at the hearing." She seemed sincere. That gave me the encouragement I needed.

I was gratified when Bert did make his appearance. I felt a huge sigh of relief. Waiting for the board's decision seemed like an eternity. The mental strain and eleven months of anguish finally came to an end when we heard their favorable decision. She would be released from confinement on December 12!

What a moment of joy! I felt my world open up before me. What a beautiful sight it was for our family to see Becca walk out of the facility a free woman, just in time to celebrate the Christmas holiday with us.

As was customary upon release, Becca was obliged to wear an ankle bracelet and be in home confinement for the following two weeks. No problem. Finally, her family was happily reunited and living comfortably together in their own home. I sent a letter of apology to Bert's office for being a nuisance. They understood my concern.

I hadn't thought too much about my age until I got a special surprise. As I lay on the couch visiting with Becca, Tayla covered my eyes with a bandana. I asked her, "What are you doing?"

She answered, "I have a special surprise for you, Nan. I'm going to take you for a short ride. You have to trust me."

"Tay, I don't like surprises. Stop this foolishness."

She insisted, "Please, Nan, trust me," assuring me it was in my best interest.

I knew her intentions had to be good so I went along with her charade mostly to make her happy. My grandchildren are my life. I would do anything to please them.

She walked me out to the car blindfolded. I had no idea what game she was playing. The short drive kept me in suspense. In my mind I thought she was taking me to church to thank God for answering my prayers. Pleasurable thoughts entered my mind.

At our destination, she helped me out of the car and guided me up some stairs.

When we got to the top, she removed the bandana as I walked into a screaming crowd, "HAPPY BIRTHDAY!" I was standing in front of my entire family, aunts, uncles, cousins, and friends. I was lost for words, completely surprised. I knew then that Mona planned the event because she took delight in planning successful parties.

A bountiful supply of food, steaks, and appetizers—all elaborately prepared—were served with a selection of wines and goodies. Mona knew how to make a party. She spared no horses, money was no object. Ned's greed didn't work with her. I wondered how she could have planned the surprise without me knowing. I hadn't an ounce of suspicion why Becca had insisted that I spend the day with her. It was truly one of the special moments in my life.
As we partied, I noticed one of Ned's friends paying special attention. He followed Mona's every move

and tried to make conversation with her. She seemed fascinated, made small talk, as she still tried to avoid him. It was plain to see with her perfect body and pleasing personality why men would be attracted to her. Everywhere in public she drew attention. Ned was well aware of the looks she got from men, and he tried his best to keep her to himself.

Mona was a caring friend to her next door neighbor, a fragile old lady who was tired and ready to give up her home. The house was a large Victorian with beautiful surroundings. The asking price was so low that Ned quickly jumped at the opportunity, thinking that its resale would give him a fine profit. His offer was accepted.

Being watched by Jane's lawyers, Ned had to continually prove he was financially wiped out. Nonetheless, he refused to pass up any profitable deal. My son hadn't changed. I was being primed again to be used for his needs. That was surely part of why Ned had reappeared in our lives, to keep me readily available for just this, plus of course to care for Jared while he stalked Mona.

Ned never asked, like usual, he demanded. He said, "You know I can't show any assets, Mom, you will have to sign for the mortgage." Back again with his trickery and, here again, I'm being used.

My second thought was, I am living comfortably in his house, I own nothing, I have nothing more to lose, I have no choice.

Nevertheless, his plan for profit went kaput. Ned's thoughts of making a bundle from the sale soon fizzed out. Mona had other plans that were all to her benefit.

While at dinner, I was again approached. Ned seemed hesitant. I assumed he realized he was about to use me again. Without even questioning, he said, "Mom, I'm going to open an account in your name to pay the bills here at the house." I was innocently shocked. I felt privileged that he considered me to handle his money, but that wishful thinking did not last long. I realized there had to be a motive behind this decision, there was always a method to his madness. He needed me to be his go between, to hide behind his scheme to show his insolvency to Jane's lawyers. He needed a cover up, I was the scapegoat, and I was conveniently ready.

He made sure the deposits were just enough to cover his expenses. I didn't get any free ride living in his home. I supplied the food. My son had never shown any generosity and I expected none.

Each month I was obliged to make out a more-than-deserved check of $4,000. to Jane for alimony, checks for the mortgages, a generous weekly check of $500. for Mona, and another for the current household bills. Never a small offer of devotion for me. All money spent was accounted for, he made sure of that. I followed the rules. I was never one to take advantage. In exchange, I was living a contented life.

The hostile fight with Jane didn't end there. She was aware of Ned and Mona's love affair. She continued her fight. She was certain that Ned had a hidden stash and she wanted it all. The $1.7 million was not enough, since most of that money went for her lawyers' fees. She was not giving up. Ned somehow needed to prove he had no more money to give. That was his escape, how he evaded her surveillance.

He was running ragged. It was difficult for him to concentrate on the business he was trying to promote and appear in court every day. Yet in spite of his troubles, he always walked in the door with a smile.

The months passed, I stayed prepared. I was available for his necessities, again, Ned took advantage of my kindness, using me for his escape.

Saturday morning, he and Jared were discussing the new Cadillac that Jared had chosen for his sixteenth birthday. With that, Ned said, "Mom, come take a ride with us. I want you to see the car Jared is interested in."

The car was a beautiful brand new black Cadillac. Jared was so happy to have a new car.

I was excited to be a part of my grandson's life. I went along, unaware that I was needed.

After the discussions and the transactions were

completed, the salesman presented the contract to be signed. I was stunned when Ned handed me the pen and said, "Mom, sign here."

I was trapped. What could I say? My son had again taken me for granted. I thought for a second and convinced myself that at least the car is in my name, even though it was mortgaged. That gave me closure.

Ned didn't stop there: he did the same thing again and again, to purchase a car for Lianne and a truck for himself. Still, I wasn't too concerned since technically I owned them, mortgage and all.

Because I lived in his house I felt vulnerable and trapped. He realized that I was caught, and could be used for his business concerns or whenever it was necessary. In return, I was obligated because I was living comfortably in his house, enjoying the lifestyle I once had and longed for.

He now had complete control of my identity: all my credit cards, phones, car insurances, mortgages, etc. He also knew I had some stocks, a bond, and a small sum from the sale of my home. It was all registered in my name but there was no reward for me. In exchange, he made sure all the bills were faithfully paid.

What I had wasn't enough to carry Norata and me for the rest of our lives. The fact that we were in business with lots of stock, we didn't think we needed insurance or to pay into social security for retirement. A dumb mistake we regretted.

Mona had thoughts about the new home that Ned had purchased. She admired her neighbor's Victorian home for many years. She was thinking of the potential of turning that new home into a bed and breakfast. She remembered how much she had enjoyed managing the family restaurant that unfortunately had been closed for lack of funds. However, she remembered operating it successfully. She had catered to some Hollywood celebrities; she hung pictures of them throughout her home.

The excitement of purchasing the Victorian home was just what she wanted. Since it was convenient being next door and a great opportunity, she thought it was suitable for a new business. Even better, it was the beginning of summer, a perfect time to fulfill her bed and breakfast dream.

Ned encouraged her to continue with her plans, suggesting that she place ads online as well. She knew it was a seasonal venture but it was what she wanted to do. They furnished the home with lovely furniture. It was well decorated, with small round tables set up in the large living room area, covered with white linen tablecloths and lovely stemware. It was picture-perfect.

She was up by five a.m. to prepare the morning breakfast for her guests.

It was working out just as she expected, except that the season was short and the summer months were coming to an end, she was not going to give up yet, she continued advertising until the reservations gradually diminished.

She left the home as it was, fully furnished, ready for operating next season. Ned turned the house over to her in her name.

The three-hour travel time back and forth was too hectic. Ned tried desperately to get Mona to come live with us. But it was out of the question for her. Mona refused to live in the same house that Jane had to vacate. However, she did spend many days and weekends with us. I never heard her complain or comment about the travel time. The distance wasn't a problem for her.

Two years past, my dear sister Sue began to suffer stomach pains. She was always afraid of doctors and hadn't been to one for many years. She thought that being seen by a doctor was out of the question. Food was never enticing to her. She ate to live, nibbling on a sandwich as if it were an obligation.

While driving one afternoon to a bingo session, she began coughing and was soon ready to vomit. I stopped the car, opened the door, and held her head as she began spitting up what looked like a stream of chocolate. We returned home and I said, "Sue, after all these years it is time for a checkup." That put some fright in her because she made no denial.

Susan, her caring daughter, immediately made arrangements with Judy, a dear friend and a registered nurse at the hospital.

After many tests, blood work, x-rays, and scans, the prognosis was stomach cancer. The surgery did nothing but shorten her life, from maybe a year to two months. Each day we could see the cancer progress. She began losing interest in everyday activities. She made no effort to help herself. I tried to comfort her, planning things to keep her busy, but tragically, she just gave up. Her loving and devoted children watched over her. She passed away with her son James's arm around her.

It was a deep loss to me. I couldn't get through a day without shedding tears. She was my confidant, my teacher, my friend, always correcting me to do what's right. I respected her guidance, despite our occasional disagreements. I deeply miss the relationship we had. We trusted each other with our deepest secrets. Since her passing, Susan and the boys have been especially kind, relating to me as their substitute mom. They include me in all their functions and social affairs. Many times I have refused their invitations because of the feeling that I didn't belong among the young people. I reminded them that I feel like a weed among the flowers. They refused to take no for an answer. They showed an abundance of love and attachment.

On one occasion James invited me and his siblings to dinner at the Ocean Cliff Restaurant. I can't find the words to express how special he made me feel. "Auntie, you sit next to me and choose whatever you like on the menu,"

I said, "Jim you make me feel so special."

His reply struck my heart, "Auntie, you *are* special. You are all we have left." I cried silent tears.

Pat's Life

My sisters were gone, Pat, my brother, was the last of my siblings. He was my idol. All through my life he watched over me, always reminding me to rely on him if I was ever in need. Pat was extremely generous but I never took advantage of his generosity.

I was indebted to him because he taught me all there was to know about the jewelry business. He, his wife Nikie, and their son Andie, worked together building a successful business. However, he made a crucial mistake.

Flora was his employee. She was illiterate and had a reputation for shoplifting. She lived on welfare in government housing. In Pat she saw the potential of wealth. She did her best to lure him into a sexual relationship.

She was destitute, having nothing but the clothes on her body, she was determined to take him away from his family. His wife, Nikie, saw the attraction but could do nothing to stop it. Soon Flora and Pat were together all the time.

Nikie filed for divorce, but she couldn't bring herself to sign the divorce decree. She still loved Pat dearly and hoped he might come to his senses and realize that Flora wanted his money.

Pat left the business to Nikie and Andie and moved into a small apartment. I was concerned about the stupidity of his decision. I asked him, "Why would you leave your family for this gold digger?"

His answer hurt my heart. "She pleases me sexually and does to me what my wife would never do." I was stunned. I realized that sex was more important to him than his family. Then he said, "Don't worry, Mae, I will keep her but I will never marry her."

The relationship between them continued with no respect for her. Their arguments always ended with him thrashing her out. She was usually stranded, and would call me to drive her home. She took daily abuse from him, but she always returned for more.

My holidays were always special with my brother, I always included Flora in our celebrations for my brother's sake.

One Sunday we were sitting together and he handed me a stack of EE bonds, $30,000 worth, made out in my name and his. I was shocked. I asked him, "Why are you giving them to me?"

He answered, "Because I want you to have them." I knew my brother loved me, but that much? Imagine my surprise.

Then he said, "I need you to drive me to the hospital for my appointment tomorrow."

I asked, "Why? What's wrong?"

He said, "Flora is oversexed, I can't keep up with her

desires so she asked me to have a penal implant."

I was speechless. I couldn't imagine him wanting to go through that sacrifice for a woman he didn't love. Why would he make such a stupid decision to mutilate his body? Was he not thinking of the circumstances? I wasn't about to chastise him because he had already made the decision.

The surgery was difficult. The pain was excruciating. I could see the tears falling. He was suffering, swearing, and cursing at her for making him do this. Listening to him cursing I thought, why did he think it would be a simple procedure? Was he so naïve? Did he think there wouldn't be a problem?

Pat had a temper and could be violent at times, so Flora was careful and kept her distance until Pat got over the pain and suffering.

As time passed, Pat's health began to fail. He suffered two strokes in his past, his glaucoma was growing worse, and he was forgetting simple things like taking his medications. He missed appointments, and was afraid of getting Alzheimer's.

I had the responsibility of taking him to all his medical appointments in Boston and at the VA. Flora had no experience driving, but she soon learned. When his evaluations were done, Pat was diagnosed with dementia, PTSD, and depression.

Flora saw an open opportunity and suggested if Pat would buy a house, she would move in and take care of him. Although Pat stated he would never marry her, he did need her at this time in his life. I convinced him to take the offer. He had been with Flora so long there was no indication that he was ever going back with his family.

Pat purchased a lovely three-bedroom home in Pawtucket in his name only. Flora wasted no time either. She chose very fine furnishings and made many changes to her liking. Pat begged me to come live with them. I told him how much I loved him but how impossible that would be. I was living a sumptuous life now, happy and contented.

The doctors advised that he not drive. Flora took more driving lessons and convinced Pat that she needed a new car. She chose the best, a Nissan right from the showroom. Since Pat was incompetent, she filled out the paperwork, putting her name on the bill of sale. I was aware of her manipulations but it wasn't my life. He was obligated to her and he still had his senses and awareness.

I made daily visits, mostly bringing food—usually Pat's favorite steaks from the nearby restaurant. Flora was extremely lazy. Since she had lived alone, she had no cooking experience. She didn't even try. She looked forward to my visits to make a pot of coffee. I tried to teach her how to cook. She had no interest. All their food was take-out.

Pat discussed his will with me, asking me to be the executor. I simply refused. I felt I would be betraying his family. He then said he would have his attorney do it. He felt an obligation since our dad passed away and left Pat, his only son, the six-apartment complex plus all his stocks and bonds. Pat felt it was unfair for Dad to eliminate us girls from his will. He felt guilty about the inheritance. (We all knew that Italian men favored their sons, especially if they carried the same name.)

Flora accompanied him. I'm sure she had some influence in the will's preparation. I did not know how it was stated at that time. Pat kept no secrets from me and I could have found out just by asking, but I was not interested. I knew my brother.

The arguments were constant. Pat was frustrated; he couldn't tolerate her. He noticed her taking his money. He told her to get out. He spent two months trying to do without her, but it was impossible. He was depressed, feeling alone, and with his health failing progressively. He needed constant care.

Dave, Pat's longtime and devoted friend, kept him company and cared for him almost daily. My commitments and trying to care for both Pat and Norata were impossible. It simply took too much time.

On May 3, unable to live on his own, Pat checked in at the VA. He was immediately hospitalized with suicidal ideation and admitted to the mental ward. A neuropsychological evaluation was ordered. Every visit I made was sad. It hurt so much to see my brother in that state of panic. He begged me, "Get me out! Call a lawyer. Do whatever you have to do but get me out!" Before I could make inquires he was discharged.

Even though Flora was living with her sister at that time and complained about Pat's disrespect for her, she moved back in.

His Alzheimer's was progressing rapidly. Because his legs were weakening, a wheelchair was ordered. In his younger days, Pat was a gambler and he owned and raced horses. So gambling became their only pleasure. Flora was addicted and soon learned her way to the gambling casino in the next town. She relied on me to care for Pat while she gambled. Now she had complete control.

Andie tried desperately to reach his dad but Flora refused to let that happen. She would hang up on him and change the phone number. Pat would ask "Who was that?" She would answer, "Wrong number."

I found it cruel and asked her why she would not let him see his dad. Her answer was "He will never set foot in this house."

Pat was unaware of the phone calls and would ask, "Why doesn't Andie come to see me?" I wanted so desperately to tell him what she was doing but I feared what she would do if he knew. She had become a demanding controller. I knew how mean and malicious she could be.

Andie was on probation for a drug charge. He and his

dad had been very close working together in their business. Pat once asked, "Do I have a family?" He would have been so happy to see his son. I wished I could have explained Flora's cruelty but Pat was losing his memory and discussions were impossible.

Flora was heartless and took advantage of that charge sending Andie a restraining order of lies stating he tried to kill her.

Since the Alzheimer's had taken control of his life, I had no influence. My interference would accomplish nothing. Being deceptive, she would resent me, and talking to Pat was useless. He forgot easily and couldn't comprehend what was said. Pat reminded me often, "Don't trust her, she can't be trusted." Sometimes she resented him saying that in her presence. He was so right.

In July 2002, being incompetent and with his Alzheimer's worsening, Flora took advantage of Pat's affliction and acted fast. She persuaded Pat to marry her. She asked if I would witness. I had no choice and agreed. He wasn't capable of making decisions. She wanted full control of his wealth.

Since his divorce was never finalized, Flora paid the judge $500 to sign the divorce decree from Nikie. I could have easily prevented this from happening but I would find myself in a bad predicament. What could I do? Pat was obligated and needed her to care for him. He wasn't capable of making decisions; dementia controlled his mind. Her determination was genuine. She would surely find a way.

She became a Mrs. She found financial freedom and she wanted to take a trip to Las Vegas. I noticed the three bank statements were addressed in her name only. It didn't take her long to control his assets. She asked if I would be willing to take the trip with them, all expenses paid, since Pat would only be comfortable with me. I tried to make her understand that it was a bad choice. Pat had a fear of flying and sometimes got violent and out of control. But she was determined and looking forward to her first flight. She insisted that it would be Okay. I accepted, with much regret.

Pat was uncontrollable on the plane. He was fidgety and refused to be buckled in. He tried to get up from his seat, yelling. I struggled to calm him down. I kept asking myself, why did I let myself be put in this position?

Caring for Pat while she gambled was frustrating. I had the responsibility of cleaning him whenever he had an accident. I was embarrassed at having to clean his private parts. The three-day ordeal was a nightmare.

Dave was visiting often. He was more than a friend. Pat had depended on him for guidance in everything he did before he was afflicted. Flora the schemer asked him to live with them to help care for Pat, especially while she gambled. Dave accepted since he had no commitments, although he was frustrated seeing her spend thousands of dollars gambling.

Pat sometimes came to his senses. Dave said Pat was disgusted with her. He was cursing and accusing her of sleeping with men and spending his money. Yet at this time, having control, Flora was immune to his accusations and remarks.

Dave said that Pat had confessed that he was tricked into the marriage and he wanted out. He asked Dave to drive to his lawyer's office to sign for the divorce. But by the time they got to the office, Pat had forgotten what he was there for and they returned.

Besides Pat's fortune, the fiduciary pension awarded to him (with Dave's help) was estimated at $170,000. No longer needing Dave, she insisted he move out. Obsessed with this windfall she inherited, she didn't know how to handle this much wealth. She showed her inexperience to me when she said, "I never made out a check in my life. I do not know how. I guess I will have my brother show me what to do." She had very little contact with her family. (Pat had refused to recognize them throughout their courtship years, but since his affliction they were slowly being accepted.)

Too much money to an illiterate is wasteful and lavishly spent. One-hundred-dollar bills were passed out like candy to her family when they visited (which was almost daily). She was seen cashing checks at the casino with her sisters standing by waiting for the take.

One morning she called me, her first words were, "Mae, did you know that Pat left you $25,000?" I didn't answer. She could not tell the difference between 25,000 and 25%, which was stated in his will. I ignored the question. I refused to discuss my brother's will with her.

Having full control, she began treating Pat rudely. He wore baggy sweatpants every day. While visiting with him, Pat tried to get up from the couch. She grabbed him by the seat of his pants and literally threw him back on the couch. "Now I can do that," she said, "and he can't hit me back." I was sickened by her cruelty, but I stood mute.

Although Flora and I had a sister relationship though the years, since her family came back into her life she no longer treated me with respect. She was beginning to resent my visits, being rude and sarcastic. Apparently I did not fit in her devious plan. On one visit Pat said, "She is making me sign papers, I don't know what I'm signing." I suspected an underhanded plot. How could I tell him she was scheming and manipulating all his assets at her discretion? She probably had him sign everything over in her name. He was not capable of signing his name. What could I say to him? Discussing any situation with him was hopeless because he would forget from one minute to the next. She would deny any wrongdoing and I would be accused of instigating. I couldn't let that happen. Without me, my brother would have no one to visit or oversee the treatment he was subjected to. She needed to make it comfortable for herself.

For her convenience she had a hospital bed delivered

from the VA and had him confined to bed 24/7. It made me sick to see him restricted. He was still physically healthy. I heard him say, "I don't want to go to bed."

Without compassion, she crudely said, "You have to go to bed."

Pat's diet was pancakes and bananas twice a day every day. She paid her brother forty dollars daily to bring two orders from McDonalds. I was concerned and I told her that Pat wasn't getting enough nourishment, that he needed more food. Her answer was, "That's all he will eat. The VA said that he is healthy and his heart is good."

Flora forbid me from bringing any food or drink. She told me, "He will get sick."

On one occasion Aunt Maimie came with me to visit Pat. When she offered him a cookie, Flora angrily said, "Don't give him that!" I asked her why can't he have a cookie, and she replied, "Because he will mess and I will have to clean him." We concluded that she was not feeding him for fear of having to clean up later. During the six months that he was confined I never noticed any food or drink anywhere near his bed or in the kitchen.

Maria, a young girl in her twenties, was hired to care for Pat from early morning until two thirty in the afternoon while Flora, now a habitual gambler, spent time at the casino with her sisters.

One morning I defied her orders and brought Pat's favorites, coffee and doughnuts. I asked Maria what he had eaten for breakfast. She said "Oh, I don't know, I only give him juice."

I stayed with Pat purposely until Flora came home at two thirty. She brought no food. Obviously Pat had had no lunch and possibly no breakfast either. She was furious at finding me there asking questions. Her resentment toward me was escalating. She was consumed with guilt. She asked, "Why are you asking questions?"

This extremely wicked woman was exactly as my brother had portrayed her. She turned from one extreme to the other. I had been her only loyal friend. I could have hurt her many times when she manipulated my brother and his money but I had closed my eyes. Now I had become her enemy.

On one particular visit, with money on her mind, she stupidly said, "You know that's our money now." I simply ignored that stupid, uncalled for remark. It was obvious that she had been told that Pat's wealth was hers as well.

Cousin Anne received a call from her to specifically tell her that no one is getting any of Pat's money when he dies. She said, "If I go before him everything is going to my brother." How cruel of her to even think that way about my brother's death.

She was evidently preparing me since twenty-five percent of Pat's estate (according to his will) was supposedly awarded to me. But obviously she and her attorney conspired to eliminate me from the will since it stated that there were no assets left after Pat passed on.

Pat earlier had an opulent fortune: savings in three banks, $7,000 a month from social security, a veteran's pension of $170,000, a home mortgage-free, a collection of diamonds, and much more. He also had those bonds worth $30,000 that he intended for me, which she probably cashed in.

Becca was disturbed at the abuse her uncle was suffering. I was not aware that she had made a complaint to the Elderly Affairs Office.

Assuming that I had made the complaint, I received a disturbing call from them chastising me and saying that I needed some lessons about Alzheimer's. I was offended that they were so disinterested. I personally went to the Elderly Affairs Office and spoke to the two women in charge.

I was under the impression that Elderly Affairs was a protector for the elderly so I mentioned the neglect, the two meals a day of pancakes and bananas, the lack of nourishment, her not letting me bring food, and Pat's constant confinement to bed. But they showed no concern; they said nothing to satisfy my complaint. They were ignorant of what was happening, as was obvious on their daily progress reports. Flora had poisoned their minds against me with false accusations.

I personally made a complaint to the Veterans Affairs

nurse, explaining the cruelty my brother was suffering. There too, it was ignored.

I was in hot water. Flora had been told of my complaints. She put me on a cross and began tormenting me. The next two visits were hell. She harassed me and called me an SOB. "What are you doing here? You don't belong here!" she shouted. I completely ignored her. Not gaining any satisfaction from me, she furiously said, "In the future you call before you come."

I thought, how could she be so mean and evil? I was her only friend for many years. My innocent mind didn't fathom what she was planning. Pat's money turned her into a despicable monster.

On my next visit Maria refused to let me in. She said "Flora gave me orders not to let you in." I called the police and explained that I wanted to see my brother, but because Flora was not home, I was not allowed in.

I explained her cruelty and the officer said, "I will check on your brother."

With that, as I was about to leave, Flora pulled up, jumped out of her car like a maniac, and yelled, "Didn't I tell you to call before you come?"

I said, nicely that, "I had tried to call but you have no phone."

She said, "I do have a phone."

"What's the number?" I asked.

She answered, "I'm not telling you." Officer Duffin looked at her stupidity with a grin, then asked if she would allow me in. "Not without me," she said. Pat was asleep; he was always asleep. I'm certain she kept him drugged for her satisfaction.
I tried a second time and again I was refused. The next week I took a chance that this monster would have a change of heart. As I pulled up she was at the window. Her face in the window had the look of a beast. Instead of shooing me away, she called the police, I was asked to wait while the officer went in. A few minutes later he came out and handed me a paper. I asked, "What is this?"

"A restraining order," he said. I had never seen a restraining order so I asked him to explain. "She claims you tried to kill and poison her on April 3," he replied.

Oh my God, how far will this evil creature go to stop me from seeing my brother? She stated that she cannot sleep at night for fear of my threats to kill her. She also said that I had threatened Maria!

I cannot fathom these vicious lies. I have a reputation of walking on water. I consider myself an intelligent woman with very high standards, so these accusations were very damaging. With her reputation she would never understand honesty. She had gone to the extreme with her fabricated lies to be rid of the only three people in my brother's life:

Andie, Dave, and me. Now she feels free to do away with Pat in her own way.

Her lie on April 3 backfired. Susan, our niece, had the day off from work at the Marriott Hotel that Monday and asked to see her uncle. We met at the Ground Round. Pat was so happy to see her he said "You made my day." Sometimes Pat would talk sensibly. Susan was sick to see the condition Pat was in, unshaven, the cluster of hair protruding from his nose, his eyebrows overgrown, and his teeth coated with food. It made her shudder. She said, "Auntie, go get me a scissor. I need to cut the hair in his nose."

Obviously, Flora had picked the third of April at random.

I refused to let her keep me from seeing my brother. She wasn't going to get rid of me that easily. Through counsel, I was allowed to make my visits every Thursday from five to six p.m. The judgment specified that the defendant is restrained from contacting, assaulting, molesting, or otherwise interfering with the plaintiff at home or otherwise. She also specified that I was not to discuss finances with Pat. (No doubt because her thievery would be disclosed.)

At every visit I made thereafter, she complained. I was either too early or too late. She was trying desperately to find me in violation of the injunction. Clearly, Flora was full of rage for my defying her court order. She could not control her bitterness, bursting out at me, swearing, "You are a SOB." I ignored her. I refused to play her hand.

On September 28, Flora was giving him valium. At one point I assumed she had overdosed him. She thought Pat had expired and called 911. The hospital report stated, on arrival, "Acute worsening of mental status, according to his wife, abdomen flat distended. Wife states she fed him pancakes and bananas for breakfast and dinner."

On September 29, "Patient continued to improve clinically, patient is discharged in FAIR condition."

I visited with him after his discharge. Unbelievably, Pat was sitting up in bed, singing with me, and joking like he never had an affliction. I was so happy to see him in normal condition. Flora stood by with an evil look of hatred. (She never allowed me to be alone with my brother.)

A few days later, I received a cordial, pleasant call from her. She was so very nice, like there was no animosity between us. She invited me to her home the following morning, to a presentation. I wondered what possessed her to be nice to me unless she had a plan.

Senator Kennedy with his staff was there to honor Pat with distinguished medals for his service in Iwo Jima. The two women from Elderly Affairs whom I had had words with also were present. My complaint to them had meant nothing. For at least five minutes, the senator bent over Pat praising and honoring him about the hero that he was. Pat didn't hear a word. He never even blinked an eye; it was obvious he was overly drugged. I could only determine that Flora was in fear that Pat might expose her wrongdoings, so she had kept him drugged. Crafty. She had to prove to the staff that she was a person of honor. She looked at me in a very friendly manner, camera in her hand, and said, "Mae stand next to Pat. I want to take a picture of you with him." I wondered how she could easily mask her hypocrisy and pretend to be nice.

I felt frustrated at her deceit, watching her being exceptionally pleasant. I couldn't stay another minute. I thanked Senator Kennedy and immediately left. The very next day I wrote my story of abuse and sent it to the senator, exposing Flora and explaining the drugged state Pat was in, asking if he had noticed? I got no response. I tried my best to expose her wrong doing but no one listened.

On October 11, two weeks after his discharge from the hospital and two weeks before he died, at my last visit with Pat I could see the neglect. He was incoherent, covered with blankets, a pillow on each side of his head, wearing a sweatshirt, and clammy like Vaseline from perspiration when I kissed him. The room was overheated. Pat was suffering. When I took his hand and looked at his fingers, Flora yelled, "What are you looking at?" I was not happy at what I was witnessing.

Obviously, Pat was in a narcosis condition. I had to pull the words out of his mouth. I asked him to please talk to me. I asked Pat, "Did you eat?"

He answered a faint no. Flora nodded her head yes.

I asked, "Are you hungry?"

He answered, "Yes" and then he said, "My crotch."

"What's wrong with your crotch?"

"It hurts."

With that, Flora said, "Oh, his crotch is red."

I fumed, "Take these blankets off him and let the air get at it. It's eighty degrees in here. Can't you see he's suffering?"

I began taking the blankets off when she stopped me and pulled them from my hands. This heartless creature said, without compassion, "No, then he will be cold." She made no effort to comfort him. I asked him again if he had eaten. When he said no again, this time Flora didn't answer. This heartless creature passed it on as if it meant nothing. How could she deprive him of food? It was easy to feed him McDonalds pancakes and bananas twice a day. Her lazy ass had no conscience. I was furious. I had to be careful since I was ordered by the court to visit without any confrontation. She waited to get rid of me. I didn't want to give her that opportunity.

It was evident that she had deadly intentions. The following Tuesday Pat died, I'm certain from neglect and malnutrition. The death certificate stated colitis. She had constantly said he was in good health. I know he died unnecessarily. I talked to the undertaker and recommended an autopsy. He said I should talk to the medical examiner at the VA hospital. I gave up. What use would it be after the fact?

To add to her greed, she bought the cheapest casket, with no draping flowers as is customary. I was sick at her deceit. I asked her, "Why are there no flowers draped over his casket?"

This cruel despicable, lying, illiterate answered, "Oh they don't do that anymore."

Andie visited his dad at the funeral parlor before visiting hours. He cried hysterically. His heart was broken. He wanted so desperately to see his father before he died. He sobbed, "I don't even have a jacket to remember him by." My heart so ached for him.

I hoped Flora would examine her heartless conscience and have a slight bit of compassion and give this grieving boy his wish. As we sat to receive friends, I asked her if she would have it in her heart to give Andie his dad's medals. This despicable, heartless, uncaring creature bluntly said "No." Sadly, Andie died broken-hearted at a young age a few months later.

Nikie is now living alone in government housing afflicted with Parkinson's disease. Pat's wealth would have easily supported her had he been aware of her condition and not afflicted with Alzheimer's. He was extremely wealthy. Flora's scheming trickery fraudulently transferred all his assets to her. Her attorney conspired with her too, stating there was nothing left from the estate.

After Pat's death, Flora moved to a lovely apartment complex. She left the house to her nephew to live in. My attorney, offered by the bar association, Jaffry Pearlo, promised me results into performing an autopsy. Months later I received a registered letter stating that he was withdrawing from my case at my request, which was a downright lie. I was exhausted. The fight was not worth the aggravation. Realizing I was no match for an attorney, I just gave up. He did, however, give me the complete file with proof of Flora's manipulations and thievery.

My story was sent out to the Washington VA. I got no response. I suspect my brother was denied his life.

I was alone in my sorrow, with the last of my siblings gone. I had a sad feeling of isolation. I was determined to put that part of my life behind me.

Norata, although independent, needed me to arrange his doctor visits, keep his appointments on schedule, and care for all of his special needs. I made sure he wasn't neglected. I never let him feel abandoned even though he was partly to blame for the failure in our lost life.

My conscience sometimes was my enemy. I always had the feeling that I was obligated to do what's right for everyone, but that wasn't always how it worked. I made so many uncalled for mistakes that I regret.

Ned and Mona were inseparable, traveling and spending much of their time together in spite of the stressful distance between them.

Her time spent with us was pleasant. The children were also happy being with us. I had the feeling that Mona didn't have many friends, just her mom and brother. Her life was rather private.

Our family of cousins, nieces, and nephews were fun-loving people. We were close and spent all of our holidays together. It was clear that Mona liked the gatherings, and the fun times with them.

Normally we spend all special days together at the Marriott since Susan, being an employee, got us special treatment.

Easter was planned for us to celebrate together. Everyone chose their special dish on the menu. The excitement of Jimmy telling his special jokes made our dinner exciting.

Come time to pay the bill, we usually shared the entire sum. However, when the waiter placed the bill on the table, Mona reached over, picked it up, and handed it to Ned. It was obvious that he had no intention of paying the bill, but then he graciously handed the payment to the waiter.

Money was no object for Mona. She thought nothing of inviting her friends to join them for dinner. No matter how many there were, she always made sure Ned paid the bill. I've seen him spend as much as $900 on a dinner. She made sure he never got away with being a cheapskate. Mona made certain his generosity flowed.

Many times while we were shopping she would ask me to choose whatever I wanted. If I happened to look at something with the minimum of interest, Mona would snatch it from me and include it with her purchase.

Once when we were shopping I noticed that Mona's credit card was in my name. I assumed from that, Ned was using my name as well to pay for all her credit card purchases.

I was careful not to take advantage, even though it was my hard earned money they were spending. At least Ned never left me responsible for paying off those cards.

It was impossible to get Mona to live with us. The relationship was becoming tiresome. Ned very rarely spent dinnertime with us unless Mona was visiting. Ned's wanting me to live with him was for a definite purpose, he needed me to care for Jared.

In truth, I welcomed it. Every day was a pleasure

preparing his lunch for school and caring for his needs. I was happy being with my grandson. It was a special time for him as well. He was an honest, outgoing kid who never held any secrets. He was an open book. He shared all of his interests. Dinnertime for us was extra special because we talked about his needs and his future.

Norata was a stickler, never wanting to leave his apartment. I had to insist at times just to get him to join us for dinner.

Intracoastal

Saturday, after breakfast, just before Ned was to leave the house, he was fumbling with some paperwork when he turned to me and said, "I'm thinking about buying a house in Florida. I found this particular one on the west coast that I liked very much. What do you think?" he asked, as he proudly handed me the picture.

I was stunned, surprised. He never showed any interest in property searching. I looked at the picture impressed at the spaciousness of the house on the Intracoastal Waterway. I answered, "It's nice."

I was lost for words. My mind was racing with the thought, could he be planning to move to Florida with Mona and her children? Could this be the end of my happy life here? I suddenly felt sick. It boggled my mind. I wanted to ask about his intentions but I was afraid of getting the wrong answer.

I tried to put the thought out of my mind. Maybe he might keep this house and continue to have me live here with Jared; then again, he might want to sell the house and leave me out in the cold. I was frightened.

He asked me again, "Do you like it?"

I had to show concern so I answered "Beautiful." He described the structure and the fine qualities of the house while I just listened. He never gave me any clue as to what he was planning.

Months passed. Ned and Mona were busy, taking small trips. I had a suspicion that they were planning to make their home in Florida.

I expected that my son was playing the confidence game again. It came natural to him. But I was very disappointed in Mona because she and I had a trustful relationship. We confided in each other. Nothing was held back. I could never have imagined her being secretive, not disclosing their plans with me. I lost complete confidence in her.

As I thought about her secrecy, I noticed the change in her since our first meeting. She wasn't the same person.

One morning, after breakfast, Ned seemed nervous. He had the contract in his hands, and he had his usual grin. It looked like he was going to use me again. He was hesitant, and then said, "You know my circumstances, Mom. I can't show any assets. You will have to sign for the mortgage."

It suddenly came to light, as long as I continue to live in his house he will continue to use me for his own selfish needs. He never changed. He was the same manipulator using me for his dirty work. I asked myself, what can I do? He's got me over a barrel. I had to do his bidding. I was still living under his roof but I wasn't sure of his plans.

I looked at him. But he didn't ask if I wanted to sign, he simply said, as he always did, "You will have to sign."

What else could I do? I had to take my chances wondering what my fate and my future would be. Maybe I was drawing false conclusions. At least I wanted to think so. Still, it stuck in my mind: I have no choice. I'm completely obligated. How can I refuse?

His mortgages, credit cards, and all the current bills are in my name. I'm a fool—I own nothing. On the other hand, I had nothing to lose, so, again, I signed. With no legal rights to his possessions and my name on all his properties, I realized that my job was done. He was planning to move to Florida. He doesn't need me anymore. He got all he wanted from me.

Anyhow, I gave it a second thought. I'm being irrational. He's shown some degree of caring. Besides, Mona has complete control over his decisions—maybe, just maybe, she will use her influence and surprise me with some consideration.

I had to trust her—she was my only salvation. She might take some interest in my manner of living. She knew my circumstances, my struggle to survive despite lack of funds. She was a controller. She could make him do anything that she wanted. He'd crawl on his knees if she asked him to.

Time passed, weeks, months, with no sign of his planning to move.
Occasionally they would take time off and fly to Florida for whatever requirements were needed, in preparation, I thought, for their move.

After months of travel, the time had finally come, though they hadn't discussed any plans with me. Ned put the house up for sale. He didn't have the decency to tell me. He didn't care what I was going to do or where I was going. It was like I didn't exist.

I expected nothing more from my unmerciful son. As always, he cared only about himself. Mona too had changed; she kept their move a secret. That gave me ill feelings. I had thought she was my dear friend who would never deceive me. The intimacy we once had was gone.

Jared had innocently filled me in on their plans, about what was happening. As for my son, nothing surprised me. He was the same user.

My dream world came to an end, I thought. I had

served his purpose and his selfish advantages. He doesn't need me anymore. My job is done. I am thrown back into impoverishment.

I was devastated. My life taken from me again, a second time.

I was back in a stressful position. Three years living in his home had finally come to an end. The home I was enjoying was taken from me. I was very disappointed.

I had to make a decision, go back and live with Norata or find another apartment. But where can I go? My social security paid a bare minimum, not even enough to pay a normal rent. Still, I searched and searched for a decent place to live.

A housing complex was being constructed some distance away. I liked the fact that the complex was new but I wasn't happy with the surrounding area. I had to decide.

Moving back in with Norata wasn't feasible. Two people living in a one-bedroom apartment wasn't comforting. As long as he was independent and caring for himself, there was no need to move in with him. Plus the fact that he was still intolerant.

I was sad, talking to myself, trying to find a solution to my misfortune. I had so many disappointments in my life, I'm sure I could survive another one. So I made the only feasible decision, to move into the new complex. I was surprised that Ned helped me get situated in my one-bedroom subsidized apartment.

Though I wasn't about to let him get away with it so easily. I kept the furniture and all necessities I needed to furnish my apartment. It turned out that it didn't matter anyway. He couldn't have cared less. Mona wasn't interested in taking any of Jane's possessions. She needed to furnish their home at her own discretion.

I was startled when I signed my lease. Ned put up the security deposit and paid a third of my monthly income (just under $300). I was amazed at his sudden generosity. It was the one and only time I had ever experienced him making a kind gesture to me. It was such a small sum that I suppose it didn't bother him. His generosity stopped there.

Although I found some contentment in my new apartment, I lost the freedom of having the spacious living conditions as well as the social gatherings with my family and friends. I had to adjust again.

The months passed. Ned made no contact. I didn't expect any, really. But after I assume they had settled in, I received a surprise call from Mona. She wasn't happy with the suburban area of Florida. It was too private for her—she hadn't realized how dreary it really was. And she asked me to fly down for a visit.

I mentioned how hard it was at that time. Money was an issue. But I sometimes did feel a need to get away.

Ned purposely chose a very private town with little activity on Florida's west coast. That sure would keep her away from the excitement of Florida's nightlife. Mona still had an attractive face and body, plus the fact that she was fourteen years younger and continued to draw attention. He was not going to expose her. He wasn't going to take the chance of losing her.

With so little activity in the area, her boredom set in. Her extravagant shopping passion meant she'd have to travel north to the next town. The furniture she chose was elegant. It was unlike any normal design. Price was no object. Ned did everything to please her to keep her happy.

The golf course across from their house was also an attraction that Mona couldn't resist. She suggested they join the club and do some golfing. Ned made excuses as to why he couldn't golf. He was just afraid of her being exposed to the male golfers.

Store shopping and dining became a drag. Ned had to find something else to do to fill their days with excitement.

Mona liked to entertain. She made new friends while attending the new church nearby. She was eager to show off her new home, also being a great cook, she enjoyed entertaining and having dinner parties, mostly with her church friends. Sometimes she invited them over right after the church services.

Ned and his cousin Dan spent many of their young days riding their cycles. It was their favorite pastime on Sunday.

Ned thought how exciting it would be for Mona, if he bought motorcycles for their pleasure and taught her to ride, mostly, to motivate her and help to eliminate the boredom of their dull town. It would be fun. They would also have the pleasure of riding together.

"Teaching her to ride will be easy," he said. She had never been on a cycle but she was ready to try. He didn't think twice. He purchased two beautiful new Harley Davidson's, white for her and red for himself. He had to impress her with his and her number plates: 'One' and 'Two.'

Mona was really eager. She bought all that she needed for riding: a jacket, a helmet to match, and new sneakers. All was in place as she prepared to take her first ride. Unfortunately, it didn't work out as well as expected. Ned's instructions hadn't sunk in. He obviously wasn't a good teacher.

With the engines started and in gear, they were ready to roll. But as Mona took off, she suddenly lost control and the bike fell directly on her leg. The hot engine cover burned her leg badly. She needed medical treatment for painful second-degree burns.

After months of healing, Ned encouraged her to give it another try. That wasn't going to happen. She had lost interest. That was the end of her adventurous undertakings.

The bikes just sitting in the garage were a temptation for Jared. Like all teenagers, he was impressed with the idea of riding. He decided to give Mona's bike a try. The girls in the family threatened him for taking it without asking. There had always been a certain amount of jealously where Jared was concerned. He ignored their warning and took it out for an hour's spin. What a fury that caused!
Mona had made drastic changes since moving to Florida. Ned spoiled her to the point of selfishness. All decisions and desires had to be met with her approval. Ned was afraid of her. He lived, as I said, "like two feet in a shoe."

Jared's actions annoyed her. She wasn't happy with him. Like all boys he was sometimes careless about conforming to her rules. Complaining had no effect. He sometimes didn't follow orders either.

Angry as hell at Jared for taking her bike without asking, she chastised Ned for not reprimanding his son. She tolerated nothing. Ned was the go-between. He took her side every time. She had become spoiled and dominating, who knows what transpired between her and Ned.

She was so frustrated she packed some belongings and left with her girls to spend the next few days with her friends from up north. They too were living nearby.

Ned was sick and destroyed at her leaving. Afraid to

hurt her, he apologized for his son's behavior, he would never take his son's side against her.

Jared was a well-mannered, refined boy, respectful in every way. When I lived with him he was a pleasure. He never raised his voice or showed signs of frustration. But living under Mona's rule was unfortunate. He was never able to satisfy her demands. He was attending the college nearby his education was affected. He was unhappy and began to lose interest.

Ned, who was obviously in fear of losing his precious Mona, told Jared, "Be nice to her. I don't want to lose her."

Mona was far from the fine person I once knew. She had become spoiled to the point of being dominating and in complete control.

The good boy that Jared was, loving his dad and trying to keep him happy, tolerated her moods and tried hard not to overstep his bounds. Mostly, he kept to himself.

But it was never enough. Everything Jared did upset her. Ned, always in fear of losing Mona, had to do something to make the tension go away. To keep peace, he rented an apartment not far from their home for Jared to live in.

That wasn't what Jared wanted. With no other family member nearby, he was unhappy, he needed his dad. Hurting and disappointed, he dropped out of college in his junior year and refused to continue his education.

Ned was a poor example as a dad. He was a huge disappointment. His only concern was his new family.

Mona was lonesome; she needed someone to confide in so she called several times asking me to come visit. As I said, I was lonesome too so I welcomed the invitation

I was happy to get away from my own loneliness. The town where they lived had little activity. Our time spent together was always the same: shopping and more shopping. We usually went to the next town, about thirty miles away. Sometimes Ned would take us boating down the Intracoastal.

Mona kept her girls now grown up, in luxury, with beautiful cars, lovely designer clothes, and the best that money can buy. They were never deprived. Although they praise their mother for their fine upbringing, it makes me cringe to think that Ned gets no credit for their luxurious, extravagant lifestyle genuinely provided for them.

Missy and Maggie came first in their mom's life. They had a life of luxury with anything and everything to make them happy. However, their dad was never mentioned. It was like he was forgotten, with no desire to see him. I wondered why. He had been a good father, according to their grandmother Yasha, who adored him and had great interest in trying to save the family.

The years passed with Ned caring only for his new family.

The girls, eighteen and nineteen, attended the college of their choice. Missy was deeply devoted to her religion so she chose a college far from their dull town. She majored in theology.

Maggie, the younger of the two, had an expensive appetite like her mom. Florida's west coast was too dull for her, no excitement. She chose a college on the East Coast where it was livelier and more exciting. She lived in the most exclusive and richest part of town. It paid off because she was introduced to the right people who could advance the career she wanted to pursue.
What she liked to do best was professional dancing. She practiced daily. Her first thought was to teach dance to children in Kenya, but people advised her that a much better choice was to make her career in her own country.

As young as she was, she opened a dance studio. She attended all the functions that would enhance her business. She vowed that one day she would fulfill her dream of teaching in foreign countries.

Lianne also lived on the East Coast. She loved her brother dearly, they had a very strong bond all through life. She was disturbed, full of contempt at her dad's decision to remove Jared from his home to please Mona. She was bitter and refused to visit her dad, except rarely and only when it was necessary.

Ned was indifferent toward Lianne. He cared less about her survival. Her refusal to accept Mona had changed his attitude. If you didn't accept Mona, you were an outcast.

Lianne was independent and proud. She never depended on her dad for help. She made the mistake of giving up her exclusive, well-paying job. She left college in Boston to continue her life in Florida, a mistake she regrets. She struggled, trying desperately to keep up with her expenses. Her real estate position wasn't very successful. As a result, she became severely depressed.

She shared her apartment to help pay the rent. She had troublesome tenants: partying, destructive, they would come and go. She suddenly found herself financially distraught and in a deeper state of depression. Paying all of the rent was impossible. She was in a bad situation, in real trouble.

Even though she had never asked her dad for help, nor had she ever wanted to, he was her only hope at this time. Without a second thought, she swallowed her pride and called him, explaining her situation. To her surprise, he did help her. He paid half of the rent, but only for three months. Then he stopped, explaining that she'd have to find her way thereafter.

Luckily, her new boyfriend, Bill, loved her and offered to share his apartment with her. Against her better judgment, she accepted. Again, he was her only choice.

It was too much to cope with. She was in despair. She became so severely depressed that she needed professional help. Her doctor was worried and advised her to admit herself for evaluation to a medical facility. She was in luck, for a while. Ned had health insurance that covered his new family, with she and Jared included. But after three weeks of therapy, Ned informed her that the insurance had run out. She moved back in with Bill.

Although she graduated with high honors, she had difficulty finding a job. She tried job after job but her depression kept bringing her down. She was having difficulty making payments on her new Lexus, so it was repossessed. It seemed that everything was against her, no family, no funds, and no transportation. All the pressure was taking effect.

Lianne was an intelligent girl but she was totally lost. There was no hope, to continue to ask for help was out of the question.

Bill was very disturbed at Ned for turning his back, he threatened to call him, but Lianne was against his interfering, so she made the decision to move back home with her mom. She did call Ned and explain her plan. She also mentioned that if she had a car, she might be able to drive home with some of her belongings. At the time Ned had a dealer's license because he had an interest in foreign cars. She was hoping her dad would take the hint. He did and was somewhat generous; he gave her the car that Maggy had outgrown. It came with an insult, though. The car was offered with a vanity plate still attached that read "Maggy." More mental pain for Lianne. She packed up what possessions she had and moved back home with her mom.

Becca and Dean

Becca was living in Boca. Embarrassed at her confinement, she needed to forget that part of her life and start anew in Florida. She met Dean who helped to fill the void in her life. He was kind, generous, and very devoted. He lived with his sister in Washington, but he was determined to court Becca. He flew out every weekend to be with her, always with a gift of flowers or candy—never empty-handed.

As the months passed, the stress mounted. It was expensive, and flights every weekend were costly. He loved Becca and sometimes refused to leave, putting his job in jeopardy. On his last visit, he proposed with a one-caret diamond. He left Washington and immediately transferred his job to Boca. They married and were quite happy.

Becca was anxious for us to meet her new husband. Our first meeting with him was impressive. He was pleasant, very courteous, and a gourmet cook. He prepared a meal especially for us. I was happy with Becca's choice. Dean immediately called me Mom. Very respectful.

At bedtime, Norata was so tired he couldn't stay up

any longer. Dean, very courteously and surprisingly, said, "Come on, Dad. I will help you get ready for bed." With that, he walked him to the bedroom, helped him get ready for bed, and kissed his forehead, wishing him a good night. It was so unusual; we were very impressed. Norata was deeply affected by his kindness and respect.

It was too good to be true. Dean's only flaw was alcohol. He was addicted. Becca tried coping, but the nightly drinking became chronic. Her threats had no effect. He was a different person on his binges.

Mona invited Becca and Dean to spend the following Sunday with them for dinner. Becca welcomed the invitation, happy to have a chance to see her brother. The almost three-hour ride across town was a bit hectic, but not to offend her, Becca accepted. To be with her brother was a special treat. The day went quite well, with a full course dinner.

In the early afternoon Becca noticed the interaction between Mona and Dean. They were overfriendly, obviously attracted to each other and conversing softly. Becca heard Dean ask if she was married to Ned. When she answered no, he remarked that she should wait for him. Ned also noticed the flirtatious attraction between them but he closed his eyes, as usual, and said nothing. With that, Becca, humiliated, couldn't stay another minute. She excused herself, and she and Dean left immediately.

Becca was mortified and disgraced. She wasn't about to accept being degraded. She couldn't wait for the opportunity to pay back the insult.

The long ride back was the perfect opportunity to return the hurt. When they left, Dean needed cigarettes, so he stopped at the station a few blocks from Ned's house. Great! Becca thought. Now is payback time. As he exited the car, Becca stepped on the accelerator, threw his cell phone out the window, and left him stranded on the highway with no way to communicate.

Becca was a kind and very personable person, but she wouldn't tolerate being used or hurt. There was no way she was going to accept the shame and painful loss of dignity.

Dean walked in the door three hours later. Excuses were not accepted.
She filed for divorce. The incident was never mentioned again.

Mona was lonesome. She needed someone to confide in other than Ned. Oftentimes she would invite me to come spend time with them. I welcomed the invitation; I was lonely and living alone.

Mona maintained her perfect body. She had everything desired in a woman. She had some surgery done to enhance her beauty and her breasts stood out to perfection. Once she mentioned that she had surgery on her mouth and chin. I never questioned her. It wasn't a subject to open up to. Ned loves her, he is happy, he cherishes her, and nothing else matters.

Maggy was proud of the fact that her mother was attractive to men.

I remember her coming home one afternoon when I was visiting and proudly saying that one of her male friends had asked her, "Is that your mother?" When Maggy said yes, he replied "She is a beauty." He was totally impressed with her good looks. Mona was proud and infatuated, she knew she had the magnetic power to attract men, it lifted her ego. The following morning, I noticed Mona dressing exceptionally nice, makeup and all, something she never did in the morning, and drove Maggy to school.

When I visited I saw the many drastic changes Mona had made. She was not the same person, whether Ned had spoiled her, or it was the taste of luxury.

However, she had been good to me in the past, delighting me with gifts she bought with Ned's credit card (that had my name on it). It was her treat. It eased her boredom. Nonetheless, she never encouraged him to help me financially. She was well aware that I was living a pauper's lifestyle and that almost everything Ned had was rightfully mine.

There were times she would change her attitude with sudden outbursts of frustration. Her aggravation hurt my feelings, but I understood.

Their property commitments in New England had to be met. The occupied rental Ned bought for Mona was a nuisance. Her tenant was delinquent with the rent and she was frustrated that she couldn't be there to supervise. Thus, she had to take unwanted trips up north.

The bed and breakfast and the home she left behind were unoccupied but ready when needed. As a result, my apartment was very convenient and necessary for their overnight stopovers before continuing to their obligations.

Mona spent a few nights with me while Ned took care of business in Newport before traveling north. She was ready to have some fun. She looked forward to spending a day at the casino.

She never came empty handed. She always had a goody for me. I was happy to see her extravagance because it made Ned get rid of some of his money. That was all that I ever got from him.

With money on his mind, Ned made another try to make use of a section of his building. He tried recycling the abundant supply of leftover hair products he had in stock. It went fairly well. It brought in a small profit.

Every day he used me to assemble and package the product to make it ready for shipping. I welcomed the much needed income, whatever he felt necessary to pay me. Ned never overpaid. He was cheap but I needed the money. There was no way I could get a job at my age.

One afternoon, while I was filling orders, he was

talking on the phone. He handed it to me without telling me why. The lady asked me questions about my credit. Evidently, Ned was using a credit card in my name to buy a $22,000 diamond for Mona. Fortunately for me, with my wrong answers, the purchase was denied.

Soon afterwards, Mona was overjoyed wearing a three-caret yellow diamond that she had wanted. I never asked where that purchase was made. The same taker who refused to take no for an answer all his life once again got just what he wanted. Of course, he didn't stop there. His plan to buy the house on the Intracoastal, with a private dock, was for a purpose.

Norata never believed in buying on credit. He had never had a credit card, until Ned changed that.

The newest surprise was finding in his mail a Visa statement in Dad's name. It showed a $33,000 balance for a newly purchased boat.
Ned was up to his old tricks. We discovered that he had bought the small yacht for his own pleasure.

I remember Sundays, their usual family day for boating. It was easy access from the house and the boat was always ready to enjoy. Ned frowned on boating too often because taking it out meant filling it up with gas. That cost at least $800.

Maggie cared less about the cost. Sometimes she invited her friends for a day of boating. Ned was concerned about the fuel consumption, but he didn't dare make a comment.

The traveling to and from Florida for monthly rent collections and other necessary business was becoming a costly habit for Ned. He was beginning to tire of the habitual stress, so he decided to relieve himself of the responsibility by taking what he could from the building and moving on.

As for Mona, she was delighted, and welcomed the travel up north for her commitments. Besides keeping focus on her property, she looked forward to being back to the old neighborhood she grew up in. To see Malia and her church friends made her happy.

Ned usually rented a truck when he traveled up north; there was always some needed equipment for the routine work around the property, plus the fact that Mona enjoys the stops along the way for her shopping pleasure.
My savings were slowly diminishing, my social security was a bare minimum, and I was still living in subsidized housing on low income. Luckily my rent was still one third of my income, which wasn't much. I used up what little savings we had.

Norata's health was beginning to fail. The VA was taking good care of his needs. He was well equipped for his daily requirements: a nurse, a caretaker, and a therapist. I went every morning to be with him, to fix his meals, and see that he kept his doctor appointments.

One night I prepared his favorite special pot roast

dinner with all the fixings. We relaxed, watched television, conversed, and reminisced about our past life together. The next morning Norata felt ill, real ill, vomiting consistently. I called rescue and he was transported to the hospital. His body broke down beyond any hope of survival.

His stay was long and he was constantly on life support. There was no cure. The hospital doctors begged me to allow them to cut off the supply. "Let him go," they said. "There is no chance for recovery." I agreed, but I couldn't bring myself to make that decision. His body had failed but his mind was still sharp.

Finally, my three months of daily visits came to an end. Norata had enough. He was tired and he knew that he was never coming home. He wanted to end the suffering. I was relieved too. The pressure from the doctors for my final permission ended when Norata asked to have all measures of life support taken away.

His last wish was to have a cup of coffee. In fact he said, "Get me a bucket full," so sad. Any liquid he swallowed would lodge in his lungs and cause him to choke. After an hour, with his family beside him, he peacefully took his last breath.

I made all the funeral arrangements. Ned's only contribution was a special mahogany casket. It was so heavy it took eight struggling men to carry. He made no other offer to help me with the expenses.

After the funeral, everyone was invited to our community restaurant to choose from the menu. I was hoping my son would show some feelings for me and be responsible for the bill. He played his part, though, by telling everyone to have whatever they wanted—"Open bar!"

I had no intention of offering an open bar. It was an added expense I couldn't afford. I assumed, since he gave the order, he might show some measure of generosity by paying the tab. It was wishful thinking. I was presented with the entire bill. Even in death my conniving son was a taker.

When I questioned the bill as we were leaving, Mona became so angry that she snatched the bill from my hand, crushed it, and threw it away. I was shocked at her sudden anger. She was well aware that I was struggling financially. I had hoped for some support from her, but she had no compassion. I lost confidence in her completely.

After Norata's passing, I found two letters with misspelled words that he had written crudely in his dying condition on the last page of a pad. I guess he needed to relieve his conscience before he died. He needed to express his feelings in writing on his dying bed. Too bad he didn't have the courage to confront his son in person.

They read, in his own handwriting:

Letter #1

After 45 years I could not wait any longer to write my book, hurting me so badly, my hurt would carry on for the world would know, Being almost end of my life at a very old age. Being just married, I went into the jewelry business working hard and raised a family with two children into a very lucrative business. I formed 2 companies me as president of one and, my son the other, that was the start of my downfall.

Letter #2

Jewelry to Norm,

Borrowed $25,000.00 and $50,000.00 for government order and chemicals, weekends up New Hampshire I went for hotel and eating, $300.00 hour for you and Earl, come every Monday for your pay, one burnt, the second I bought for $28,000.00, and sold it to Salem realty, I used to come help you and leave my business, you and Jimmy built the barn that cost me $40,000.00 you screwed me good, how much did you make? It was only worth $10,000.00, it was a shit barn. I should have realized then a Ferrari and plane working for me, now you want me to give you my stocks loss to you and your hot ones."

I gather from those letters Ned was not satisfied; his greed continued to take whatever was left of our savings. Norata had a little dementia. However, he expressed his last words to relieve his burdened state of mind. He realized what his son really was and expressed it on his dying bed. Too late. He never could approach him. He was a coward letting Ned know how he felt after his death.

After struggling for two years, I found myself with little resources.
Without Norata's help, I found myself living below poverty level. This was the opportune time to ask Ned for help.

I wrote him from my computer explaining the hardship I was having. I told him that since I lost Dad's help, I could not live on this small monthly income. The stocks, bonds, and savings gone, I desperately needed his help.

I was crushed, devastated, from his immediate response: "I CAN'T HELP YOU, I HAVE A FAMILY TO TAKE CARE OF."

My heart skipped a beat when I read that. How could he deny me when he had taken our life savings and everything else we owned?

I refreshed his memory by filling in all of the details of his skillfully manipulated thievery, his unearned possessions, and drowning us in poverty with his greed and selfishness. I hurt so much.

He completely ignored me.

I made threats. I exposed his cruelty to his friends, but it made a small impression. He sent me a $500 check for the next three months, and nothing thereafter. I've seen him spend money like a drunken sailor, hundreds of dollars on dinner with Mona, her family, and friends. I tried to shame him every which way but he refused to budge.

Mona knew how I was hurting.

I had great feelings for her. Her influence was what I needed for Ned's help. I thought she would be my salvation. But evidently she wasn't going to jeopardize her extravagant lifestyle for me, his mother.

Yasha was aging and alone. She needed her daughter. Mona was concerned. She decided to have her mom move in with them. But caring for her wasn't an easy task. Yasha interfered with their life, so after months of constant care, Mona checked her into an assisted living facility.

I felt mental grief to think that my son could care for Yasha, a complete stranger, and turn his back on me, his mother.

Maggy was still living comfortably on the east coast. Missy, still in college, lives comfortably in her own apartment in New York. Ned did a great job, living in retirement at such a young age, supporting Mona and her family with the best money can buy. Lianne is happy living back home with her mom. Jared is living with his girlfriend, struggling as well.

The fact that I was forced to put my signature on all Ned's properties when living with him, kept me from being forceful. Since I couldn't pursue my rights, there was nothing I could do.

I tried to shame him again, with one last try. His answer was, "I have no money. I owe everybody."

He opened a new café, bought two new buildings, etc., why not forfeit the bed and breakfast that was put in Maggy's name I asked? I still hold that mortgage, but he refuses to respond to my messages. I just gave up.

My Forever Friend

My dear friend Lori was back home for the summer. After spending her winters in Florida, I wait patiently every year to be with her. Our forty-three years of true friendship with Marie was very special. We were always in close contact. We managed a get-together at least once a year in spite of the miles between us.

Lori surprised me with a sudden invitation. She called and said, "Mae, I rented a house for a week in Narragansett by the ocean for us to spend time together. Marie will be coming up from Florida next week." What a surprise. I couldn't wait.

Lori was a special person. In spite of her being extremely wealthy, she was kind, generous, unselfish, and thoughtful. Five years earlier she had a heart attack. It left her with thirty percent heart function. She has never let it interfere with her life of pleasure.

I felt honored being the elder. Lori is ten years my junior and Marie, just three years younger. The difference in age didn't matter. Our thoughts were compatible. Our forever friendship was real.

I was impressed with the five-room house Lori rented. Even though we were directly across from the ocean, we never put on a bathing suit.

Our days were programmed for excitement. After breakfast we planned each day, mostly visiting the places of interest in our town. The nights were spent playing cards or reminiscing about our past experiences.

My only concern was watching Lori spread eighteen pills on the table every morning to take with her coffee. I lectured her, I wondered why her doctor over-prescribed her pills. I worried for her. I mentioned how they will cause her harm; however, she had faith in her doctor and felt they were a necessity.

How very exciting it was being together. Lori spends her winter months on the east coast, so many times I make a quick weekly visit to be with her. Every April is a special time for me. I look forward to Lori's call and time for her arrival. flying up north to her home here in Rhode Island is always a pleasure for her as well.

Marie, who lives in Naples, Florida, very often visits her daughters who live in Massachusetts. Her visits are always with a stay for two or three days with us. This time when our week together came to an end, we all went our separate ways. Marie flew back to Naples. Lori and I left for home.

I was missing my eyeglasses. I couldn't imagine how I could have been so careless, but I couldn't do without them. Then I remembered leaving them in the back seat pocket of Lori's car the previous night. I called to tell her that they were in her car.

"No problem," she said, "Let's meet on Wednesday for lunch. I'll have them with me."

"Great," I said.

Then on Tuesday night, when I was about ready for bed, I got the shock of my life when my phone rang.

Donna, Lori's daughter, said, "Mom had a stroke tonight. She's not going to make it."

I was paralyzed, devastated, I didn't believe what I was hearing. How could this have happened? She was fine when we were together. It was a great time, without complaints.

Donna was in shock as well, she couldn't continue, just a quick click.

The next morning, I went to the hospital to see her. She lay in bed in critical condition. I begged her, please don't leave me. She was my mentor. I could confide in her; she understood my problems and always had the right answers. My heart ached. I knew one day those pills would take her life, but I was ignored.

I had a sleepless night, deeply affected by the sad news. My heart hurt. I'd lost my very dear friend. She will live in my heart forever.

I've had so many heartaches in my life. I guess "God gives to those who can bear them." Without resources, my life is painful. I am aging; I have lost most of my loved ones, and live every day as if it is the last.

Now I am fighting credit card debt from the card they used for their traveling expenses in Europe. My credit score is almost zero and it makes no difference. I have no credit cards, and unable to ever buy on credit again.

I am counting my days, trying to enjoy what little time I have left. My evil son has no pity for his mom who unwillingly gave him the undeserved millionaire lifestyle that he maliciously stole from me.

I have just five words to express, "YOU REAP WHAT YOU SOW."

Ned had a commitment and left on a hunting trip. He was gone just a week. When he returned, he found almost everything gone from his home, except for a note that read, "DON'T TRY TO CONTACT ME."

I wrote this manuscript to release the pain from my past. I learned too late that by trusting our precious son with our finances, we created a creature of greed and selfishness, that which destroyed us physically and mentally, an important lesson to be learned.

Made in the USA
Charleston, SC
13 January 2017